LIFE IN GOD

LIFE IN GOD

*John Calvin,
Practical Formation,
and the
Future of Protestant Theology*

Matthew Myer Boulton

*William B. Eerdmans Publishing Company
Grand Rapids, Michigan / Cambridge, U.K.*

© 2011 Matthew Myer Boulton
All rights reserved

Published 2011 by
Wm. B. Eerdmans Publishing Co.
2140 Oak Industrial Drive N.E., Grand Rapids, Michigan 49505 /
P.O. Box 163, Cambridge CB3 9PU U.K.

Printed in the United States of America

16 15 14 13 12 11   7 6 5 4 3 2 1

Library of Congress Cataloging-in-Publication Data

Boulton, Matthew Myer, 1970-
Life in God: John Calvin, practical formation, and the future of protestant theology /
Matthew Myer Boulton.
p.   cm.
Includes bibliographical references and index.
ISBN 978-0-8028-6564-9 (pbk.: alk. paper)
1. Calvin, Jean, 1509-1564. 2. Calvinism — History.
3. Protestant churches — Doctrines.
4. Protestant churches — Forecasting. I. Title.

BX9418.B713 2011
230′.42092 — dc23

2011017692

www.eerdmans.com

Abide in me, as I abide in you.
John 15:4

Contents

Acknowledgments   x

INTRODUCTION: The Sacred City   1

I. Storming the Sanctuary

1. **The City a Desert**   11
   The Rule of Life   12
   Christian *Paideia*   22

2. **Calvin's Geneva**   29
   The Sacred Schoolhouse   29
   Singing the Psalter   33
   Prayer and the Supper   38

3. ***Summa Pietatis***   45
   Pietas   46
   The Role of the *Institutio*   50
   Pietatis Doctrina   53

Contents

II. Rereading the *Institutio*

4. **Six Kinds of Knowledge**	61
"The Knowledge of God and of Ourselves"	63
Intimacy and Speculation	70
Creator and Redeemer	76
5. **Radiance and Oblivion**	83
Creation	86
Providence	88
Oblivion	91
6. **Seeing through Scripture**	96
Scripture and the Spirit	98
Scripture in the *Institutio*	105
7. **God with Us**	112
Us without God	112
The Mediator	117
In Christ's Image	128
Flesh and Faith	131
8. **Doxology and Destiny**	138
Humility and Hope	139
Sheep out of Wolves	149
A Church beyond Our Ken	156
9. **Prayer and Communion**	166
The Communion of Prayer	167
The Sacred Supper	180

Contents

III. On the Future of Protestant Theology

10. Reforming Calvin	191
Quietism	193
Masochism	199
Misanthropy	202
11. Life in God	210
Calvin's Ideas	211
Calvin's Approach	215
Reforming Formation	222
Reforming Church	228
Bibliography	233
Index	239

Acknowledgments

Many people read and commented on early drafts of this book, or made suggestions to improve the argument, including Mark Jordan, Jonathan Schofer, Ron Thiemann, Kevin Madigan, Susan Abraham, Dan McKanan, Martha Moore-Keish, William Wright, Christopher Elwood, John Witvliet, Todd Billings, Robert Saler, Chad Smith, Joel Rasmussen, Malcolm Young, Wayne Boulton, Elizabeth Myer Boulton, Bram Briggance, Michael Motia (who also tirelessly chased down both books and typos), Emma Crossen, Scott Dickison, and Jocelyn Gardner. Much of what is useful in these pages, and none of what isn't, is properly credited to them.

My son, Jonah, who turned five this summer, and my daughter, Maggie, who turned three in April, somehow didn't get around to reading even a single page. But when it comes to some of Calvin's most important theological themes — the art of living as beloved children of God, for example, or the idea that discipleship means, among other things, learning to grow up and into that childhood — I have had no better teachers. This book is dedicated, with thanks, love, and a wink, to them.

MMB
August 20, 2010
Harvard Divinity School

INTRODUCTION

The Sacred City

Sometime near 1483 in Nuremberg, church leaders faced an intriguing question: What work of art should grace the prestigious Krell altar in Saint Lawrence Church, the city's signature, twin-towered colossus?

Their decision, as it turned out, was an unlikely herald of things to come. In 1525, just a few years after Martin Luther's excommunication, the people of Nuremberg declared themselves allied with the emerging reform movement. And when they did, the picture hanging over the Krell altar, as it had by then for over forty years, was a portrait not of Christ's crucifixion, or the last judgment, or the feeding of the five thousand, or indeed any other scene found anywhere in Christian Scripture.

It was a portrait of Nuremberg itself. It is a sunny, ordinary day. Nestled into the surrounding hills, shops and houses huddle together, and rising up out of their midst, the two spires of Saint Lawrence point toward heaven. In the heart of a landscape, a city; in the heart of the city, a church; in the heart of the church, an altar; and over the altar, a picture of — that very landscape, and that very city. Hanging in what was arguably the most extraordinary, exceptional, holy setting in all of Nuremberg, a most ordinary, familiar, earthly sight.

Which was, no doubt, the point. As one historian has put it, the picture portrayed "the sacred city," a vista meant to remind disciples that "their worship had to do with the whole of their life," and that "the life of the city was accountable to God."[1] Accountable to God, to

---

1. See Peter Matheson, ed., *Reformation Christianity* (Minneapolis: Fortress, 2007), plate H.

Introduction

be sure, but also shot through with God's presence and power, related to God in every respect, even and especially the workaday details of ordinary life. The Christian church had its central, indispensable role to play, but the essence of that role, on this view, was not to arrogate the status of "sacred" to itself alone, that is, to ecclesial holy things and holy men. Rather, the church's role was to call attention to the fact that in everything we do, as John Calvin would later put it, we have to do with God.[2] Not the sacred church alone, then, but rather "the sacred city." Not a special spiritual precinct, class of experts, or set of operations, but rather an integral world, in all its variety and ruin, divinely called to both holiness and wholeness.

The sixteenth-century European reformations did not invent this basic idea, but many of their driving principles represent attempts to recapture it anew. Those movements were spirited battles over beliefs, but even more, they were battles over embodied disciplines, social patterns, and ways of life. In this sense, they were battles over Christian discipleship and formation, over who properly had access to the church's key formative practices, and on what terms those practices were properly carried out.

The monastery, the cathedral, the clerical class — each institution in its own way drew a kind of sacred circle on the late medieval landscape, a privileged sphere in which certain spiritual goods were widely supposed to be especially or exclusively available. Many Protestants variously argued, to the contrary, that in fact there are no such spheres — or, rather, that creation as a whole is the single, unbroken sphere of human life with God, and that every faithful disciple in the Christian church, ordinary and extraordinary alike, is equally a beneficiary of divine gifts through Jesus Christ and the Holy Spirit. Whatever sanctifying, formative exercises marked and edified monks and clergy, then, to the extent that those practices were grounded in Scripture, they should be made available to all Christians everywhere, *mutatis mutandis*.

In other words, these reformers insisted that, properly under-

---

2. See, e.g., John Calvin, *Institutes of the Christian Religion*, ed. John T. McNeill (Philadelphia: Westminster, 1960), 3.7.2: "the Christian must surely be so disposed and minded that he feels within himself it is with God he has to deal throughout his life." Or again, as he pondered whether or not to return to Geneva after his expulsion, Calvin wrote in a letter to William Farel: "I am well aware that it is with God that I have to do [*mihi esse negotium cum Deo*]." See *Letters of John Calvin*, ed. Jules Bonnet (New York: B. Franklin, 1973), 1:281.

stood, religious disciplines are not rarefied recommendations for cloistered or ordained virtuosos in training. Instead, they are the disciplines of discipleship itself, divinely and apostolically bequeathed to the whole church, and in that sense, to the whole human family. To the extent that reformers declared a "priesthood of all believers," then, they thereby undertook two tasks at once. They sought, on one hand, to demote supposedly superior priests to a level on par with the laity, and on the other hand, to promote the supposedly inferior laity to the holy office of priesthood — a role that in late medieval Europe was by no means abstract, but rather was quite tangibly constituted in and through particular practices and patterns of life.

Scriptural study is an iconic case in point. In fourteenth- and fifteenth-century Europe, say, Bibles were typically housed behind ecclesial, monastic, or academic walls, written in Latin, and so read almost exclusively by trained specialists. By the dawn of the sixteenth century, however, scattered vernacular translations had already begun to appear (the Koberger Bible, for example, was published in Nuremberg in 1483, roughly contemporary with the Krell altarpiece), and a common reformed motif — in woodcuts, pamphlets, and other polemic material — was the image of a layperson outwitting a religious official in a debate over biblical interpretation.[3] Thus an eminently prized Christian practice was, at least in the ideal pictures promoted by Protestant propagandists, wrested back into lay hands.

Indeed, such images were not only expressions of anticlericalism, or emblems of the idea that the Word of God is meant for the whole people of God — though each of these sentiments surely played its part. The image of a cobbler interpreting the Bible more adeptly than a clergyman also made the vivid, compact case that laypeople were in fact fully capable of being formed in and through the Holy Spirit's scriptural curriculum and illuminating pedagogy. The point was not merely to expose and upstage the allegedly corrupt monk, the arrogant bishop, or the hapless priest; the point was also to cast the cobbler, and with him the seamstress, the peasant, and people of all other trades and types as intelligent, educable disciples in their own right.

Even the history of the term "clergy" (from the Old French, *clergié*,

---

3. See, e.g., Argula von Grumbach, *Argula von Grumbach: A Woman's Voice in the Reformation*, ed. Peter Matheson (Edinburgh: T. & T. Clark, 1995), p. 72; and Matheson, *Reformation Christianity*, plate G.

Introduction

"learned men," and *clergie*, "learning, knowledge, erudition") indicates something of the ground on which this battle was joined. Reformers argued, in effect, that ordinary disciples, too, could become "learned" men and women — if not in the academic arts and sciences, then certainly in the art of knowing God. They too could gain, demonstrate, and convey religious knowledge. They too could live in and with God, day in and day out. The church's pedagogical apparatus, then, its distinctive practical repertoire handed down since the earliest disciples and apostles, properly belongs to the church universal, not to any elite group within it. Formative disciplines often associated with monastic or clerical life — scriptural and theological study, daily prayer and worship, regular psalm singing, frequent reception of the Lord's Supper, renunciation of "the world," rigorous moral accountability, and so on — are in fact, reformers claimed, divine gifts meant for the church in general, and for each child of God in particular. If the monk's organizing vocational goal was union with God, so too was the cobbler's. In short, if the whole city was sacred, so too was each disciple's whole life. And accordingly, to live into such a life, each and every Christian required this training, this sacred instruction, this program of embodied, regular, formative practice.

In this book, I read John Calvin's theology — and in particular, his most well-known and influential text, the so-called *Institutes of the Christian Religion* — as a framework of ideas designed to serve precisely this sort of practical program. I argue that for Calvin, Christian doctrine is properly conceived and articulated in the first place for the sake of Christian formation, particularly the immersive, embodied, restorative training that may take place, God willing, by way of the church's disciplinary treasury. At every turn in Calvin's work, he sought to clarify the intellectual conditions of this pedagogical, practical life in God, and today's Protestant theologians, I contend, should do the same.

My argument proceeds in three parts. First, I sketch the outlines of Calvin's reforming work, highlighting how he positions himself both against and alongside monasticism, at once a critic and a fellow heir to the distinctive suite of practices that make for Christian life. For Calvin, discipleship is *paideia*, "formative education," a sanctifying, disciplinary, recuperative path, and in that sense a humble and humbling return, little by little, to full humanity in Christ's image. In a variety of ways, Calvin attempted to put this vision into practice in the "sacred city" of Geneva, laying out a holistic program of ideas and exercises,

4

training and study, all meant to form disciples toward genuine *pietas:* the grateful love and reverence for God induced by relational, pragmatic knowledge of divine benefits.

Second, in part II, with this historical and theological sketch as a backcloth, I reread seven key loci in Calvin's doctrinal work: first, theological knowledge; second, the thematic cluster of creation, providence, and sin; third, Scripture; fourth, Christology; fifth, predestination; sixth, prayer; and seventh, the Lord's Supper. All the way along, I contend, Calvin consistently crafts his ideas for the sake of practical formation, and so ultimately for the sake of ongoing companionship and union with God in Christ.[4] In this section, I focus primarily on the *Institutio*, not only because Calvin himself considered it a "sum of religion in all its parts," but also because of its reputation today as a monumental statement of Christian doctrine in the Reformed tradition.[5] Since I aim to explore how, for Calvin, doctrine itself is fundamentally formational, and then to recommend that today's Protestant theologians follow suit, I treat the *Institutio* — Calvin's doctrinal classic — as a kind of case study. To be sure, as Richard Muller, Elsie Anne McKee, and others have shown, the *Institutio* stands in what McKee calls a "symbiotic relationship" with Calvin's biblical commentaries and, more in-

---

4. Charles Partee has argued that "union with Christ" functions as a "central dogma" for Calvin; Richard Muller has persuasively countered that Calvin's thought contains no single "central dogma," while at the same time denying that Calvin's work is therefore "unsystematic," as William Bouwsma has claimed. In my view, Calvin's theology is both architectonic and deeply pastoral, and on both counts, it is a carefully organized, interconnected composition (thus resisting the "unsystematic" label) that relies on a diverse constellation of indispensable ideas (thus resisting the "central dogma" claim), and to be sure, one such idea, among others, is the church's "union" or "participation" in God. Like a well-designed house, Calvin's theology is meant to be lived in, and so (1) its architecture is intended to "hold together" as a whole, without leaks or structural hazards; (2) its layout is designed to serve various human needs on the ground, some of which occur in apparent tension with others; and (3) its overall construction includes several weight-bearing walls and supports, the removal of any one of which would cause a significant collapse, potentially rendering the house unlivable. See Charles Partee, "Calvin's Central Dogma Again," in *Calvin Studies 3* (Davidson, N.C.: Davidson College, 1986), pp. 39-46; Richard Muller, *After Calvin: Studies in the Development of a Theological Tradition* (New York: Oxford University Press, 2003), chapters 4 and 5, and *The Unaccommodated Calvin* (New York: Oxford University Press, 2000), chapter 6; and William Bouwsma, "Calvin and the Renaissance Crisis of Knowing," *Calvin Theological Journal* 17, no. 2 (1982): 208.

5. Calvin, *Institutes*, "John Calvin to the Reader," p. 4.

Introduction

directly, with his preaching, so any comprehensive assessment of his thought requires an investigation across all three of these bodies of work.[6] In what follows here, however, though I do refer occasionally to Calvin's commentaries and sermons, I deal principally with the final Latin edition of the *Institutio* (1559) as an influential example of Protestant doctrine, and thereby lay groundwork for my argument that fresh readings of Calvin may help chart a more explicitly formational approach to Protestant doctrine today.

Third and finally, then, in part III, I briefly propose a range of ways in which twenty-first-century theologians might critically retrieve aspects of Calvin's work. After outlining what I take to be some important hazards in his thought, I point toward some of its most compelling features, not the least of which, I contend, is the governing idea that Christian doctrine should be conceived, delimited, and developed

---

6. See Elsie Anne McKee, "Exegesis, Theology, and Development in Calvin's *Institutio*: A Methodological Suggestion," in *Probing the Reformed Tradition: Historical Studies in Honor of Edward A. Dowey, Jr.,* ed. Brian G. Armstrong and Elsie A. McKee (Louisville: Westminster John Knox, 1989), pp. 154-72, and Muller, *The Unaccommodated Calvin,* pp. 29, 102ff., especially p. 106. The methodological idea that, to understand Calvin on any particular subject, one should pursue that subject by way of, as Muller puts it, "careful historical and contextual study of Calvin's exegesis, preaching, and theology," is a welcome correction of approaches to Calvin's thought that read the *Institutio* ahistorically, or eisegetically, or in any case to the exclusion of his biblical commentaries and sermons. From this it does not follow, however, that the only way to read the *Institutio* is in this historically and generically comprehensive sense — a conclusion that would, after all, rather awkwardly claim for historical theologians the role of magisterial interpreters, if not the sole interpreters, of Calvin's work. To be sure, the more a reader has read of Calvin's writing and preaching, the better sense she may have of the nuances in any particular text in his oeuvre. But each particular text, too, has its own structure, substance, and limits, and so may be read and assessed in its own right, albeit with at least a general view to its peculiar context and purposes. Moreover, among Calvin's writings, the *Institutio* is something of a special case, since Calvin himself considered it a *summa*: a catechetical *summa pietatis* in its first edition, and by its final edition a *summa religionis* fit for training theological students to read Christian Scripture — but in any case a *summa*, a synopsis, an overview of Christian thought and life, and so a text with its own integrity as a work of Christian doctrine. Indeed, the fact that Calvin both produced French editions of the *Institutio* and permitted it to be translated into Spanish, Italian, Dutch, and English during his lifetime indicates that he, too, thought the book could be properly and profitably read without simultaneous study of his commentaries and sermons. See Muller, "Directions in Current Calvin Research," in *Calvin Studies IX: Papers Presented at the Ninth Colloquium on Calvin Studies,* ed. John H. Leith and Robert A. Johnson (Davidson, N.C.: Davidson College, 1998), p. 87.

The Sacred City

on behalf of the church's formative program. Indeed, in broad strokes, we may put the case this way: though Calvin has long been recognized as a key transitional figure into the modern period in the West, the extent to which he drew upon the church's premodern disciplinary heritage, carrying it forward by transposing it into a renewed, relatively democratized key, has too often been de-emphasized or overlooked.[7] For John Calvin, the Christian reformations of his age had everything to do with formation, and for many Protestant theologies and communities today, *semper reformanda*, revisiting Calvin's work from this angle may well open up promising new patterns of thought and life.

In the end, this book is a critical, constructive retrieval of Calvin's reforming project, always with a view to how that project may be inherited and developed by Christian communities today. Though the argument is grounded historically, part I is by no means a comprehensive historical sketch, but rather a partial, strategic one, highlighting particular aspects of Calvin's work that his recent interpreters typically have left in the shadows.[8] Likewise, part II is a close, constructive read-

---

7. Max Weber famously argued that the sixteenth-century European reformations involved forms of "inner-worldly asceticism" *(innerweltliche Askese)*: "The religious life of the saints," he wrote, "as distinguished from the natural life, was — the most important point — no longer lived outside the world in monastic communities, but within the world and its institutions." Similarly, in *The Theology of John Calvin*, Karl Barth wrote that "the Reformation was at least also an extension of the monastic line," indeed nothing less than monasticism's "most powerful offensive" by which it "broke out of the cloister and became a universal matter." And more recently, Charles Taylor has put the idea this way: "with the Protestant Reformation . . . [m]onastic rules disappear, but ordinary lay life is now under more stringent demands. Some of the ascetic norms of monastic life are now transferred to the secular." Calvin's chief interpreters, however, have by and large declined to read his work through this kind of lens, electing instead to emphasize the disjunctions between Calvin and monasticism, rather than the striking parallels between them. Weber's quip that the Protestant reformers "slammed the door of the monastery" comes to mind as an apt slogan for much of this scholarship. See Max Weber, *The Protestant Ethic and the Spirit of Capitalism* (London: Routledge, 1992), pp. 100-101; Karl Barth, *The Theology of John Calvin* (Grand Rapids: Eerdmans, 1995), pp. 50-51; and Charles Taylor, *A Secular Age* (Cambridge: Harvard University Press, Belknap Press, 2007), p. 266.

8. For relatively recent work calling attention to formational dimensions of Calvin's thought, see, for example, on contemplative and experiential aspects of Calvin's doctrine, Randall Zachman, *John Calvin as Teacher, Pastor, and Theologian* (Grand Rapids: Baker Academic, 2006), especially pp. 77-102; on the "virtue-shaping" function of Calvin's doctrine, Ellen Charry, *By the Renewing of Your Minds: The Pastoral Function of Christian Doctrine* (New York: Oxford University Press, 1997), pp. 199-221; on eucharistic di-

Introduction

ing of key themes in the *Institutio,* framing them as examples of Calvin's formational approach to doctrine. And in part III, of course, my constructive designs for contemporary Protestant theology come front and center, but in fact, they set the terms of analysis and discussion from the outset. Christian theology in the Reformed tradition, I contend, among other streams of Christian thought, should take a more explicitly, more decisively formational turn in the twenty-first century — and in this respect, we may find no better guide than John Calvin.

---

mensions of Calvin's thought, Brian Gerrish, *Grace and Gratitude: The Eucharist in John Calvin's Theology* (Minneapolis: Fortress, 1993); on Calvin's rhetoric, Serene Jones, *Calvin and the Rhetoric of Piety* (Louisville: Westminster John Knox, 1995), and David Willis, "Rhetoric and Responsibility in Calvin's Theology," in *The Context of Contemporary Theology,* ed. Alexander McKelway and David Willis (Atlanta: John Knox, 1974), pp. 43-64; on creation and law, Serene Jones, "Glorious Creation, Beautiful Law," in *Feminist and Womanist Essays in Reformed Dogmatics,* ed. Amy Plantinga Pauw and Serene Jones (Louisville: Westminster John Knox, 2006); and on spirituality, Lucien Richard, *The Spirituality of John Calvin* (Atlanta: John Knox, 1974). With the exception of Richard, however, these scholars treat neither the distinctive suite of formative practices Calvin had in mind for Christian discipleship nor the ways in which, in his doctrinal work, he sought to serve that practical program.

PART I

Storming the Sanctuary

And so there were on the mountain monastic cells like tents, filled with divine choirs of people singing psalms, reading and praying.... They appeared to inhabit an infinitely large area, a town removed from worldly matters, full of piety and justice.

Athanasius, *The Life of Antony* 44

CHAPTER 1

The City a Desert

On a late summer day in Geneva, 1535, a violent mob stormed the Convent of St. Clare. As one sister later described it in her polemic memoir, the intruders numbered well over one hundred men, wielding "arms and weapons and all kinds of swords and dreadful instruments." Outbreaks of iconoclastic violence were on the rise in the city, and so the nuns had already removed and hidden the most precious "objects of piety" the mob had come to destroy. But the wild-eyed throng, not to be denied, forced the doorman to lead them to the secret cache, and once there, they set about their brutal work. "Like enraged wolves," the sister wrote, "they destroyed those fine images with great axes and hammers, especially going after the blessed crucifix, which was wonderfully handsome, and the image of Our Lady." As the hammers fell, the women withdrew to the chapel, "cried out for mercy without ceasing, and a terrible cry could be heard faraway; the whole convent resonated with the violence."[1]

Less than a week later, the Poor Clares abandoned Geneva for good, and the city council took possession of the convent, eventually converting it to a hospital. That same month, the council seized all other church property within and around the city walls, and by the spring of 1536, Geneva had formally declared itself an "evangelical" stronghold. Priests and monastics converted, or fled. The coins minted that year in Geneva bore a new motto, a slogan that would soon be-

---

1. See Jeanne de Jussie, *The Short Chronicle: A Poor Clare's Account of the Reformation of Geneva* (Chicago: University of Chicago Press, 2006), pp. 138-40.

come a rallying cry for sixteenth-century reformers across western Europe: *post tenebras lux*, "after darkness, light."[2]

The Rule of Life

And so when the young French lawyer and theologian John Calvin first set foot in the city, just three months after the council's declaration, the tides of reform had already turned against monasteries and monastic life — and not only in Geneva. That very year, five hundred miles to the north and west, the English Parliament authorized Henry VIII to disband hundreds of monasteries across England, Ireland, and Wales, confiscating fantastic amounts of land and treasure for the royal coffers. Analogous precedents for these maneuvers, each driven by its own mixture of motives, had recently appeared in Denmark, Sweden, and the Swiss city-states. For their part, reform-minded theologians took aim at monasticism in sermons, songs, pamphlets, broadsheets, and books, including tracts by Martin Luther, the audacious Augustinian monk who denounced monastic vows as unscriptural and unchristian.[3] It comes as no surprise, then, that Calvin, too, over more than twenty years of teaching, preaching, and writing in Geneva, developed his own critique of monasticism in what would become his signature theological work, *Institutio Christianae Religionis*.[4]

What may come as a surprise, however, is the basis of Calvin's critique in the first place. Put briefly, in the *Institutio* Calvin grounds his quarrel with monasticism — in an endorsement of monasticism. That is, his argument hinges on a contrast between contemporary and ancient forms of monastic life, and a close reading of his case illuminates

---

2. Robert M. Kingdon, ed., *Transition and Revolution: Problems and Issues of European Renaissance and Reformation History* (Minneapolis: Burgess, 1974), p. 67.

3. See, e.g., Luther's *Method of Confessing* (1520), in *Dr. Martin Luthers Werke* (Weimar: Böhlau, 1883-1993), 6:167ff.; *Topics on Vows* (1521), in *Dr. Martin Luthers Werke*, 8:313-66; and *On Monastic Vows* (1521), in *Dr. Martin Luthers Werke*, 8:564-669.

4. This title is typically translated into English as "Institutes of the Christian Religion," though as I shall argue, this translation is unfortunate in several respects, not least because it obscures the formational dimensions of Calvin's overall approach. In any case, while the *Institutio* became the work for which Calvin is most widely known, it was by no means his only major theological project. See above, my introduction, pp. 5-6.

not only his views on the cloister, but also his overall vision of Christian discipleship as an immersive path of practical formation. For Calvin, monastics are mistaken only insofar as they make elite, difficult, and rare what should be ordinary, accessible, and common in Christian communities: namely, whole human lives formed in and through the church's distinctive repertoire of disciplines, from singing psalms to daily prayer to communing with Christ at the sacred supper.

Thus Calvin positions himself not only *against* monasticism as a critic, but also alongside monasticism as a fellow heir to the church's practical treasury. He argues that this inheritance belongs as much to the common laity as to monastics, and that the time has come for the whole church to reclaim what is rightfully hers. In this sense Calvin, too, sought to storm the privileged sanctuaries of late medieval Europe, though in a way quite different from the violent invasion of the Convent of St. Clare. For while the mob meant to destroy the "objects of piety" they understood as idols, Calvin's principal aim was restorative: he set out to recover the objects and practices of piety he understood as fit not for an exceptional class, but for the whole people of God without exception. For Calvin, even ordinary Christian life is a disciplined life, a life of discipleship formed in and through a particular suite of disciplines, and so at every turn in his theological and reforming work, Calvin sought to serve the church's broad program of practical formation.

On one hand, in the *Institutio* Calvin casts his monastic contemporaries as models of corruption, men "polluted by all sorts of foul vices; nowhere do factions, hatreds, party zeal, and intrigue burn more fiercely."[5] Moreover, he diagnoses the ailment as finally institutional, not merely personal: "I have spoken rather of monasticism than of monks, and noted not those faults which inhere in the life of a few, but those which cannot be separated from the order of living itself" (*ICR* 4.13.15).[6] But on the other hand, at the same time, Calvin frames his cri-

---

5. John Calvin, *Institutes of the Christian Religion*, ed. John T. McNeill (Philadelphia: Westminster, 1960), 4.13.15 (hereafter cited as *ICR*; section references cited in parentheses in the text).

6. David Steinmetz opens his incisive essay "Calvin and the Monastic Ideal" by quoting this sentence from the *Institutio*, thereby leaving the misleading impression that Calvin's critique applies to monasticism per se. In context, however, the sentence actually conveys a quite different idea, since the "order of living" in view here is the monasticism of Calvin's own day *as opposed to* ancient monasticism, an order of living for which

tique by way of a fundamental contrast: on one side, the "present-day monasticism" he condemns, and on the other, what he calls the "holy and lawful monasticism" of an earlier age. Thus with every blow Calvin strikes against the corrupted descendant, he thereby commends the venerable ancestor. For in the days of Augustine, Calvin contends, "a far different mode of living once prevailed in monasteries," and this mode of living had at least two advantages (4.12.8, 10).

First, ancient monasteries were strongholds of spiritual "severity" and "discipline." "They slept on the ground," Calvin writes, "their drink was water; their food bread, vegetables, and roots," and their time was spent (here Calvin quotes Augustine directly) "'together, living in prayers, readings, and discussions. . . . Brotherly love especially is kept: diet, speech, clothing, countenance — all are conformed to it'" (4.13.8, 9).[7] But these living conditions and everyday practices were not ends in themselves, but rather, formative "preliminaries" by which the monks "prepared themselves for greater tasks": namely, the pastoral and episcopal leadership of the church. In other words, "the monastic colleges were, so to speak, seminaries of the ecclesiastical order," preparing and forming such "great and outstanding men" as "Gregory of Nazianzus, Basil, and Chrysostom" for the pastorate or bishopric, precisely so "they might be fitter and better trained to undertake so great an office." Thus for Calvin, ancient monastic life was commendable first of all because it took place for the sake of the fitness and formation of church leadership, and in that sense for the sake of the church universal (4.13.8).

The second advantage follows from the first, since as Calvin conceives it, a shepherd's practical piety should never surpass the capacities of his flock. "Augustine requires a kind of monasticism," he writes,

---

Calvin has considerable respect. Here is the sentence in context (emphasis added): "These differences which I have so far recounted *between the ancient monks and the monks of our time* are not in morals but in the profession itself. Let my readers accordingly remember that I have spoken rather of monasticism than of monks, and noted not those faults which inhere in the life of a few, but those which cannot be separated from the order of living itself." Thus the contrast Calvin draws in this passage is actually between "the profession itself" practiced by (1) "the ancient monks," for whom Calvin has qualified praise, and (2) "the monks of our time," for whom Calvin has little but condemnation. See David Steinmetz, "Calvin and the Monastic Ideal," in *Calvin in Context* (New York: Oxford University Press, 1995), pp. 187-98.

7. Here Calvin quotes and summarizes Augustine, *On the Morals of the Catholic Church* 31.67; 33.70-73.

"which is but an exercise and aid to those duties of piety enjoined upon all Christians" (4.13.10).[8] Far from a special, independent class of Christian virtuosos, these monks were taught to serve so that "by their example they may shed a light" for other Christians in their own education and development, the better to help "preserve the unity of the church" (4.13.10). Accordingly, an ancient monk's piety was typical and accessible, not extraordinary. If he spent his time "living in prayers, readings, and discussions," if he let neighborly love form even his "diet, speech, clothing, countenance," he merely modeled the kind of training and discipleship to which "all Christians" are called.

From this angle, then, Calvin commends ancient monastic life not only because it helped form church leaders, but also because it was consistent with Christian formation generally, prescribing, developing, and demonstrating the very "duties of piety" that apply to every disciple, bar none. In this way, Calvin extols ancient monasticism for what he takes to be its service to the wider church on the one hand, and its spiritual accessibility on the other. And precisely here, in clear view of this allegedly "holy and lawful monasticism" of Augustine and Gregory and Basil and Chrysostom, Calvin delivers his critique of "present-day" monastic life.

Rather than building up spiritually fit church leaders, Calvin contends, "our monks" orchestrate "a conspiracy by which a few men, bound together among themselves, are separated from the whole body of the church." And likewise, rather than building up exemplary disciples for "all Christians" to imitate, "our monks are not content with that piety to which Christ enjoins his followers to attend with unremitting zeal. Instead, they dream up some new sort of piety to meditate upon in order to become more perfect than all other people." Thus Calvin charges contemporary monasticism with separatism on the one hand and elitism on the other — contrasting perfectly with the sup-

---

8. The term "piety" is central to Calvin's whole theological approach, and we will examine the term in more detail in chapter 3. For now, suffice it to say that at the outset of the *Institutio* (1.2.1) Calvin defines the term this way: "I call 'piety' [*pietas*] that reverence joined with love of God which the knowledge of his benefits induces." For an overview of how flexible and wide-ranging the term is in Calvin's work, see Sou-Young Lee, "Calvin's Understanding of Pietas," in *Calvinus Sincerioris Religionis Vindex: Calvin as Protector of the Purer Religion,* ed. Wilhelm H. Neuser and Brian G. Armstrong, Sixteenth Century Essays and Studies, vol. 36 (Kirksville, Mo.: Sixteenth Century Journal, 1997), pp. 225-39.

posed ecclesial service and spiritual accessibility of its ancient counterpart (4.13.10).[9]

On both counts, then, Calvin's fundamental concern is to reject what he calls "double Christianity," conceived either as two separate camps side by side or as two separate ranks in a hierarchy of discipleship. By setting up a "private altar," he argues, sixteenth-century monastic communities "have both excommunicated themselves from the whole body of the church and despised the ordinary ministry," thus creating two camps or kinds of Christianity. And by inventing and vowing to carry out a "new sort of piety," these monks claim that "a more perfect rule of life can be devised than the common one committed by God to the whole church," thus creating a two-tiered ladder of Christian perfection (4.13.10, 12).

Against all this, Calvin sets not a vision of a world without monasticism, but rather an appreciative portrait of the ancient monastic approach. In those days, he writes, there was but one "rule of life" common to all Christians, one set of "duties of piety," and monasteries served as laboratories of "exercise and aid" for learning how to follow that rule and discharge those duties, all in the service of forming the piety of the wider church. As long as monks remained what Calvin calls "part of the people," the monastic office was an honorable one, and the monastery was a useful showcase and training ground for practical formation.

The historical accuracy of Calvin's portrait of ancient monasti-

---

9. Revealingly, Calvin pursues an analogous line of criticism against the Anabaptists, whom he took to be attempting to establish an unduly separatist, perfectionist, elitist form of life set against and apart from the world. As Susan Schreiner has argued, Calvin objects to such "otherworldly perfectionism" both because it claims for itself a specious ecclesial and spiritual purity and because it presents a divisive, disruptive danger to the common social order. For Calvin, Christians are called to live in and among the world, where every human heart (even and especially Christian hearts) and every human institution (even and especially the Christian church) are a mixture of good and evil, righteousness and wickedness, humility and hypocrisy. See Susan Schreiner, *The Theater of His Glory: Nature and the Natural Order in the Thought of John Calvin* (Durham, N.C.: Labyrinth Press, 1991), especially pp. 83-85. Cf. Calvin, *ICR* 3.3.14. See also Bruce Gordon, *Calvin* (New Haven: Yale University Press, 2009), p. 277: "Society for Calvin was mixed. The faithful . . . are called to live in communities, not to exclude themselves. This was at the root of Calvin's objection to the Anabaptists and to any suggestion of moral perfection in this world." Building up from Calvin's position here, in part III, I briefly critique the argument advanced by Stanley Hauerwas and William Willimon in *Resident Aliens: Life in the Christian Colony* (Nashville: Abingdon, 1989); see below, chapter 11, note 8.

cism is, for my purposes here, beside the point. The point is this: Calvin's critique of sixteenth-century monasticism is taken up from a position sympathetic to what he takes to be the original, authentic monastic mission, namely, to manifest and facilitate the practical formation of individual disciples and, crucially, the church as a whole. In a characteristic move, Calvin arraigns the corruption of the present by commending the allegedly sound, exemplary, bygone practices of the past.

And so we might expect him to complete this familiar rhetorical pattern with a call for restoration. That is, in a typical Protestant polemic, comparing the present unfavorably with the "holy and lawful" past is prologue to an appeal for a contemporary renewal, a modern recovery of the older, "original," bona fide way of life. But Calvin issues no such appeal. He does not recommend a return to the fourth-century monastic model. For as it turns out, in one key respect, his critique applies even to the days of Augustine: "I grant that they were not superstitious in the outward exercise of a quite rigid discipline, yet I say that they were not without *immoderate affectation and perverse zeal*. It was a beautiful thing to forsake all their possessions and be without earthly care. But God prefers devoted care in ruling a household, where the devout householder, clear and free of all greed, ambition, and other lusts of the flesh, keeps before him the purpose of serving God in a definite calling" (4.13.16, emphasis added). Ancient monasticism may have been a commendable, "beautiful thing," but something else is more beautiful still — and so God "prefers" it. Without withdrawing his praise for the alleged ecclesial service and spiritual accessibility of ancient monasticism, and in fact extending the logic underpinning this praise, Calvin argues that God prefers the "devoted care" of a householder managing his possessions to that of a monk who has forsaken his. For while both may be "devout" — that is, suitably disciplined and therefore "free of all greed, ambition, and other lusts of the flesh" — the householder's devotion is properly tempered and formed, neither "immoderate" nor "perverse." That is, the devout householder "keeps before him the purpose of serving God in a definite calling," and so his life is not set apart such that he may live "without earthly care." On the contrary, his cares are decidedly earthly, and he thereby serves God in heaven through the nit and grit of a particular vocation on earth.

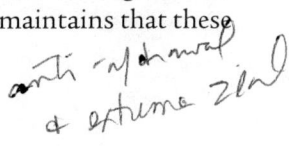

Thus Calvin not only rejects the idea that cloistered life "is the best way of all to attain perfection" such that "all other callings of God are regarded as unworthy by comparison." He also maintains that these "other callings of God" are actually preferable to the cloister as venues for Christian formation. In this way, like so many sixteenth-century reformers, Calvin seeks to overturn some long-standing tables of vocational prestige — and to do so, he mounts arguments on both scriptural and moral grounds (4.13.11).

First, since on his reading of Scripture many "other callings" are mentioned and approved "by God's own testimony," and the call to the cloister is not, Calvin concludes that these "other callings" are in fact the higher ones. "I should like to ask [the present-day monks]," he writes, "why they dignify their order alone with the title of perfection, and take the same title away from all God's callings," particularly since "their order" is "an institution nowhere approved by even one syllable" of Holy Writ. Calvin stops short of disputing the monks' claim to being on a path of "acquiring perfection"; his point is that they have no right to claim this title for themselves alone, since the status applies to "all God's callings." As we shall see, this expansive, relatively democratizing logic is a key signature of Calvin's approach. But at the same time, by invoking the divine "testimony" of Scripture, Calvin lays the standard Protestant groundwork for nevertheless discrediting the supposed call to the cloister (4.13.11).

Second, now arguing on broadly moral grounds, Calvin contends that a formational path lived in and through the world of "earthly care" is more in keeping with Christian humility, philanthropy, and responsibility: "It is not the part of Christian meekness, as if in hatred of the human race, to flee to the desert and the wilderness and at the same time to forsake those duties which the Lord has especially commanded." Calvin leaves these special commands unspecified, but for him they presumably run the scriptural gamut from Genesis ("be fruitful and multiply") to the Decalogue ("honor your father and mother") to any number of works of mercy ("care for the widow and the orphan"). In a word, Calvin indicts the ancient monks for being overzealous, manifesting an "immoderate affectation and perverse zeal" that in practice cut them off from a range of Christian virtues and obligations. And accordingly, in direct contrast to such intemperance, Calvin insists that Christian "meekness" and love for humanity are better incarnated in the ordinary spheres of household and city than in the extraordinary seclusion of the desert (4.13.16).

In the end, then, Calvin's critique of ancient monasticism turns out to be a logical extension of his praise for it, in effect a charge that the ancients did not go far enough along their own admirable path. If a monastery in Augustine's day was a laboratory and showcase for training church leaders and, by example, helping to form "all Christians," Calvin commends the early monks for their ecclesial service and spiritual accessibility — and then critiques them for not sufficiently living up to their own standards. For, after all, the monastic way of life would be most widely and effectively exemplary for "all Christians" precisely to the extent that it is made (1) maximally available within the wider spheres of church and society, not secluded from them, and (2) maximally compatible with common vocational circumstances — say, those of a "devout householder," or indeed those of "all the kinds of life ordained by [God] and praised by his own testimony" (4.13.11).

Is this an attack on monasticism, even in its ancient form? It is, and it strikes at the very root of the idea that in order to pursue Christian perfection, an individual or group of disciples should set themselves alone and therefore apart from common human life ("monastic" and "monk" derive from the Greek *monos*, "alone").[10] But at the same time, Calvin grounds the attack in a profound affirmation of the basic formative project undertaken by the ancient cenobitic (i.e., communal) monks: to live lives of comprehensive religious discipline, immersed in "prayers, readings, and discussions" such that even the most mundane, everyday activity — "diet, speech, clothing, countenance" — is formed by love (4.13.9). Far from condemning this kind of life, Calvin commends it, not only for an elite class of spiritual savants, but even for every Christian man and woman without exception, since all properly live under God's single "rule of life" revealed in Scripture.[11]

Calvin critiques monasticism, then, chiefly in its sixteenth-

---

10. It is a matter of some debate whether the root *monos* (alone) should be etymologically interpreted to indicate (1) monasticism's *contra mundum* withdrawal, (2) the single-mindedness of the monastic vocation, or (3) both at once. This debate itself reflects the considerable historical variety among so-called monastic forms of life, many of which involve significant engagement with the nonmonastic world. Nevertheless, the idea of withdrawal is both historically and intellectually bound up with Christian monasticism to a considerable degree, and in his critique, Calvin makes this idea his principal target.

11. In a sermon later published under the title "The Word Our Only Rule," Calvin makes a compact homiletical version of this point, arguing that since God provides all Christians with the only proper "rule of life" in the word of God revealed in Scripture, all other rules amount to "robbing God of His honor, and giving it, as a spoil, to mortal men." See John Calvin, *The Mystery of Godliness and Other Sermons* (Morgan, Pa.: Soli Deo Gloria Publications, 1999), pp. 69-80.

century but also in its ancient form, for making elite, difficult, and rare what should be ordinary, accessible, and common across the Christian church. According to this view, monastics are not mistaken in their attempt to live out lives of immersive formation by means of the church's disciplinary treasury. Their mistake, Calvin contends, is to do so at arm's length — geographically and spiritually — from the wider spheres of church and society. Parallels and precedents for this line of criticism may be found among Calvin's contemporaries,[12] and indeed scattered throughout the varied history of Christian monasticism itself.[13] In

---

12. Among sixteenth-century precedents, Desiderius Erasmus's preface to his *Enchiridion* (1518) and Philip Melanchthon's *Loci Communes Theologici* (1521) are representative: after an appreciative portrait of ancient monasticism, Erasmus writes, "Such were the first beginnings of monasticism, and such its patriarchs. Then gradually, with the passage of time, wealth grew, and with wealth ceremonies; and the genuine piety and simplicity grew cool. . . . And yet because of their dress, or because of some name they bear, they claim so much sanctity for themselves that compared with them they think other people hardly Christians." Melanchthon puts it this way: "At one time the monasteries were nothing but schools, and the unmarried scholars voluntarily spent their time there as long as they liked. They had all things in common with their fellow students. . . . They sang, prayed, and discussed matters together. The whole manner of life was not regarded as some peculiar type of Christianity or a state of perfection, as they now speak of it, but rather as a discipline and training for the immature. Would that this were the condition of the monasteries today!" See *The Correspondence of Erasmus*, trans. R. A. B. Mynors and D. F. S. Thomson (Toronto: University of Toronto Press, 1982), vol. 6, no. 858, p. 89, and Wilhelm Pauck, ed., *Melanchthon and Bucer*, Library of Christian Classics, vol. 19 (Philadelphia: Westminster, 1969), pp. 60-61.

13. In Christian monasticism's inaugural days in fourth-century Egypt, eremitic (solitary) monks were unmatched in spiritual prestige, widely admired for braving the desert's demons in a kind of living martyrdom; but even as early as John Cassian's *Institutiones*, more communal forms of monastic life began to emerge as the more typical, recommended norm, if only as necessary preparation for solitary spiritual battle. From there, it was a short step to the exaltation of cenobitic (communal) monasticism in its own right, in effect expanding the hermit's prestige to encompass the whole cloister. And in later centuries, the circle of those living under a "rule of life" expanded further, first to include not only cloistered monks but also secular priests ("canons regular"); again in the twelfth century to include orders of Christian knights; and again in the thirteenth century to include mendicant orders of friars (Franciscans, Dominicans, and others) who emphasized not so much geographic withdrawal from the world as apostolic immersion in it, the better to preach the gospel and serve the poor. All the while, of course, traditional cloistered life continued apace in countless monasteries, with varying levels of religious prestige and social power; even eremitic solitude enjoyed an occasional renaissance. But amid all this flux and variety among monastic movements, a relatively democratizing, relatively inclusive impulse is discernible here and there,

fact, the expansive, relatively democratizing logic underpinning the critique is a characteristic pattern of thought among reformers in sixteenth-century Europe, many of whom often sought not to eliminate a given practice or institution (e.g., priesthood, the Mass, and so on), but rather to expand access to its key privileges and responsibilities. In his *Institutio,* Calvin makes this approach his own, and it illuminates not only his views on monasticism, but also his overall vision of Christian discipleship as an immersive path of practical formation fully engaged in ordinary, "earthly" life.

To sum up: in Calvin's view, the best features of ancient monasticism point toward their own fulfillment in a pervasive mode of life, a mode in which the formative project often associated with monasteries and monks — "acquiring perfection" through lives of practical formation in and toward union with God — is reclaimed as the work of the whole Christian community, and so of every individual Christian disciple. In this new world, which Calvin believed was dawning in his day, all forms of "double Christianity" would be set aside. As in the fabled days of old, a single "rule of life" would prevail among Christians, not writ small into a particular cloister, but rather writ large across the broadest

---

sometimes overt (as in certain passages in Augustine, for example, on which Calvin seizes; or among early followers of Francis of Assisi, who emphasized the spiritual stature of lay monks within his order), sometimes implicit, but in any case constituting one side of an abiding, creative tension within monastic evolution and development. Some medieval lay movements, too, moved in similar directions: in Italy, for example, the Patarines pursued a simple, quasi-monastic life together of sharing and prayer; in Germany, the Hirsau reform sought to establish a domestic lay lifestyle inspired by monastic ideals; and in Lombardy, the early Humiliati, as Lawrence Cunningham has put it, "were groping toward some kind of life in which all classes could share in the gospel life," insisting that "ordinary lay life and work were compatible with the reforming impulses once almost exclusively found within the traditional religious orders." Even Bernard of Clairvaux (whom Calvin admired and often quoted in the *Institutio*), while frequently insisting that a monk's proper place was in the cloister, also taught that within the cloistered world, a life of contemplative, mystical union with God was an attainable ideal not only for a few virtuosos, as was commonly thought, but also for large numbers of monks. As we shall see, Calvin's work on "mystical union" with God as available (and necessary) for all Christians may be interpreted as a move along an analogous trajectory. See, e.g., R. A. Markus, *The End of Ancient Christianity* (Cambridge: Cambridge University Press, 1990); Christopher Brooke, *The Age of the Cloister: The Story of Monastic Life in the Middle Ages* (Mahwah, N.J.: Paulist, 2003); and Lawrence S. Cunningham, *Francis of Assisi: Performing the Gospel Life* (Grand Rapids: Eerdmans, 2004), pp. 27-28. For Bernard's relatively expansive view of the mystical life, see Brooke, pp. 170-71.

patterns of society, the better to clarify and renew the common "duties of piety" originally "committed by God to the whole church" (4.13.12).

Christian *Paideia*

Is John Calvin, then, best understood as a kind of crypto-monastic theologian, criticizing monks and monasticism while simultaneously advocating an expanded "monkhood of all believers"? As a rhetorical figure, the idea of an inclusive monastic office was by no means unheard of in Calvin's day. Desiderius Erasmus, for example, put it this way in the preface to the 1518 edition of his *Enchiridion,* itself a formation-oriented primer on Christian life: "Why do we so closely confine [to monks] the professed service of Christ, which he wished to be as wide open as possible? If we are moved by splendid names, what else, I ask you, is a city than a great monastery [*magnum monasterium*]?"[14]

As we have seen, however, for Calvin the term "monasticism" signals an order of living too zealously differentiated from church and society, and so to call Calvin "monastic," or even to interpret him as standing within an explicitly "monastic" stream of development, can only muddy the terminological water. Moreover, the rhetorical choreography of Calvin's case — appealing first to the "ancient monks" of the fourth century against the "present-day monks," and then critiquing the ancients, too — indicates that Calvin understood himself to be drawing on Christian traditions of practical formation both deeper and wider than their monastic incarnations. That is, Calvin did not conceive himself as an heir to a distinctively *monastic* treasury of formative practices, but rather to an even older, distinctively *scriptural and early ecclesial* treasury of such practices, the original well from which the monastics themselves originally drew, and continued to draw, in their own various ways.

In other words, Calvin's argument with monasticism is over how to properly live out the ancient Christian panoply of formative disci-

---

14. *The Correspondence of Erasmus,* vol. 6, no. 858, p. 89; see also vol. 2, no. 296, p. 297: "How much more consonant with Christ's teaching it would be to regard the entire Christian world as a single household, a single monastery as it were." Indeed, Erasmus's critique of monasticism — and clericalism generally — in the epistolary preface to the 1518 *Enchiridion* is in several respects strikingly resonant with Calvin's case. For a brief discussion of Erasmus's figure of the *civitas* as a "great monastery," see Diarmaid MacCulloch, *The Reformation: A History* (London: Penguin Books, 2003), p. 104.

plines as an integrated, holistic way of life, and so in this sense, at its heart the argument is over Christian *paideia* (formative education). In the New Testament, the term *paideia* is typically translated as "training," "discipline," or "instruction,"[15] and in the Greek-speaking ancient world, *paideia* referred to a formative program by which a person was educated and acculturated into a particular kind of human being and human life.[16] In the late modern West, the underlying concept is perhaps most familiar in connection with child rearing, that is, with the all-encompassing regimen of "raising" children into a particular style and constellation of values, virtues, manners, capacities, and know-how. In a similar way, the earliest monastic movements were attempts to apply this approach to Christianity, to "raise" Christian disciples via a distinct disciplinary program carried out within a distinct disciplinary society. But the approach itself is not identical with those movements; it is not essentially "monastic" in the first place. Rather, it is essentially paideutic, in the New Testament and early ecclesial sense of the term *paideia,* "formative education." And likewise, it is essentially

---

15. The word *paideia* features prominently in three New Testament passages: (1) Eph. 6:4, where the term is linked to humane child-rearing: "Fathers, do not provoke your children to anger, but bring them up in the discipline and instruction [*paideia*] of the Lord"; (2) Heb. 12:5ff., where the term is again linked to child-rearing, though this time with an emphasis on God's disciplinary role as parent: "My child, do not regard lightly the discipline [*paideias*] of the Lord"; and (3) 2 Tim. 3:14-16, where the term is linked to training in righteousness, and to the role of Scripture in such training: "All scripture is inspired by God and is useful for teaching, for reproof, for correction, and for training [*paideian*] in righteousness."

16. On *paideia*, see Werner Jaeger, *Early Christianity and Greek Paideia* (Cambridge: Harvard University Press, 1961) and *Paideia: The Ideals of Greek Culture* (New York: Oxford University Press, 1943-45); see also H. I. Marrou, *A History of Education in Antiquity* (New York: Sheed and Ward, 1956). On *paideia* in the context of Christian theological education, see David Kelsey, *To Understand God Truly: What's Theological about a Theological School* (Louisville: Westminster John Knox, 1992), and Edward Farley, *Theologia: The Fragmentation and Unity of Theological Education* (Philadelphia: Fortress, 1983). The term *paideia* is appropriate to an analysis of Calvin's work for at least three reasons: first, the term's New Testament and patristic pedigree; second, its Hellenistic association with a practical, life-encompassing pedagogy in which the student is formed toward an ideal image of humanity; and third, the fact that the term has often indicated a style of formation grounded in a literary canon: in the ancient Greek context, Homeric epics and, later, a range of philosophical texts; and in the Christian patristic context, the canon of Christian Scripture. In each case, proper paideutic formation was thought to result from extensive and intensive engagement with the respective (oral or written) tradition — and in his theological and reforming work, Calvin takes up this idea in his own distinctive way.

ascetic, in the original athletic sense of the term *askesis*, "exercise" or "athletic training," a word borrowed from the Greek gymnasium.

Thus Calvin and the monastics generally agree that Christian life is fundamentally paideutic and ascetic, a life of formative education, practical training, and spiritual discipline. Moreover, as we will see, they largely agree on which early church disciplines constitute the proper paideutic repertoire: scriptural study, daily prayer and worship, psalm singing, moral accountability, the Lord's Supper, and so on. Where they disagree is over precisely how — and by whom — this *paideia* is properly lived out. And so if Calvin's preferred suite of formative practices bears a remarkable resemblance to certain monastic repertoires, this does not, Calvin would insist, indicate any direct dependence on monasticism. Rather, it indicates that both Calvin and the monastics are dependent on what they take to be the church's ancient disciplinary treasury laid out in Scripture and other early Christian texts. To put the point briefly: Calvin is no son of monasticism, but he is close kin, and the family resemblance is striking.

For if we set aside those aspects of monasticism that Calvin found objectionable — the alleged separatism and spiritual elitism that produced forms of "double Christianity" — we may then ask: What are the broad distinguishing marks of an ideal monk in medieval western Europe? He is literate and educated, able to carry out extensive, intensive study of Scripture and liturgical texts; his day is structured according to a regular daily prayer regime and frequent, mandatory worship; he chants the Psalms regularly and frequently, so as to be formed by them; his moral life is closely regulated and intensively surveyed by those around him, his brothers and especially his superiors; and above all, his governing telos, the underlying goal that organizes everything else, is a life of practical sanctification and, ultimately, mystical union with God. His whole day, his whole life, his whole being — body, soul, mind, and strength — is ideally implicated in this scriptural-liturgical-moral program, all the way down to "diet, speech, clothing, countenance." Accordingly, he lives "in prayers, readings, and discussions" — or, as Athanasius puts it in his *Life of Antony*, a text at the headwaters of Christian monasticism, he lives "singing psalms, reading, and praying" in a community "removed from worldly matters, full of piety and justice."[17]

---

17. Athanasius, *Life of Antony* 44, in *Early Christian Lives*, trans. Carolinne White (London: Penguin Classics, 1998), p. 36.

How does this ideal vision compare with Calvin's vision for Geneva? Unlike Athanasius and Antony, of course, Calvin endorses no retreat into the wilderness. He does not seek to make "the desert a city."[18] But in an intriguing sense, Calvin sets out to effect the opposite transformation: that is, to make "the city a desert" in which Genevans, like Israelites newly freed from Egyptian slavery, might undergo a paideutic, ascetic journey of liberation, sanctification, and renewed intimacy with God.[19] For more than a millennium, Christian monastics had found the wider world's ways and conditions to be variously inhospitable to this kind of rigorous Christian formation — and with this much, Calvin wholeheartedly agrees. He too finds the conventional everyday life of his time deeply at odds with the needs of Christian piety: "the world, according to the depravity of its own disposition, has always repelled with such obstacles as it could the helps by which it ought to have been led to God" (*ICR* 4.13.1). And accordingly, he too calls for a "rule for regulating life well," an ascetic rule that begins with "renouncing our former life," that is, our "impiety and worldly desires."[20] But rather than design an alternative society set off within or apart from "the world" of Geneva, Calvin sets out to remake the city itself — or rather, he sets out to participate in God's remaking of it.

---

18. This phrase, which derives from Athanasius's *Life of Antony* 14, has become iconic. See, e.g., Derwas J. Chitty, *The Desert a City: An Introduction to the Study of Egyptian and Palestinian Monasticism under the Christian Empire* (London: Mowbrays, 1977).

19. Again, this basic idea is by no means unique to Calvin. In fact, as Paul Bradshaw has argued, the whole history of urban cenobitic monasticism may be fruitfully interpreted, in part, as a kind of hybrid between the eremitic disciplines of the desert on the one hand and the communal "cathedral office" piety of townsfolk on the other, in effect bringing the spirituality of the desert together with the spirituality of the city. Similarly, as Calvin himself points out in his portrait of ancient monasticism, early monasteries often served as training grounds for church leadership, and for many monks who became bishops, the project of translating monastic ideas and disciplines into versions practicable for laypeople throughout the church became a driving, influential mission. See Paul F. Bradshaw, *The Search for the Origins of Christian Worship: Sources and Methods for the Study of Early Liturgy* (New York: Oxford University Press, 2002), especially pp. 171ff.; *Early Christian Worship: A Basic Introduction to Ideas and Practice* (Collegeville, Minn.: Liturgical Press, 1996), especially pp. 72-74; and *Two Ways of Praying*, rev. ed. (White Sulphur Springs, W.Va.: OSL Publications, 2008). See also Markus, *End of Ancient Christianity*, especially chapter 13, "The Ascetic Invasion," pp. 199-211.

20. Calvin, "Commentary on Titus 2:12," in *Calvin's Commentaries,* vol. 21 (Grand Rapids: Baker, 1981), p. 318. For Calvin, of course, that "rule" is to be found in Holy Scripture.

And yet for Calvin, Christian life does involve being set apart, not via a geographical, social retreat to a monastic campus, but rather via a moral, existential brand of practical withdrawal from "the world" and "the depravity of its disposition." That is, Calvin envisions a reformed way of life robustly engaged in ordinary affairs that is nevertheless unconformed to their prevailing patterns and protocols, in effect a dispositional defection from the world while remaining ensconced within it. Christian life is fundamentally a life of "self-denial," of renouncing the world's ways of "self-interest" and "self-love": "Let this therefore be the first step," he writes, "that a man depart from himself in order that he may apply the whole force of his ability in the service of the Lord" (*ICR* 3.7.1, 4).[21]

Likewise, Calvin continues, Christian discipleship means a reformation of life ultimately manifest in *pietas,* the reverence and love for God "which joins us in true holiness with God when we are separated from the iniquities of the world" (3.7.3). This separation, then, is no escape into the desert, but it is a withdrawal from the world's "iniquities." It is a moral, existential, and practical separation, a kind of engaged detachment vis-à-vis the world, a renunciation that involves neither resentment nor retreat. It is a style of "contempt of the present life," as he puts it, that "engenders no hatred of it or ingratitude against God" (3.9.3). And in Calvin's view, precisely this kind of *contemptus mundi* should characterize the lives not merely of a special elite class, but also of each and every Christian disciple living in — but not of — the created, fallen world.

Thus in the heady, apocalyptic atmosphere of sixteenth-century western Europe, a world that popular preachers and placards declared was being "turned upside down," Calvin discerns a divine hand turning Christian piety, in effect, "inside out."[22] Cloistered monastics, by many

---

21. Calvin titles this well-known chapter, "The Sum of the Christian Life: The Denial of Ourselves."

22. The idea that Christians "turn the world upside down" derives from Acts 17:6. As a refrain picked up in the sixteenth-century European reformations, see, e.g., Peter Matheson, *The Imaginative World of the Reformation* (Edinburgh: T. & T. Clark, 2000), especially pp. 15, 18. Henry Cohn sketches several incidents of enforced "role reversal" during the Peasants' War, episodes in which peasant armies took possession of monasteries and compelled monks (or nuns) to wear peasants' clothes and carry out peasants' tasks outside the monastic grounds, while the victorious occupiers themselves donned monastic habits and furs — a vivid, brutal performance of a world turned both "upside down" and

considered the consummate "insiders" with respect to Christian formation and intimacy with God, are now driven "outside." Lay citizens, by many considered relative "outsiders" in these same respects, are now ushered in — that is, they are now enrolled, as Calvin envisions it, in a citywide paideutic program of practical formation. Now every Christian, rooted in her own particular calling and context, is to live out a life formed through disciplines only speciously reserved to cloistered specialists: Scripture reading, daily prayer regimes, psalm singing, and so on. As Erasmus might have styled it, now the monastery's perimeter would at last extend out to the city walls, and Geneva as a whole would become a *magnum monasterium* — or, in terms Calvin would have preferred, now Geneva as a whole would become a training ground for Christian sanctification and Christian life.

In other words, Calvin's ideal "devout householder" does not eschew the disciplines of the monastery, but rather reclaims them as a birthright to be lived out at home, in church, and in the marketplace. He too spends his time "living in prayers, readings, and discussions," precisely so that he might become and remain "clear and free of all greed, ambition, and other lusts of the flesh." He too lives a life of Christian *paideia*, walking a rigorous road of Christian practices, formation, *contemptus mundi*, and ongoing asceticism. But as he does so, the householder does not inhabit the traditional monastery's campus and cowl; instead, he lives abroad in the city, and in street clothes. He does not pore over Latin, Hebrew, or Greek scriptures in the cloister's library, or chant Latin psalms in the cloister's chapel; instead, with new vernacular Bibles and Psalters in hand, he studies and sings in his own mother tongue, in church and at home. He does not live under the moral surveillance of his brothers and his abbot; instead, he lives under the surveillance of his lay peers and elders, and under the authority of the city's consistory. And ultimately, he does not pursue and pray for mystical union with God by withdrawing into a narrow society of specialists. Instead, he pursues and prays for mystical union with God — "*unio mystica*" is Calvin's phrase in the *Institutio* (3.11.10) — in all things

---

"inside out." See Henry J. Cohn, "Changing Places: Peasants and Clergy 1525," in *Anticlericalism in Late Medieval and Early Modern Europe*, ed. Peter A. Dykema and Heiko A. Oberman (Leiden: Brill, 1993), pp. 545-57. For comparison with the seventeenth-century English context, see Christopher Hill, *The World Turned Upside Down: Radical Ideas during the English Revolution* (New York: Viking Press, 1972).

and with the whole church, preeminently and paradigmatically gathered at the table of the Lord's Supper.

John Calvin was no monastic.[23] But alongside and against monastics ancient and contemporary, he sought to reinterpret and restore the Christian paideutic tradition as the charter for all Christian discipleship. Understood this way, Calvin's project of religious and civic reform in Geneva amounts to an attempt to retrieve for all disciples the ascetic, disciplinary, paideutic approach to Christian life, and in particular to retrieve the distinctive practices that in his view constitute the *paideia* of the early church. Scripture reading, prayer regimes, psalm singing, moral surveillance and accountability, mystical union with God via the Lord's table — each one of these disciplines, along with the integrated program they constitute together, is refigured and returned in Calvin's work to what he considers its proper place: the fundamental, immersive, life-forming work of every Christian. Thus for Calvin, the Genevan reformation meant not so much the closing of the cloister as its grand reopening, in effect reclaiming the challenges and privileges of the monastic office — like the priestly one — as appropriate and available to "all believers."[24]

---

23. In fact, it is worth noting that among the major figures of the sixteenth-century European reformations (Erasmus, Luther, Zwingli, et al.), Calvin stands out as having been neither a monk nor a priest prior to his reforming work. He received theological and legal training in those early days, but was then a layman. On the other hand, however, as T. H. L. Parker has shown, Calvin's early schooling included studies at the College of Montaigu in Paris, which Parker describes as "an educational monastery" of "poor clerks who, under the most severe rules, were preparing to become priests and 'reformed' monks." The daily office was recited; feasts of the church were observed; and a "strict control of moral life" was kept, including intensive self-examination and "denunciation of one another" when appropriate. This early experience with an ascetic, liturgical, quasi-monastic style of education may well have been formative for the young Calvin and his developing ideas about Christian life. See T. H. L. Parker, *John Calvin: A Biography* (Louisville: Westminster John Knox, 2006), especially pp. 23-25.

24. "The priesthood of all believers" is a formula that derives from similar language in Luther's writing, not from Calvin's, but the basic idea is variously discernible in the latter's work, albeit couched in other terms. See, e.g., *ICR* 2.15.6 on the "priestly office": "For we who are defiled in ourselves, yet are priests in him, offer ourselves and our all to God, and freely enter the heavenly sanctuary." See also 2.7.1: "For all have been endowed with priestly and kingly honor, so that, trusting in their Mediator, they may freely dare to come forth into God's presence."

CHAPTER 2

Calvin's Geneva

The Sacred Schoolhouse

The concrete reforms Calvin sought to realize in Geneva are best considered against the broad background of late medieval European life. Up through the fifteenth century, Christian Bibles were relatively rare sacred objects, typically controlled by clergy, housed behind ecclesial, monastic, or academic walls, and in any case were written in Latin, a language few Christians could read, speak, or aurally understand with ease. Likewise, Latin was the exalted ceremonial language of late medieval Christian worship, spoken or chanted by priests or clerical choirs, often from behind a rood screen that architecturally — and theologically — established a key separation: on one side, the church's chancel or "sanctuary," the elevated area up front where the clergy celebrated the Mass; and on the other side, the long, wide corridor of the nave below, where the laity stood (there was no fixed seating) observing, listening, and performing their own parallel, individual devotions.

The liturgy's choral music, also often (though not always) in Latin, was typically a complex, polyphonic braiding of voices, sometimes including different texts simultaneously sung at different tempos, so even those parishioners familiar with the language being sung could not easily understand all the lyrics, much less sing along. This was music made not for congregational singing but rather for congregational listening, prayerful meditation, and devotion, as well as for enveloping the gathered assembly in a liminal atmosphere redolent of heaven. In most parishes, preaching was a special seasonal or occasional event, often held not in a church but in a friary or public building, and when sermons did happen, they were normally broad topical reflections, not intensive expositions or close commentaries on a particular passage of Scripture. The climax of the worship service was the eucharistic rite, reverently admired by the congregation, but not usually received by them. On a typical Sunday, only the priest received the elements; most of the laity communed once a year (as was mandatory), often at Easter, and even then laypeople were permitted to receive only the body, not the blood, presumably since the latter was vulnerable to spilling.

Thus for most ordinary Christians in late medieval Europe, at its best worship could be a rich, reverent, engaging blend of visual, kinetic, aural, olfactory, and tactile experience, always framed and pervaded by a strong sense of the distinction between clergy and laity. It was the clergy who had access to the most exalted language of Christian worship, the language of Scripture, psalm, and above all the Eucharist itself, the rite in and through which Christ's presence became tangible up on the altar. It was typically the clergy (or lay specialists) who sang psalms and spiritual songs, at once joining and mediating heaven's angelic choirs. For the laity, intellectual modes of scriptural, doctrinal, or even broadly verbal analysis were not central to their experience of the church's official worship, couched as it was in a language they could not easily or fully understand.

But this does not mean, as Protestants are too often fond of claiming, that late medieval lay worship was merely spectatorial or passive; on the contrary, for many it could be richly participatory and engaging. Doctrinal catechesis and rigorous knowledge of the sacred text, however, were not the principal goods such worship aimed to provide, nor was the opportunity to sing with the angels. In the main, those were tasks thought appropriate to the trained clergy — though even here, laypeople participated in these acts vicariously, since, after all, the very idea of a priest hinges on the notion of one person carrying out tasks on behalf of another. Over time, the status of vicarious lay participation in clerical acts of worship began to break down in certain respects, and both Protestant and Roman Catholic reformers eventually reshaped Christian worship accordingly. But for many late-medieval Europeans, traditional forms of Christian worship struck the right balance between lay participation on one side of the rood screen and the clergy's special mediating, representative role on the other.[1]

The sixteenth-century reformers, of course, saw things rather differently. No sooner had Genevans declared their allegiance to the reforming movement than they dismantled and removed the rood screen from the city's cathedral of Saint-Pierre. Moreover, in the 1540s, Calvin oversaw the building of a new pulpit in the heart of the cathedral; the complete whitewashing of the walls, covering all remaining images; and the relocation of the choir stalls down into the cathedral body, now designated as special worship seating for the members of the city council.[2] One of the most telling innovations in Reformed worship spaces was what amounts to the invention of the church pew: fixed benches were installed throughout the cathedral, the better to facilitate the scriptural and doctrinal learning that the laity, reformers argued, had so long been denied.[3] When critics dismissed Reformed churches as resembling secular schoolhouses, the criticism might as well have been a compliment.[4] The very idea of what the church is, and what it is for, was undergoing a striking shift toward a more explicitly pedagogical model.

Presiding over this transformation, Genevan pastors left aside the colorful priestly vestments made for each liturgical season, opting instead for a plain black robe — indeed, as plainly black as the walls were plainly white — topped off with a starched white collar, the so-called

---

1. The foregoing portrait is drawn from Bruce Gordon, *Calvin* (New Haven: Yale University Press, 2009), especially pp. 136-37; Robert Kingdon, "Worship in Geneva before and after the Reformation," in *Worship in Medieval and Early Modern Europe: Change and Continuity in Religious Practice*, ed. Karin Maag and John Witvliet (Notre Dame, Ind.: University of Notre Dame Press, 2004), pp. 41-60; Elsie Anne McKee, "Reformed Worship in the Sixteenth Century," in *Christian Worship in Reformed Churches Past and Present*, ed. Lukas Vischer (Grand Rapids: Eerdmans, 2003), especially pp. 6-8; and Virginia Reinburg, "Liturgy and the Laity in Late Medieval and Reformation France," *Sixteenth Century Journal* 23 (1992): 526-46.

2. Gordon, *Calvin*, pp. 136-37; Kingdon, "Worship in Geneva," p. 52.

3. See Raymond A. Mentzer, "The Piety of Townspeople and City Folk," in *Reformation Christianity*, ed. Peter Matheson (Minneapolis: Fortress, 2007), pp. 23ff.

4. McKee, "Reformed Worship," p. 20; Mentzer, "Piety of Townspeople," p. 23. Mentzer cites the report of one Catholic critic who in the mid-1550s reviewed Reformed worship space in Lausanne, a city just thirty miles from Geneva: "It is exactly like the interior of a school. Benches are everywhere and a pulpit for the preacher in the middle. The women and children are seated on low benches in front of the pulpit, while around them the men are on higher ones, without differentiation of status."

Storming the Sanctuary

bands of Geneva. To his contemporaries, a reformed pastor did not look like a clergyman; he looked like a lawyer, or an academic. In a sense, these were civilian clothes, the customary attire of an educated man; so here, too, we glimpse another way in which reformers tended to dismantle sharp distinctions between sacred and secular, church and world.[5] With the rood screen removed, the walls whitewashed, vestments discarded, and fixed seating oriented toward the new, centralized pulpit, supposed distractions were at a minimum, and the transformed cathedral was ready for a newly restored, fundamentally pedagogical function: the scriptural, doctrinal, and spiritual formation of the church, and by extension, the city as a whole.

Accordingly, now sermons were scheduled in Geneva at least once a day, and now each sermon was unmistakably a close, methodical exposition of a biblical text. The traditional lectionary — assorted selections from the Psalter and various New Testament books — was set aside, and in its place, preachers used a method of *lectio continua* in which successive selections from a single book in the Old or New Testament were expounded consecutively, eventually preaching that entire book from start to finish. These sermons were not brief. Calvin was one of the most economical among Reformed preachers, arguing that sermons should be no longer than one hour (he is said to have preached, typically without notes, with a large hourglass beside him in the pulpit).[6] Not surprisingly, Genevans commonly referred to the worship service as a whole as a "sermon."[7]

These daily preaching services were typically held in the mornings; on three afternoons a week, Calvin delivered more technical lectures on Scripture.[8] Genevans could attend as many of the daily services and lectures as they wished, but attendance at worship was

---

5. See Kingdon, "Worship in Geneva," p. 53. The ironic tenacity of sharp sacred/secular, ordained/lay distinctions is demonstrated nicely by the fact that in many Protestant churches today, the plain black robe inherited from revolutionary Geneva now serves as the distinctive, classifying costume of the clergy.

6. Elsie Anne McKee, *John Calvin: Writings on Pastoral Piety* (New York: Paulist, 2001), see p. 14.

7. McKee, *John Calvin*, p. 20. See also Kingdon, "Worship in Geneva," p. 48. As Kingdon suggests, calling the whole service a "sermon" was both a sign of the sermon's importance in Reformed worship and a way to distinguish such services from their Roman Catholic counterparts, which were typically referred to as a *messe*, that is, a Mass.

8. Philip Benedict, *Christ's Churches Purely Reformed: A Social History of Calvinism* (New Haven: Yale University Press, 2002), p. 91.

mandatory for the whole city on both Sundays and Wednesdays. Ideally at least, reformed Geneva was awash in Scripture and instruction. If medieval European liturgies had not emphasized the verbal, catechetical, intellectual dimensions of Christian life, now the pendulum swung decisively in the other direction: Reformed worship was in the first place a matter of verbal, catechetical, intellectual engagement with God's word revealed in Scripture and expounded from the pulpit.

Singing the Psalter

But that is not all it was. The invigorated intellectual dimensions of Reformed worship were intended to be corrective, not reductive, and in any case were set within a broad, multidimensional program of Christian formation. For example, under Calvin's leadership, ecclesiastical discipline was overseen by a consistory of pastors and elders, a body that presided over cases related to Genevan religious and moral life. When it came to Christian behavior, then, the city became a jurisdiction under consistorial control and accountability: sermon attendance, doctrinal opinion, worship conduct, alleged sexual and other improprieties, and, quite commonly, interpersonal disputes (especially family quarrels), among other matters, were subject to consistorial oversight and regulation. Likewise, Geneva's ruling councils instituted a wide range of moral legislation meant to effect, along with the consistory's work, what many historians call a "reformation of manners": an overall shift in religious and moral conduct that, over time, emboldened some to claim Geneva as "a Citie counted of all godly men singularly well ordered."[9]

Less widely known, perhaps, is that one of Calvin's lifelong passions — and arguably one of his most influential triumphs — was what eventually became known as the Genevan Psalter, a compilation of all 150 psalms, the Ten Commandments, and the Song of Simeon, all translated into metrical French and set to new tunes composed not for specialist choirs but for the whole congregation. Indeed, as early as the opening paragraph of one of Calvin's first acts as a reformer in Geneva, the 1537 *Articles for Church Organization,* he calls for congregational sing-

---

9. *Lawes and Statutes of Geneva,* iii, quoted in Benedict, *Christ's Churches Purely Reformed,* p. 108; see also pp. 96-109; and Robert Kingdon, ed., *Registers of the Consistory of Geneva in the Time of Calvin* (Grand Rapids: Eerdmans, 2000).

ing of psalms "for the edification of the church" — a phrase that in this context signals an upbuilding not so much of sound doctrine as of warmth, liveliness, and zeal.[10] "Certainly as things are," Calvin explains, "the prayers of the faithful are so cold, that we ought to be ashamed and dismayed. The psalms can incite us to lift up our hearts to God and move us to an ardor in invoking and exalting with praises the glory of his Name."[11] Calvin wanted to sharpen the minds of the faithful, but at least as much, he wanted to engage and enliven their hearts.

Thus psalm singing became an indispensable discipline in Calvin's paideutic plans for Geneva, both for public worship and for private life. In his view, psalm singing offered a middle way between the anxious exclusion of music from public worship on the one hand, a position advanced by reformers such as Huldrych Zwingli in Zurich, and the embrace of popular music in worship on the other, advocated by the likes of Martin Luther, who put selected folk tunes to use as melodies for new hymns. For Calvin, newly composed settings of the psalms provided a moderate alternative to both of these options, capturing music's marvelous power to "bend customs" and "move morals" by harnessing it within the trustworthy lyrical bounds set by Scripture itself.[12] Calvin was nevertheless wary of music's seductive potential, and perhaps for this reason insisted that congregational psalm singing be strictly a cappella and in unison. Whatever the rationale for this practice, singing the new vernacular psalms in "a joyous unaccompanied roar," as one historian has put it, no doubt contributed to its communal power.[13]

Accordingly, for many in the sixteenth-century reform movements, the psalms became identified as the music of the people, God's Word once only accessible to a few, now sung by one and all. Indeed, in an era when women's voices were prominently heard in public worship only in convents, and children's voices only in specialist choirs, the joyous roar in Genevan churches rose from the entire assembly, men,

---

10. Calvin, *Articles for Church Organization*, in Calvin, *Theological Treatises*, trans. J. K. S. Reid, Library of Christian Classics, vol. 22 (Philadelphia: Westminster, 1954), p. 48.

11. Calvin, *Articles for Church Organization*, p. 53.

12. Calvin, "The Form of Prayers and Songs of the Church," trans. Ford Lewis Battles, *Calvin Theological Journal* 15 (1980): 163-64.

13. Diarmaid MacCulloch, *The Reformation: A History* (London: Penguin Books, 2003), p. 590. Accordingly, MacCulloch writes, the metrical Psalter was "that secret weapon of the Reformation."

women, and children singing together — with children often leading the way, teaching the adults the new psalms, a method Calvin recommended.[14] Both the music and the singing practices met with enthusiastic acceptance, as well as enthusiastic resistance, well beyond Geneva: Queen Elizabeth I is said to have dubbed the new psalms "Genevan jigs."[15] For both adherents and detractors, psalm singing became a distinctive signature of the Reformed movements. Soon after the complete Genevan Psalter was published, the congregation at Saint-Pierre was singing through the entire Psalter in twenty-five weeks of public worship, or roughly twice a year — a clip of more than thirty stanzas per week.[16]

Thus by the late sixteenth century, not only were monastics regularly singing through the Psalter as a defining, formative discipline, but ordinary Genevans were, too, in their own joyous unaccompanied roar. "In one of the ironies of Reformation liturgy," writes historian John Witvliet, "the Genevan church adopted a regimen of psalm singing not entirely unlike that of Benedictine monasticism."[17] If we bear in mind Calvin's paideutic approach to Christian life, however, as well as his keen interest in reappropriating the disciplines of the early church, this parallel may appear less as an irony and more as a revealing sign of kinship and common cause — or indeed, more contrastively, as a reclamation of the practice itself, wresting it back into lay hands.

Nor did Genevans sing psalms only in church. The Genevan Psalter was a publishing phenomenon, and in literate Reformed households all over Europe the vernacular Psalter and the vernacular Bible soon became the twin pillars of domestic worship. Around the hearth and the dinner table, fathers ideally functioned as a kind of "lesser pastor" of the household, leading morning and evening devotions typically consisting of prayer, a reading from Scripture, and psalm singing.[18] While prohibited in church, sung harmony was permitted and encouraged at home,

---

14. John Witvliet, "The Spirituality of the Psalter in Calvin's Geneva," in *Worship Seeking Understanding* (Grand Rapids: Baker Academic, 2003), p. 211. For Calvin's recommendation about children leading the singing, see Calvin, *Theological Treatises*, p. 54.

15. Mentzer, "Piety of Townspeople," p. 46.

16. Witvliet, "Spirituality of the Psalter," p. 210. Witvliet concludes from this data that for the Genevan church, "psalm singing was a discipline, a discipline of sung prayer."

17. Witvliet, "Spirituality of the Psalter," p. 210.

18. Mentzer, "Piety of Townspeople," pp. 36-38.

and composers provided four-part settings by the thousands for the new Genevan texts and tunes.[19] Students at the Genevan academy rehearsed psalms for an hour a day.[20] Across Europe, reformers sang the new psalms as battle hymns, protest songs, and rallying cries: in 1559, for example, more than three thousand French Calvinists occupied the left bank of the Seine in Paris, parading and singing psalms as a bold political act.[21]

When he first began compiling what would become the Genevan Psalter, Calvin recruited the poet Clement Marot to translate the psalms into metrical, singable French. In 1539, echoing Erasmus, Marot wrote of "the time approaching when a laborer at his work, a driver in his cart, a craftsman in his shop, lightens his toil with psalm and canticle."[22] By 1543, Calvin's own thinking about music and the psalms had evolved in a similar direction: "Even in houses and in the fields," he wrote in his preface to the Genevan liturgy, singing is "for us an incitement and as it were an organ to praise God, and to raise our hearts to him for him to console us, as we meditate upon his power, goodness, wisdom, and justice."[23]

But Calvin then extended and intensified this line of thought to a striking, even astonishing, degree. Not only are psalms entirely fitting for Christians to sing "in houses and in the fields," he argued, but psalms should also replace *all other songs on earth* that do not "arouse us to pray and praise God, to meditate on his works, in order to love him, fear, honor, and glorify him." Music is so powerful, Calvin contended, both for good and for ill, that it must be enjoyed strictly in the service of piety, not only in church but also out in the wider world — indeed, everywhere.[24] And since the ultimate author of the biblical psalms is

---

19. Witvliet, "Spirituality of the Psalter," p. 224.

20. See Karin Maag, "Change and Continuity in Medieval and Early Modern Worship: The Practice of Worship in the Schools," in *Worship in Medieval and Early Modern Europe: Change and Continuity in Religious Practice*, ed. Karin Maag and John D. Witvliet (Notre Dame, Ind.: University of Notre Dame Press, 2004), p. 123.

21. Witvliet, "Spirituality of the Psalter," pp. 222-23.

22. Clement Marot, *Oeuvres complètes*, pp. 303-9, quoted in Allen Cabaniss, "The Background of Metrical Psalmody," *Calvin Theological Journal* 20 (1985): 201.

23. Calvin, "Form of Prayers," p. 163.

24. Indeed, for a brief period in 1546 Calvin unsuccessfully attempted to extend this logic into the Genevan taverns, closing and replacing them with five religious public houses. These establishments sold food and wine on a nonprofit basis, and kept a French Bible prominently displayed on the premises. Swearing, slandering, dancing,

none other than the Holy Spirit, "we will not find better songs" than the psalms to harness music's unwieldy, "secret power, almost unbelievable, to move morals one way or another."[25]

In other words, by 1543 Calvin envisions not only the church but also the whole world resounding in songs that "arouse us to pray and praise God," with the Psalter at the heart of the repertoire: "let the world be so well advised," he writes, "that in place of songs in part empty and frivolous, in part stupid and dull, in part obscene and vile, and in consequence evil and harmful, which it has used up to now, it may accustom itself hereafter to singing these divine and celestial hymns with the good King David."[26] With ambitious language implicitly evoking the eschaton, Calvin calls for a world in which the only music anywhere is music that kindles piety — in short, a world full of psalms, hymns, and spiritual songs (Eph. 5:19), a kind of quasi-liturgical world at least proleptically manifesting the perpetual doxology portrayed, for example, in the book of Revelation (e.g., Rev. 4:8).[27]

---

and obscene singing were prohibited in these houses — but psalm singing was strongly encouraged, as was saying grace before and after eating and drinking. Curiously and suggestively, these houses were called *abbayes* (abbeys). They were notoriously unpopular, and it was only a few months before the old taverns were permitted to return. See T. H. L. Parker, *John Calvin: A Biography* (Louisville: Westminster John Knox, 2006), pp. 127-28, and Benedict, *Christ's Churches Purely Reformed*, p. 98.

25. Calvin, "Form of Prayers," p. 164.
26. Calvin, "Form of Prayers," p. 165.
27. In a nonetheless groundbreaking and helpful essay, "The Origins of Calvin's Theology of Music: 1536-1543," Charles Garside overstates Calvin's case, arguing that in the 1543 preface to "The Form of Prayers and Songs of the Church," Calvin "proceeds to urge the universal adoption of the psalms to the exclusion of all other songs." In fact, Calvin's claim in that text is that "we will not find better songs nor ones more appropriate for this purpose [i.e., praying and praising God] than the Psalms of David, which the Holy Spirit has spoken to him and made." Thus he contends that the psalms are the best and most appropriate of all songs, but from this it does not follow, as Garside claims, that "all other songs" are thereby excluded. Identifying the best does not necessarily entail excluding the second-best. Indeed, new settings of the Decalogue and the Song of Simeon are examples of approved songs included in the Genevan Psalter itself. On the other hand, however, in the 1543 preface Calvin does argue that, given the susceptibility of music to being misused, the only songs appropriate for singing are those that "arouse us to pray and praise God." After detailing the difficulties and dangers surrounding music, Calvin puts it this way: "What then is to be done? We must have songs not only honorable but also holy, which are to be like needles to arouse us to pray and praise God, to meditate on his works, in order to love him, fear, honor and glorify him." Again, of these "honorable but also holy" songs Calvin deems the "Psalms of David" to

Storming the Sanctuary

Like so many of his contemporaries, Calvin was convinced that the world was "now declining to its ultimate end," and in his reforming work, he set out to make Geneva a vanguard, psalm-soaked city, an audible sign of God's incoming, transformative grace.[28]

Prayer and the Supper

Likewise, in Calvin's view, not only would this dawning, sanctified, and sanctifying world be full of psalms; it would be full of prayer of all kinds. The mandatory Wednesday morning service, for example, was principally a prayer service, a so-called Day of Prayer distinctive to the Reformed tradition, and particularly to Strasbourg and Geneva. A robust engagement with Scripture and doctrine was still present in this service, and a pastor's prayer could be as influential a mode of catechesis as a sermon. But the Day of Prayer in Geneva was primarily devoted to prayers of penitence, intercession, and at times thanksgiving, and so it aimed to cultivate not only the participant's mind but also her affections, her conscience, and her basic stance toward God, her neighbors, and the wider world — in short, her life as a whole, as well as the common life of the church community.[29]

---

be the most excellent and reliable, and it is worth remembering that Calvin's vision for music in public worship is almost entirely dominated by the Psalter. But at the same time, he does leave the door open to other songs, both in church and particularly "in houses and in the fields," as long as they serve to "arouse us to pray and praise God, to meditate on his works," and so on. Thus Calvin's actual call is for a world whose music is limited not to psalms alone, but also to psalms and other songs that "arouse us to pray and praise God" — which is to say, in the language of the Epistle to the Ephesians, "psalms, hymns, and spiritual songs" (Eph. 5:19). Nevertheless, to limit *all* music to such songs is an extraordinarily ambitious position, and Garside helpfully highlights it. It is so extraordinary, in fact, that it casts Calvin's vision for reform in an eschatological — even apocalyptic — light, since a world in which there is no music whatsoever except "psalms, hymns, and spiritual songs" is a world strikingly transparent to the endless praise sometimes associated with the eschaton (e.g., Rev. 4:8). See Charles Garside Jr., "The Origins of Calvin's Theology of Music: 1536-1543," in *Transactions of the American Philosophical Society*, vol. 69, part 4 (Philadelphia: American Philosophical Society, 1979), p. 24; and Calvin, "Form of Prayers," p. 164.

28. John Calvin, *Institutes of the Christian Religion*, ed. John T. McNeill (Philadelphia: Westminster, 1960), 1.14.1 (hereafter cited as *ICR;* section references are cited in parentheses in the text).

29. On the "Day of Prayer," see McKee, *John Calvin*, especially pp. 27-29 and 157-77.

Indeed, as important as preaching and formal catechesis are to Calvin in his work as a reformer, in the *Institutio* he argues that a life of prayer is no less than "the chief exercise of faith" — the very thing, in other words, that preaching and catechesis are supposed to prompt and inspire (3.20). Accordingly, Calvin insists that although "we should ever aspire to God and pray without ceasing," a disciplined, daily round of dedicated times for prayer is nonetheless necessary, and so Calvin proposes a daily prayer cycle, in effect a version of the divine office designed to be practicable to all Christians. As historian Herman Selderhuis has noted, this cycle amounts to "virtually a monastic rule."[30] Each and every disciple, Calvin writes, "should set apart certain hours" for daily prayer: "when we arise in the morning, before we begin daily work, when we sit down to a meal, when by God's blessing we have eaten, when we are getting ready to retire" (*ICR* 3.20.50).[31] Thus with its hours tied not to a timepiece or the tolling of cathedral bells but rather to common daily practices (waking, working, beginning a meal, finishing a meal, and retiring for bed), Calvin's proposed office was both pragmatic enough to accommodate everyday Genevan life and robust enough to help shape it.

He judged the proposal so practical and important, in fact, that he appended model versions of these five prayers to his 1542/45 *Catechism*, and notably, he drew language for these prayers from (where else?) the Psalter.[32] Add to all this the recommendation that family devotional liturgies be used at home every morning and evening,[33] and an

---

30. Herman J. Selderhuis, *John Calvin: A Pilgrim's Life* (Downers Grove, Ill.: IVP Academic, 2009), p. 161.

31. If we assume a typical pattern of two sit-down meals a day, Calvin's cycle is a sevenfold pattern roughly parallel to the common sevenfold version of the divine office: matins, lauds, terce, sext, none, vespers, and compline. Tellingly, immediately after the sentence listing his proposed "certain hours" in 3.20.50, Calvin distinguishes this daily cycle from what he takes to be its corrupt counterparts — no doubt including its clerical counterparts — with a warning: "But this must not be any superstitious observance of hours, whereby, as if paying our debt to God, we imagine ourselves paid up for the remaining hours." Thus for Calvin, the question was not whether to pray the hours, but rather (1) precisely which hours to pray, and (2) with what motive, and on what theological basis, to pray them.

32. McKee, *John Calvin*, pp. 210-14.

33. McKee, *John Calvin*, p. 210: "In 1561 the printer Jean Rivery used a number of Calvin's prayers to create a family devotional liturgy to be used morning and evening, and added this to his publication of [Calvin's] catechism. . . . It is not clear how much

ideal picture emerges of Genevan life as a life lived in and through liturgical, disciplinary, paideutic forms and formation: twice-weekly mandatory worship in church among the gathered assembly (Sundays and Wednesdays), as well as optional public worship on all other days; daily morning and evening devotions at home among the household (parents, children, and servants); and over the course of each day, a regular cycle of dedicated times for individual or small-group prayer.

Not that all — or even most — Genevans actually lived such a life. As the city's consistory records vividly make clear, worship may have been mandatory twice a week, but Genevans showed remarkable (and for Christians today, quite familiar!) creativity in coming up with reasons why, alas, they could not attend this or that Sunday or Wednesday service — and the same undoubtedly held true of household devotions and daily prayer.[34] The point, then, is not that Genevans universally or impeccably followed this paideutic program, but rather that Calvin envisioned it in the first place as the regimen toward which and through which Genevan Christians ought to practice, strive, and grow. To be sure, Calvin's vision was only imperfectly realized in Geneva, but that vision is nevertheless a crucial key to understanding the basis and direction of his reforming work.

A case in point is Calvin's argument about the role of the Lord's Supper in Genevan life. The city council eventually established a pattern of celebrating the supper four times a year — which was four times more often than the common custom in late medieval Europe.[35] And

---

Calvin had to do with developing this, but he certainly approved of parents and family heads leading their respective households in worship."

34. Gordon, *Calvin*, pp. 138-40, 276-77, 294; Kingdon, "Worship in Geneva," pp. 53-54.

35. In one of the ironies of nearly five hundred years of Reformed historical and liturgical-theological development, prevailing arguments about the proper frequency of communion have, at least in one key respect, undergone an almost perfect reversal since the sixteenth century. In Calvin's day, reformers consistently (though to varying degrees) demanded more frequent communion for the laity, arguing that the Roman Church was withholding from laypeople an important spiritual good — whereas today, many Reformed Protestants resist more frequent communion (say, monthly instead of quarterly, or weekly instead of monthly) on the grounds that it seems to them "too Catholic," or in any event is somehow at odds with what is distinctively essential about the Reformed tradition. At the same time, there are encouraging signs today in some Reformed circles that such attitudes are giving way to new openness toward more frequent communion, and this is a welcome step forward — not only because of its potential to help build ecumeni-

moreover, in keeping with the relatively laicizing, relatively democratizing direction of reform in Geneva,[36] the supper was not only received generally by the laity, it was also in certain respects administered by them: lay elders supplied the sacramental elements, ushered the congregation, and sometimes distributed the cup of wine, the very thing medieval communicants were not permitted even to receive, much less serve.[37] And yet Calvin's vision for reforming the supper went even further: he called for no less than weekly celebrations of the meal, both on scriptural grounds and on the grounds that the sacrament's manifold benefits — not least its role as a clear and potent symbol of the "mystical union" *(unio mystica)* between Christ and the church — recommend it as a frequent, regular part of Christian life.[38]

---

cal bridges among Christian communities, but also and especially because it represents a recovery of the founding Reformed impulse with respect to the Lord's Supper, that is, the desire and demand for the laity to receive it more frequently, not less.

36. The democratizing direction of reform in Geneva was always only a relative one: even as some social hierarchies and distinctions were broken down in certain respects (say, some aspects of the distinction between laity and clergy), others were at the same time maintained and even fortified (say, various class distinctions among the laity). As they so often are, communion practices were an epitome of this kind of social complexity in Geneva: even as lay elders sometimes served laypeople the cup (surely a democratizing development), they typically served them according to a standard order of reception that both indicated and reified a pecking order of social and spiritual prestige (just as surely a classificatory, hierarchical practice): the pastor received first, followed by the elders, local nobles, members of the judiciary, city consuls, and, finally, the remaining laity. At least in Geneva, sixteenth-century reform was by no means an outbreak of unalloyed egalitarianism — though it did involve particular, limited changes in relatively egalitarian, relatively democratizing directions. See, e.g., Mentzer, "Piety of Townspeople," p. 35.

37. There was significant variation among Reformed churches across Europe with respect to this practice: in some, the pastor distributed both the bread and the cup; in others, an elder or deacon ceremoniously handed the cup to the pastor, who then distributed it; and in others, elders or deacons themselves administered the cup directly to the people. Geneva appears to have followed the latter method. In a list of "indifferent" alternatives, for example, Calvin mentions "whether [the people] hand the cup back to the deacon or give it to the next person." Calvin, *ICR* 4.17.43. Also see Mentzer, "Piety of Townspeople," p. 34.

38. In fact, Calvin indirectly suggests in the *Institutio* that "the Sacred Supper" should be "set before believers every time they meet together." He then explicitly recommends that the meal be celebrated "at least once a week," and that the whole congregation be "urged and aroused" to receive it, so that "all, like hungry men, should flock to such a bounteous repast." See Calvin, *ICR* 4.17.44-46.

Storming the Sanctuary

Calvin failed to persuade the city council to adopt a weekly pattern, but the attempt itself — and the fact that he preserved his arguments for frequent celebration in the *Institutio* even in its last editions — points again to his paideutic, disciplinary approach. As we will see in part II, Calvin conceives Christian life as a life of intimate union with God — indeed a "life in God." That is, Calvin understands Christian *paideia,* the formative education toward genuine and full humanity, as an immersive, life-encompassing program of worship, prayer, psalm singing, catechesis, moral accountability, and scriptural study. But as a whole, the program is oriented toward union with God in Christ, and for Calvin, the sacred supper is the sacrament — which is to say, both an instance and the iconic paradigm — of that mystical union. Accordingly, Calvin placed the supper at the heart of his theological work, and called for its weekly celebration in Christian churches.

In architectural terms, then, we may summarize Calvin's reforming project in Geneva as a storming of the sanctuary — though in a very different sense than that violent invasion of the Convent of St. Clare in the summer of 1535. As we have seen, in late medieval Christian worship, the elevated chancel or "sanctuary" front and center in the church's worship space was a privileged precinct of sacred activity. There, often behind a rood screen, the clergy spoke the language of Scripture and official liturgy; clerical and lay specialists sang the psalms; priests played special mediating, intercessory roles in prayer; and above all, the whole service culminated in the priestly celebration — and typically, the exclusive priestly reception — of the Eucharist, the intimate, embodied act of communion with Jesus Christ. All this was anchored in the chancel, architecturally, socially, and theologically distanced from the laity. The key sacred instruments — the Bible generally, the Psalter in particular, the altar, the bread and wine, and so on — were all up there on the platform, situated clearly under clerical control.

What Calvin envisioned, in effect, was an array of reforms by which laypeople in several respects approached, occupied, and made that "sanctuary" their own: now Scripture and official liturgy would be spoken in French, the Genevan mother tongue; now the Psalms would be sung by the whole congregation; now the Lord's Supper would be celebrated in the midst of the people, not up on the altar but down at a table located directly below the pulpit; and now the laity would receive the supper not once a year, but (as Calvin envisioned it) at least weekly, and ideally at every worship service, just as medieval priestly celebrants had done.

But the point can also be made from the other direction. Reversing the architectural metaphor, Calvin's reforming work may be summarized as an expansion of the chancel's sanctuary to encompass the whole room, nave and all. Indeed, even today, a terminological trace of this kind of thinking is clear in the widespread Protestant practice of calling the whole worship space "the sanctuary," a designation that for some Christians still refers to the chancel area alone. But as we have seen, Calvin ultimately sought to expand the sanctuary not only out to the walls of the church's worship space, but also beyond them, all the way out to the Genevan city walls — or better, out to the limits of a Christian disciple's life and work wherever she may go, and in that sense out to the limits of creation. Just as it was for the clergymen up on a medieval cathedral's chancel, now the business of Christian discipleship would be an immersive disciplinary program for all the men, women, and children of the church, complete with Scripture reading, psalm singing, prayer regimes, and eucharistic piety, all carried out for the sake of "mystical union" with God in Christ.

Accordingly, Calvin argued that in Reformed Geneva, worship services should be frequent, and should include the Lord's Supper at least weekly; prayer should be both continual and punctuated by a daily office and a weekly day of prayer on Wednesdays; psalm singing should be pervasive, in church, at home, and in the fields; catechesis should be rigorous and grounded in both the home and the Sunday services; moral and spiritual life should be accountable, ultimately overseen by the city's consistory; and engagement with Scripture, please note, understood as hearkening to the revealed Word of God, should be the discipline that founds and forms all the others.[39] Disciples should engage the Bible as often and as deeply as they can, Calvin advised, reading it, listening to others read it, and frequently attending to preachers expounding it, putting particular passages in context and applying them to everyday life. Literate Genevans were a growing but

---

39. As we will see in chapter 6, for Calvin, the Spirit-led interpretation of Scripture undergirds the whole of Christian life. See, e.g., *ICR* 1.6.2-3: "Now, in order that true religion may shine upon us, we ought to hold that it must take its beginning from heavenly doctrine and that no one can get even the slightest taste of right and sound doctrine unless he be a pupil of Scripture. . . . If we turn aside from the Word, as I have just now said, though we may strive with strenuous haste, yet, since we have got off the track, we shall never reach the goal." Or again, in 1.7.5: "Indeed, what is the beginning of true doctrine but a prompt eagerness to hearken to God's voice?"

still small minority in the city, and so Calvin put a special emphasis on the oral exegesis and instruction provided from the pulpit.[40]

In brief, this was the Christian *paideia*, the "formative education" Calvin sought to establish in Geneva and, by example, across the reforming world. And in the midst of these ongoing efforts, and indeed as part and parcel of them, Calvin composed and revised what would become known as his theological masterwork: *Institutio Christianae Religionis*.

---

40. Calvin expected Christians to read Scripture (or listen to others read it) as often as possible, and a regular Bible study for clergy and laypeople was held on Fridays in Geneva. But overall, Calvin put less emphasis on private and small-group Bible study than on the corporate, ecclesial Bible study that constituted the daily sermons delivered in Geneva — sermons Calvin intended to be guided, of course, by the exegetical and theological orientation laid out in his *Institutio*. Accordingly, we may think of Calvin's project as a massive program of civic education, and sermons by trained preachers delivered to large assemblies (as opposed to, say, innumerable individual or small-group Bible studies) were, perhaps, the strategy Calvin deemed most efficient, disciplined, and effective for such large-scale pedagogy. See McKee, "Reformed Worship," p. 25.

CHAPTER 3

Summa Pietatis

The *Institutio* was by no means Calvin's only major project. Indeed, a strong case can be made that his biblical commentaries and preaching are crucial, complementary companions to the *Institutio*, and in any event were vitally important to his labors as a theologian and reformer. But the *Institutio* is Calvin's most well-known and influential piece of writing, widely regarded today as a classic, monumental statement of Christian doctrine, arguably the preeminent one in the Reformed tradition. And yet, in the first edition's subtitle, the *Institutio* is characterized not with the familiar medieval phrase *summa theologiae* (summary of theology), but rather as both a *summa pietatis* (summary of piety) and an account of "what is necessary to know of the doctrine of salvation."[1] From

---

1. The full title of the 1536 first edition is *Of the Christian Religion, an Institution* [*Institutio*, "instruction"], *embracing nearly an entire summary of piety and what is necessary to know of the doctrine of salvation: a work most worthy to be read by all those zealous for piety.* Over more than twenty years of subsequent editions, Calvin expanded and reorganized the text significantly, though from 1539 on he characterizes it as a "sum of religion [*religionis summam*] in all of its parts" meant "to prepare and instruct candidates in sacred theology for the reading of the divine Word" — thus specifying the *Institutio*'s relation to piety as an aid to reading and listening to Scripture. In sum: Calvin comes to conceive the *Institutio* as a gathering of *loci communes* and *disputationes* rhetorically arranged for the sake of facilitating Christian *pietas* and *religio* by preparing leaders of the church "for the reading of the divine Word," precisely so they might, through preaching and catechism, do the same for the church as a whole. See "John Calvin to the Reader," *Institutes of the Christian Religion*, ed. John T. McNeill (Philadelphia: Westminster, 1960), p. 4. For a discussion of the *Institutio*'s genre, see Richard Muller, *The Unaccommodated Calvin* (New York: Oxford University Press, 2000), pp. 102ff.

the very outset, then, Calvin signals that "piety" is a leading, central term in his theological approach. And at the same time, he introduces a key premise of his overall argument: namely, that "piety" and "doctrine" (or rather, "what is necessary to know" of doctrine) are mutually and organically related.

Pietas

What is *pietas* for Calvin? His earliest gloss on the term is in his *Commentary on Seneca's "De Clementia"* (1532), where he cites Cicero's rhetorical question, "What is piety but a grateful disposition to one's parents?" and then turns to Augustine: "Piety, properly speaking, is commonly understood as worship of God, which the Greeks call *eusebeia*. Yet this *eusebeia* is said to be exercised by way of obligation toward parents also . . . [or] when we wish to express a particularly forceful love."[2] Thus in Calvin's early work, a primary paradigm for "piety" is the relationship of children to their parents, and especially the sense in which children (ideally!) feel gratitude, love, reverence, and a consequent sense of devoted obligation toward them. Moreover, even these early references suggest that when Calvin goes on to make *pietas* a centerpiece of his theology, he thereby appropriates not only the term but also something of its classical and early ecclesial pedigree. After all, Calvin was deeply influenced by sixteenth-century humanism's esteem for antiquity, and while he no doubt judged the word *pietas* to be uniquely suited to his semantic purposes, the fact that it figures in the work of Seneca, Cicero, and Augustine could only have enhanced its standing in his eyes. Ford Lewis Battles puts it this way: "For Calvin, then, there is in the word [*pietas*] the classical overshine of filial obedience" — an obedience, that is, born of filial gratitude and "forceful love."[3]

Accordingly, in the opening pages of the *Institutio*'s final Latin edition (1559), Calvin defines *pietas* as "that reverence joined with love of

---

2. "Quid pietas, nisi voluntas grata in parentes?" Cicero, *Pro Plancio* 33.80; Augustine, *City of God* 10.1. See Calvin, *Commentary on Seneca's "De Clementia"* (1532), ed. and trans. Ford Lewis Battles and André Malan Hugo, Renaissance Text Series, vol. 3 (Leiden: Brill, 1969), p. 226.

3. Ford Lewis Battles, *The Piety of John Calvin* (Phillipsburg, N.J.: P&R Publishing, 2009), p. 29.

God which the knowledge of his benefits induces,"[4] an oft-quoted formula that deserves a close reading. Calvin does not write that *pietas* is "reverence joined with love of God" in some general or abstract sense, but rather "reverence joined with love of God *which the knowledge of his benefits induces.*" That is, the "knowledge of benefits" clause is constitutive, not merely incidental, to the inaugural definition of *pietas* in the *Institutio* — and so for Calvin, true *pietas* is always *grata pietas* (grateful piety).[5] It is always a form of affectionate thanksgiving concretely "induced" by a beneficiary's recognition of benefits received.

Hence the term "knowledge" in the definition of *pietas* does not refer to a speculative, abstract, or merely mental affair, but rather to a concrete, relational, affective, and experiential one, what we might call a *knowledge of* as opposed to merely a *knowledge about*. This all comes clear in the definition's larger context, a crucial passage in the *Institutio* worth examining in full: "it will not suffice," Calvin contends,

> simply to hold that there is One whom all ought to honor and adore, unless we are also persuaded that he is the fountain of every good, and that we must seek nothing elsewhere than in him. This I take to mean that not only does he sustain this universe (as he once founded it) by his boundless might, regulate it by his wisdom, preserve it by his goodness, and especially rule mankind by his righteousness and judgment, bear with it in his mercy, watch over it by his protection; but also that no drop will be found either of wisdom and light, or of righteousness or power or rectitude, or of genuine truth, which does not flow from him, and of which he is not the cause. Thus we may learn to await and seek all these things from him, and thankfully to ascribe them, once received, to him. For this sense of the powers of God is for us a fit teacher of piety, from which religion is born. I call "piety" that reverence joined with love of God which the knowledge of his benefits induces. (*ICR* 1.2.1)

---

4. Calvin, *Institutes of the Christian Religion*, 1.2.1 (hereafter cited as *ICR*; section references cited in parentheses in the text).

5. See, e.g., Calvin, *Christianae religionis institutio* (1536), in *Opera Selecta*, ed. P. Barth and W. Niesel, 5 vols. (Munich, 1926-36), 1:76: "We should so revere such a father with grateful piety [*grata pietas*] and burning love as to devote ourselves wholly to his obedience and honor him in everything." For an account of Calvin's "piety" as a "eucharistic piety," see Brian Gerrish, "Calvin's Eucharistic Piety," in *Calvin Studies Society Papers 1995, 1997* (Grand Rapids: Calvin Studies Society, CRC Product Services, 1998), pp. 52-65, and *Grace and Gratitude: The Eucharist in John Calvin's Theology* (Minneapolis: Fortress, 1993).

Thus the definition of "piety" at the end of this passage actually summarizes and culminates a rhetorical cascade in which Calvin describes a universe saturated in divine power and activity, and a human situation of being continuously governed, accommodated, protected, and especially sustained and nurtured by God at every turn. Indeed, for Calvin, humanity is enveloped and continuously engaged by these "powers of God," and having a "sense" of these powers is "for us a fit teacher of piety." That is, once we come to sense God's parental, gracious, loving care for us in daily life, we responsively take up a posture of filial, grateful, reverent love in return. And this is *pietas*: "that reverence joined with love of God which the knowledge of his benefits induces."

In this way, the "knowledge" in the definition of *pietas* is an appositional correlate to the "sense of the powers of God" *(hic virtutum Dei sensus)* in the sentence preceding it. For Calvin, the "knowing" that induces *pietas* is akin to a kind of "sensing," an intellectual and also quite personal, tangible, and familiar knowledge analogous to the way in which a child "knows" the manifold benefits she receives from her parents. She does not only know *about* them. She knows them. She senses them. She is intimately familiar with them, intellectually, emotionally, and physically, and this familiarity almost intuitively moves her to Cicero's "grateful disposition," to Augustine's "forceful love" — and so to Calvin's *pietas*. There may be a thousand ways to feel "reverence joined with the love of God": a philosopher might earnestly admire the divine attributes; a prophet's zeal might stir at the idea of divine justice; a parishioner might marvel at a portrait of divine beauty. But for Calvin, the only "reverence joined with the love of God" that makes for genuine *pietas* is the one provoked by the "knowledge of" — that is, an intellectual, relational, tangible "sense of" — God's benefits, a mode of knowing through which human beings "experience" *(sentio)* God as both loving parent and graceful fountain, in short, "the Author of their every good" (1.2.1). And so for Calvin, *pietas* is a concrete, relational, responsive mode of thankful reverence, love, and willingness to serve.

Is it then primarily a matter of a person's inner life? Does *pietas* belong to the sphere of dispositions and attitudes and ideas? It surely does. But just as surely, Calvin contends, does it also and ultimately belong to the sphere of action. *Pietas* may be induced in human beings by knowledge of God's gracious activity toward them and in them, and so it may initially take shape as a "grateful disposition" of filial love and reverence toward the divine benefactor. But in its full flower, *pietas* blooms not only in a filial sense of obligation, not only in a glad willingness to serve, but also in the actual discharge of that obligation, and so in whole human lives of divine service.[6]

Indeed, even in the *Institutio*'s opening definition of *pietas*, Calvin points toward its practical dimension. For when he claims that the "sense" of the gracious powers of God "is for us a fit teacher of piety," he does so having just outlined this teacher's basic pedagogical goals, namely, that "we may learn to await and seek all these things from him, and thankfully to ascribe them, once received, to him." For Calvin, this is piety in practice, and as he well understood, such learning does not and will not happen by itself. On the contrary, it requires intellectual, practical, formative training, and thus regular forms by which "awaiting and seeking" all good things from God, and then "thankfully ascribing" all good things to God, might properly take place. In brief, this kind of learning requires paideutic disciplines of prayer ("awaiting and seeking all good things from God") and praise ("thankfully ascribing all good things to God"). Done well, these formative disciplines — carried out paradigmatically in church worship services, but also at home and in the fields — may help disciples both to express and to sharpen their "knowledge," that is, their "sense" of God's gracious work in their lives, a sense that in turn serves as "a fit teacher of piety."

Thus Calvin writes of not only the "disposition" but also the "practice" of *pietas* in broad, embracing terms. As we have seen, in his discussion of monasticism, he refers to "those duties of piety [*pietatis officia*] enjoined upon all Christians" (4.13.10). And these duties pertain, it turns out, not only to each and every disciple but also to each and every aspect of a disciple's path: "The whole life of Christians ought to be a sort of practice of piety [*pietatis*], for we have been called to sanctifica-

---

6. Brian Gerrish differentiates "spirituality" from "piety" by finding the former to be "largely a performance word," whereas "'piety' is an attitude word, and in Calvin it is prescriptive: it denotes the right disposition of the human mind toward God." And so it does. But Calvin uses the term "piety" in the *Institutio* and elsewhere to indicate both right dispositions and right actions, and indeed arguably to indicate a fundamental unity of the two, especially when it comes to Christian discipleship and relationship with God. Moreover, even in those passages where Calvin characterizes piety as, say, "reverence joined with love of God," it is not at all clear that we should take him to understand "reverence" and "love" strictly or even primarily as internal attitudes and not as external performances, or indeed as both at once. See Gerrish, "Calvin's Eucharistic Piety," pp. 53-54.

tion" (3.19.2). For Calvin this practice of piety is itself a divine gift, a gracious way for disciples to participate in a life of communion with Christ. Indeed, part of what likely appealed to Calvin about the term *pietas* in the first place is the way it can be made to bridge supposed distinctions between dispositions and actions, doctrines and practices, reverence and righteousness, and so point toward a holistic, integrated way of life. In any case, Christian discipleship is nothing but *pietas:* "piety alone is able to conduct a human being to complete perfection. It is the beginning, the middle, and the end of Christian life. . . . We ought to apply ourselves altogether to piety alone; because, when we have once attained it, God asks nothing more from us."[7]

The Role of the *Institutio*

But how exactly do human beings "apply ourselves altogether to piety alone"? How might disciples live whole lives "as a sort of practice of piety," that is, as a practice of reverence, love, and service toward God? This is the same basic question, of course, that Christian monastics have variously taken with them into deserts and cities; that friars have taken with them in pursuit of apostolic perfection; indeed that countless Christian movements — and countless Christians — have taken with them in their own more or less ambitious attempts to live out lives of comprehensive discipleship and devotion. It is the question of how to live a Christian life, as opposed to merely a Christian hobby. And since most of these men and women have understood the realization of such a life to require guidance, growth, and practical training, the ques-

---

7. Calvin, "Commentary on 1 Timothy 4:8," in *Calvin's Commentaries* (Grand Rapids: Baker, 1981), 21:109-10. In his comment on this verse, Calvin briefly critiques what he takes to be monastic — and, more generally, ascetic — overzealousness, a tendency he finds seated in fallen human nature: "our nature always disposes us strongly to attribute more than we ought to austerity of life; as if it were no ordinary portion of Christian holiness" (p. 109). Indeed, for Calvin, an appropriate measure of dedicated practical discipline is precisely an "ordinary portion" of Christian discipleship, not an extraordinary one. But even here, as he critiques overzealousness with respect to both austerity itself and the tendency to esteem austerity, he by no means rejects practical discipline, but rather resituates it in what he takes to be its proper place. Thus while he opens his comment with a critique of excessive reliance on "bodily exercise," at the comment's close he sums up his case this way: "we ought to give attention to bodily exercise in such a manner as not to hinder or retard the practice of piety" (p. 110).

tion is typically posed as a matter of pedagogy and formation — that is, as a question of which *paideia* will most effectively set the course and the pace.

As we have seen, in Calvin's view, Christian life is best lived through the church's ancient repertoire of disciplines, from worship to psalm singing to a regular cycle of daily prayer, a *paideia* ultimately grounded in the sound interpretation of Scripture. But throughout his work, Calvin contends that such disciplines can be properly carried out only by the luminous, empowering presence of the Holy Spirit in and with disciples, and this is nowhere more clear than in scriptural interpretation. For Calvin, reading the Bible well is only possible in the first place by the illumination of the Holy Spirit, on which the pastors and doctors of the church depend as they expound biblical texts from pulpits and lecterns and on the printed page.[8] Day in and day out, illiterate residents of Geneva (the majority) would hear Scripture proclaimed and explained by these men; literate ones (the minority) would have their own reading of Scripture shaped and informed by them. But who would train the trainers? If the whole paideutic program — and so the whole life of *pietas* the program is meant to foster — is framed and founded in the Spirit-illumined interpretation of God's Word, then the pressing question becomes: How is Scripture best interpreted? Yes, in general, the Holy Spirit illuminates and persuades hearts and minds, but how will she provide the teachers and preachers of the church with a basic exegetical manual and orientation?

From 1539 on, this is precisely the role Calvin envisions for his *Institutio Christianae Religionis*. In his preface "to the reader," Calvin first identifies his own role as a "teacher in the church" charged to maintain "the pure doctrine of piety [*sinceram pietatis doctrinam*]," and then turns

---

8. On the role of the Holy Spirit in illuminating the interpretation of Scripture, see, e.g., Calvin, *ICR* 1.7–1.9. For Calvin, Scripture is "self-authenticating" by the "inward testimony of the Holy Spirit," but since fallen human beings are so thoroughly dulled, desensitized, and in any case untrained, even the genuinely faithful require guidance in order to read Scripture correctly — and this the church provides, primarily through the preaching of pastors, who in turn rely on doctors of the church past and present (such as Calvin) to help them interpret Scripture properly. And since presumably neither the pastors nor the doctors could succeed in their work without themselves receiving the "inward testimony of the Holy Spirit," and since in any case parishioners can only grasp the Word of God proclaimed by virtue of that same testimony, the entire choreography is, in Calvin's view, suffused with the Holy Spirit's ongoing guidance and illumination.

to the *Institutio* itself: "it has been my purpose in this labor to prepare and instruct candidates in sacred theology for the reading of the divine Word, in order that they may be able both to have easy access to it and to advance in it without stumbling." That is, the *Institutio* is meant to function as a doctrinal complement and framework for his scriptural commentaries, a "sum of religion in all its parts" arranged such that, "if anyone rightly grasps it, it will not be difficult for him to determine what he ought especially to seek in Scripture, and to what end he ought to relate its contents."[9]

In other words, Calvin understands the *Institutio* to be a guide both to reading Scripture well and to putting it to good use in Christian life. And the proper context for this reading and application, it turns out, is not a sum of Scripture in all its parts, but rather a "sum of religion in all its parts." For Calvin, the proper setting of Christian Scripture, the intellectual and practical environment within which its interpretation should be worked out, is the Christian life as a whole. The *Institutio*, then, is a basic theological framework for that life, complete with accounts of creation and fall, salvation and prayer, key doctrines and key practices, all designed to properly orient readers of Christian Scripture. Of course, Calvin also claims to have derived the *Institutio* largely from his own reading of Scripture in the first place. It is as if he has ventured up ahead into the Bible's strange new world, interpreted it in the context of the strange new life to which God calls Christian disciples, and then returned with a map to help other "pious readers" find their way.[10]

Accordingly, for Calvin, the journey into Scripture is by no means for its own sake. Rather, it is for the sake of progress and edification in Christian life, the life of "piety alone." In his "Prefatory Address to King Francis I of France," written for the *Institutio*'s first edition and then retained as a preface for all subsequent editions, even after the king's death in 1547, Calvin puts it this way: "My purpose was solely to transmit certain rudiments by which those who are touched with any zeal for religion might be formed to true piety [*formarentur ad veram pietatem*]."[11] That is, Calvin's ultimate, governing purpose in the

---

9. Calvin, *ICR*, "John Calvin to the Reader," p. 4.

10. Calvin, *ICR*, "John Calvin to the Reader," p. 5. Karl Barth famously described the Bible as a "strange new world."

11. Calvin, *ICR*, "Prefatory Address to King Francis I of France," p. 9.

Summa Pietatis

Institutio is Christian formation to true *pietas:* the embodied knowledge, filial love, willing service, and immersive intimacy with God for which human beings are made. The *Institutio* is indeed a guide to studying Scripture, but studying Scripture, in turn, is for Calvin a practice ultimately meant to form disciples toward whole lives of *pietas*. In this sense, even the 1559 edition of the *Institutio* is, as the 1536 first edition's subtitle declares, both a *summa pietatis* and an account of "what is necessary to know of the doctrine of salvation." For Calvin, these two — *doctrina* and *pietas* — belong together, not as two separate swaths of cloth more or less ingeniously sewn into one, but rather as dimensions of a single, seamless whole.

As one scholar has put it, Calvin's work in the *Institutio* is "theology within the limits of piety alone."[12] And at the same time, we may add, Calvin thereby seeks to advance what we might call "piety within the limits of theology alone." To be sure, for Calvin, no sound theological work — that is, no sound "knowledge of God" — exists apart from piety: "we shall not say that, properly speaking, God is known where there is no religion or piety" (*ICR* 1.2.1).[13] No piety, no knowledge of God. But as we have seen, in Calvin's view, piety is induced by knowledge of God in the first place. No knowledge of God, no piety.

Pietatis Doctrina

In this way, doctrine and piety together form for Calvin a kind of circular choreography, and if — and only if! — the Holy Spirit wills it, that dance can begin, and that circle can become a spiral of spiritual growth and sanctification. Accordingly, precisely insofar as the *Institutio* is a text meant to clarify and advance sound doctrine, it is simultaneously a text meant to clarify and advance Christian *pietas,* the crucial companion and corollary of sound doctrine, and the basic form of Christian life. Thus to say of Calvin's theological work, as his modern interpreters have sometimes done, that "in no system has practice been so

---

12. Brian Gerrish, "Theology within the Limits of Piety Alone," in *The Old Protestantism and the New: Essays on the Reformation Heritage* (Chicago: University of Chicago Press, 1982), pp. 196-207.

13. As we shall see in the next chapter, Calvin's point here is not that *pietas* is a precondition of the knowledge of God, but rather that genuine knowledge of God necessarily gives rise to *pietas,* and so they are always found together.

closely united with theory," or that his work includes "an essential relation . . . between orthodoxy and orthopraxy," is still to put the matter too lightly.[14] Like many theologians prior to the so-called modern period in the West, Calvin effectively denies at the outset any divide between theological theory and practice, orthodoxy and orthopraxy, doctrine and life. In his view, these are not separate or even separable items to be "closely" or "essentially" related. Rather, for Calvin, sound doctrine is always already *pietatis doctrina*, "doctrine of piety," doctrine written and read for the sake of being "formed to true piety." And at the same time, for Calvin, all true *pietas* is always already grounded and disciplined by the Holy Spirit's teaching and testimony revealed in Scripture and proclaimed in the church.[15]

In fact, from this angle we might say that Calvin's theological and reforming work is an early Protestant expression of the church's ancient formula *lex orandi, lex credendi* ("law of praying, law of believing"), a witness to the idea that liturgical-practical and creedal aspects of Christian life are not in the first instance separate spheres or components to be subsequently coordinated or fit together. On the contrary, according to Calvin's approach, liturgical-practical and creedal aspects of Christian life cannot be properly thought apart in the first place, any more than the length of a field can be thought apart from its width. Of course, we may abstractly speak of a field's "length" alone, or its "width" alone, as if each feature is somehow detachable from the other. But in doing so, we have left the actual field behind. In fact, the field is one.

Thus the question is not whether or how Calvin's liturgical-practical ideas influenced or were influenced by his creedal ideas, since the notion of "influence" implies separate spheres in the first place. Rather, as we will see in part II, Calvin's liturgical-practical ideas were al-

---

14. See Charles Partee, "Prayer as the Practice of Predestination," in *Calvinus Servus Christi*, ed. Wilhelm H. Neuser (Budapest: Presseabteilung des Ráday-Kollegiums, 1988), p. 245. The first remark, which Partee quotes with qualified approval, is from Emile Doumergue; the second is Partee's own.

15. Calvin, *ICR*, "John Calvin to the Reader," p. 4: "I have had no other purpose than to benefit the church by maintaining the pure doctrine of [piety] [*sinceram pietatis doctrinam*]." Ellen Charry puts the matter perfectly: "If we take doctrine and piety as belonging to two separate fields, one academic and the other pastoral, we will never understand John Calvin." See Ellen Charry, *By the Renewing of Your Minds: The Pastoral Function of Christian Doctrine* (New York: Oxford University Press, 1997), p. 199.

ways already creedal, shaped and colored at every turn by the "knowledge of God" revealed by the Holy Spirit in Scripture and, once revealed there, newly discernible throughout creation, even down to the details of daily life. And likewise, Calvin's creedal ideas were always already liturgical-practical, conceived and articulated in the service of prayer and praise, reverence and righteousness — in short, in the service of *pietas*.

Finally, with all this in mind, what should we make of the *Institutio's* title? The most familiar English translation, "Institutes of the Christian Religion," is unfortunate in several respects. First, the phrase "the Christian Religion" rings today as if Calvin is picking out Christianity from among the world's religions, but the modern notion of "religion" had not yet taken hold in sixteenth-century Europe, and so for Calvin and his early readers, *religio* meant something quite different. Wilfred Cantwell Smith has argued that in Calvin's work the term *religio* refers to a universal, innate "sense of piety that prompts a man to worship"; Brian Gerrish has suggested that "Calvin's use of the word *religio* comes closer to our own present-day 'spirituality.'"[16] Following these proposals, Calvin's title might be rendered today as "*Institutio* of Christian Piety" or "*Institutio* of Christian Spirituality."

Indeed, as Smith points out, for no less than a millennium in Europe, from roughly the fifth century to the fifteenth, a prevailing way the word *religio* was used was with reference to monastic life, a sense preserved today when a monk or nun is called a "religious." Calvin was likely well aware of this traditional usage and the way it set "religious" orders apart from other clergy and, most strikingly, from ordinary lay Christians, and so it is at least possible that his decision to feature the term in his title involved an implicit critique. That is, bearing in mind the common medieval usage of *religio* in connection with monastic orders, it is possible to read Calvin's title — *Institutio Christianae Religionis* — as among other things a tacit claim that the text's subject is the bona fide, singular, simply "Christian" *religio*, as opposed to the monastic varieties (the Benedictine *religio*, the Cistercian *religio*, and so on).[17] Cal-

---

16. See Wilfred Cantwell Smith, *The Meaning and End of Religion* (San Francisco: Harper and Row, 1978), pp. 36-37, 225-27; Gerrish, "Calvin's Eucharistic Piety," p. 54 n. 9.

17. In Smith's estimation, keen and substantive interest in the term *religio* largely disappears in the West around the fifth century, sometime after Augustine's *De vera religione*. Until the mid-fifteenth century, Smith writes, the "standard use of *religio*" in Europe was with regard to the *vita monastica* — and beyond this standard medieval use, the term is "little prevalent," at least as a major subject of analytical study. When it is re-

vin's use of *religio* may have been a terminological expression of his argument that all Christians, not only monastics, are called to be "religious" — or, put another way, that all Christians belong to a single "religious" order.[18] Of course, precisely what Calvin had in mind with the term must remain an open question, as must the matter of how the term's connotations resonated for his early readers. In any case, any assessment of what Calvin meant to say should include the fact that in those days the word *religio* had a long-standing and ongoing association with monastic life, and therefore with the spiritual, practical, and liturgical devotion ideally characteristic of that life.

But what of the title's leading term, *Institutio*?[19] An obvious op-

---

vived again in the mid-fifteenth and sixteenth centuries, it is by thinkers steeped to varying degrees in Renaissance humanism (Ficino, Zwingli, Calvin), and each uses the term in ways analogous to Augustine's, that is, as indicating a general human tendency toward worship and piety. Thus the sixteenth-century reappropriation of *religio* may well have been prompted by a humanist fondness for the ideas and language of antiquity: in Cicero, for example, who uses *religio* liberally, and perhaps particularly in Augustine. But even if this is so, the fact that in the intervening millennium the term very often referred to monastic life could hardly have gone unnoticed by Calvin, and so it may well be that if he reached back into antiquity to retrieve the term *religio,* he thereby also conceived himself to be wresting it from medieval monastic hands. See Smith, *The Meaning,* pp. 28-37, 211-29, and Benson Saler, "*Religio* and the Definition of Religion," *Cultural Anthropology* 2, no. 3 (August 1987): 395-99.

18. Cf. *ICR* 4.13.14, where Calvin, playing on 1 Cor. 3:4 but also, perhaps, on the term *religio* itself, declares that it is "an injustice to Christ when some call themselves Benedictines instead of Christians, some Franciscans, some Dominicans; and when they haughtily take to themselves these titles as their profession of religion [*religionis professione*], while affecting to be different from ordinary Christians!"

19. The term *institutio* has appeared in titles of instructional compendia by such classical and patristic figures as the Roman orator Quintilian (*Institutio oratoria* [ca. 90 C.E.]), the early Christian writer Lactantius (*De divinis institutionibus* [ca. 310]), and Ambrose (*De institutione virginis et sanctae Mariae virginitate perpetua ad Eusebium* [ca. 391]); and by such sixteenth-century figures as Erasmus (*Institutio principis Christiani* [1516]), Melanchthon (*Theologica institutio in Epistolam Pauli ad Romanos* [1519]), and Luther (in the introduction to his *Larger Catechism* [1529]). Calvin was probably familiar with many such texts, if not all of them, and in general, the sixteenth-century use of the term was likely at least in part a retrieval from the classical and early church period. But the term also appears in some practical manuals of monastic spirituality, including Gregory of Nyssa (*De instituto Christiano* [ca. 390]) and John Cassian (*Institutiones coenobiorum* [420-429]). This is by no means an argument for direct influence on Calvin, of course, but the parallels are intriguing. See Muller, *The Unaccommodated Calvin,* p. 104; John T. McNeill, "Introduction," in Calvin, *ICR,* p. xxxi; and Bruce Gordon, *Calvin* (New Haven: Yale University Press, 2009), pp. 57-58.

tion is "instruction," the word Calvin uses in his own French translation; likewise, Erasmus's *Institutio principis Christiani* (1516) is often rendered in English as "The Education of a Christian Prince." Thus we might translate Calvin's title, "Instruction in Christian Piety," or "Education in Christian Spirituality." But as we have seen, the pedagogical program Calvin had in mind is more comprehensively immersive and formational than what the terms "instruction" or "education" often connote in modern English. Perhaps for this reason, Christopher Elwood has suggested what may be the best translation of all: "Formation in Christian Piety."[20]

As it turns out, however, Calvin left behind one other hint, by itself inconclusive, but tantalizing nonetheless. Translating Second Timothy into Latin for his commentary on that text, Calvin makes use of the term *institutio* at a crucial juncture: the author of the epistle — whom Calvin took to be Paul — is encouraging Timothy in the life of Christian discipleship, exhorting him to "continue in what you have learned," and to remember "how from childhood you have known the sacred writings that are able to instruct you for salvation in Christ Jesus. All scripture is inspired by God and is useful for teaching, for reproof, for correction, and for training in righteousness" (2 Tim. 3:14-16). It is a passage Calvin would have found entirely congenial to his own work as a theologian and reformer, and an exhortation he himself could have delivered to the faithful in Geneva, or indeed to his persecuted comrades in France. Moreover, since both Scripture and sanctification hold such important positions in his thought, the idea that "the sacred writings" are useful for "training in righteousness" would have been for him an especially compelling claim. Indeed, as we have seen, such "training" is at the heart of Calvin's reforming project.

And for just this word — "training" — Calvin translates the letter's original Greek into Latin as *institutionem*. The original Greek term? *Paideia*. Thus taking a cue from Calvin himself, we may translate *Institutio Christianae Religionis* as "Training in Christian Piety," or indeed as "Christian *Paideia*" — or, bearing in mind the pedagogical, immersive, disciplinary overtones of the word "disciple," as "Christian Discipleship."

In part II of this book, I will read the *Institutio* in just this way — as

---

20. Christopher Elwood, *Calvin for Armchair Theologians* (Louisville: Westminster John Knox, 2002), p. 15.

a thoroughly practical, thoroughly theoretical manual for Christian paideutic formation. This reading will be representative, not comprehensive. Brief treatments of seven key doctrinal loci will fill out the case: first, Calvin's account of theological knowledge; second, the thematic cluster of creation, providence, and sin; third, Scripture; fourth, Christology; fifth, predestination; sixth, prayer; and seventh, the Lord's Supper. Calvin had other ideas, of course, but these seven are fundamental to his thought, and so their reinterpretation may help chart a course for further work along similar lines.

In all their variety, the sixteenth-century European reformations were in many respects passionate, sometimes violent arguments over formation — that is, over the role of formation in Christian life, and over who should have access to key formative goods and disciplines. While some stormed the privileged sanctuaries of late medieval Europe primarily to destroy "objects of piety" they believed to be idolatrous, others — including John Calvin — sought primarily to reclaim objects and practices of piety they believed rightly belonged to the whole people of God. Alleged purgation plays its part in all movements of reform, and Calvin's was no exception; but in the main, his principal driving motive was restorative. Indeed, just as reformers rejected the idea that a priestly class properly mediated between the rest of humanity and God, they likewise rejected the idea that a "religious" class properly had exclusive access to the paraphernalia and practices of living a life in God. In Calvin's view, the key formative disciplines of the church's paideutic tradition are indispensable to ordinary discipleship, and so should be available to all. In part III, I reflect on what implications this particular retrieval of Calvin's work might have for Protestant theology today and tomorrow. But first, in part II, I turn to a close, constructive reading of the *Institutio*, framing seven of Calvin's central ideas as doctrines meant to serve an immersive program of practical Christian formation.

PART II

Rereading the *Institutio*

For it is a doctrine not of the tongue, but of life.

John Calvin, *Institutio Christianae Religionis* 3.6.4

CHAPTER 4

Six Kinds of Knowledge

The *Institutio* as a whole is generally structured according to Calvin's fourfold exposition of the Apostles' Creed, with book 1 focused on God the Father, book 2 on God the Son, book 3 on the Holy Spirit, and book 4 on the church.[1] But this connection with the creed only makes more striking Calvin's decision to begin explicitly in terms of human knowledge. He does not title book 1 "God the Creator," but rather "The Knowledge of God the Creator"; book 2 is not "God the Redeemer in Christ," but rather "The Knowledge of God the Redeemer in Christ"; and in the *Institutio*'s famous opening pages, Calvin explores the reciprocal connections between human "knowledge of God and of ourselves." We might speak simply and directly of sunlight or stone, for example, without first having to address "the knowledge of sunlight" or "the knowledge of stone," much less the connections between these and human self-knowledge. But when it comes to God, in Calvin's view, exactly this kind of epistemological work comes first, and this sets the stage in important ways for everything that follows.

In the first place, the opening focus on human knowledge in the *Institutio* establishes the text's vantage point — that is, the Christian dis-

---

1. See, e.g., T. H. L. Parker, *Calvin's Doctrine of the Knowledge of God* (Edinburgh: Oliver and Boyd, 1969), p. 6, and Richard Muller, *The Unaccommodated Calvin* (New York: Oxford University Press, 2000), pp. 133-34. Of course, as Muller points out, there were a range of other influences on Calvin's organization of the *Institutio* over more than twenty years of revisions, from conventional catechetical models to Pauline thematic loci, but a basic (if rather loose) connection to the creed was a key factor in the final fourfold arrangement.

ciple's proper vantage point as Calvin understands it — as a theologically limited, relatively modest one, a kind of "view from below." For Calvin, human beings are in no position to survey the subject matter of theology as if from on high, professing generally or abstractly about "God the Creator" or "God the Redeemer." Rather, theologians can engage their subject matter only from a position determined by the capacities and limits of human knowledge, which itself is always dependent on the God who creates those capacities and limits, and may now illuminate and guide them.

In an important sense, then, book 1 of the *Institutio* is not strictly or even principally about "God the Creator" per se; instead, it is about human knowledge of God the Creator, and ultimately about the saving, humanizing relationship between God the Creator and humanity. Along the way, this topic includes a whole range of substantive claims about God the Creator — the point here is not that Calvin is uninterested in the truth about God, but rather that in the *Institutio* he frames the truth about God strictly in terms of human knowledge, human salvation, and human life. For Calvin, "God" is not an abstract subject. Rather, God is a relational subject, a living subject in ongoing relationship to human subjects, and in turn, human subjects are fit to know God only in particular ways. Calvin does not invent this basic idea, of course, but he distinctively underscores it throughout the *Institutio*, not least by beginning explicitly in terms of human knowledge.

Indeed, as in Calvin's account of *pietas*, here the knowledge of God is always relational knowledge, at once enabled and constrained by humanity's situation in the first place as a creature under God's ongoing care and creative command. This is humanity's actual situation, Calvin contends, and so it naturally determines the stance and bearing from which human knowledge of God may take place. The clay may know the potter, but only by way of the potter's touch and handiwork. Any more general or abstract knowledge of the potter "in herself" or outside of the studio is, for the clay, inconceivable. And so in Calvin's view, human knowledge of God can only take place from a position set squarely on the potter's wheel — which is to say, human knowledge of God can only be knowledge of a particular sort. It can only be situated, relational knowledge, fully determined from the outset by the benefits and bounds of the relationship between potter and clay, creator and creature, parent and child.

In this way, Calvin opens the *Institutio* with the idea that "knowledge" comes not in one but in several kinds, and in the text's opening pages he outlines no fewer than six — or rather, three pairs. The first pair is "the knowledge of God and of ourselves"; the second, which arises out of his discussion of the first, is not explicitly named, but for our purposes here we may refer to it as "relational-pragmatic" knowledge of God on one hand, and "abstract-speculative" knowledge of God on the other; and the third pair provides the titles for book 1 and book 2 of the *Institutio*: "The Knowledge of God the Creator" and "The Knowledge of God the Redeemer in Christ." Thus in three different, interlocking ways, three epistemological pairs frame and structure the *Institutio* as a work of doctrine serving Calvin's reformed program of practical formation.

"The Knowledge of God and of Ourselves"

The first and most famous pair appears in the text's opening sentence, what Calvin calls the "two parts" comprising all "true and sound wisdom" human beings possess: the knowledge of God and the knowledge of ourselves. Here Calvin maintains that on one hand, "no one can look upon himself without immediately turning his thoughts to the contemplation of God, in whom he lives and moves."[2] Thus self-knowledge leads into knowledge of God. And at the same time, on the other hand, "man never achieves a clear knowledge of himself unless he has first looked upon God's face, and then descends from contemplating him to scrutinize himself" (*ICR* 1.1.2). Thus knowledge of God leads into self-knowledge. In this way, Calvin argues that each kind of knowledge gives rise to the other and follows from it in turn, an interplay so intimate that "which one precedes and brings forth the other is not easy to discern" (1.1.1). Throughout the *Institutio* Calvin keeps this epistemological reciprocality in view.[3]

Beginning and proceeding this way has important consequences for Calvin's overall theological project in the *Institutio*. First, it casts the project's purpose as ultimately sapiential, since both the knowledge of

---

2. John Calvin, *Institutes of the Christian Religion*, ed. John T. McNeill (Philadelphia: Westminster, 1960), 1.1.1 (hereafter cited as *ICR*; section references cited in parentheses in the text); cf. Acts 17:28.

3. Cf., e.g., 1.15.1: "we cannot have a clear and complete knowledge of God unless it is accompanied by a corresponding knowledge of ourselves."

Rereading the Institutio

God that follows from self-knowledge and the self-knowledge that follows from knowledge of God are framed as together constituting humanity's "true and sound wisdom." Second, it positions the project within two broad, interconnected practices, namely, "scrutinizing oneself" and "contemplating God," activities that are for Calvin paradigmatically carried out via particular disciplinary forms. Third, it frames theological knowledge as an ongoing, personally contextual, processual affair, a kind of practical pilgrimage undertaken by each disciple in and through her own disciplined journey from self-examination to divine contemplation and back again. And fourth, the interdependence of these two kinds of knowledge — that is, the extent to which they depend upon and proceed from each other — renders each one an exercise properly undertaken in a way that advances its counterpart. Thus the education Calvin describes in the *Institutio*'s opening pages, far from a linear course of merely accumulating data, is rather an ongoing circle or spiral, an edifying itinerary in which scrutinizing oneself leads into contemplating God, which in turn leads into scrutinizing oneself, and so on.[4] In the end, then, neither the knowledge of God nor the knowledge of ourselves exists for its own sake alone. On the contrary, each kind of knowledge is properly pursued for the sake of both itself and the other, and ultimately for the sake of upbuilding "true and sound wisdom" — which is to say, true and sound human lives lived by true and sound human beings.

4. Whether Calvin understands this spiral to have a particular point of departure is an interesting question. On one hand, Calvin seems to give a kind of theological priority to "the knowledge of God," if only because he asserts that "the order of right teaching" requires that the knowledge of God be discussed first in the *Institutio* (1.1.3). But on the other hand, even throughout these early chapters on the knowledge of God, Calvin weaves a running discussion of human self-knowledge — and in any case, in his opening description of the spiral in 1.1.1, self-knowledge comes first: "no one can look upon himself without immediately turning his thoughts to the contemplation of God. . . . For, quite clearly, the mighty gifts with which we are endowed are hardly from ourselves." Thus we might say that for Calvin, while the knowledge of God has a kind of theological, pedagogical, and rhetorical precedence in how the *Institutio* unfolds, from an existential, experiential point of view, the epistemological spiral may begin anywhere, and may well begin with "looking upon oneself" and one's "gifts." After all, the "order of right teaching" is one thing, and the order of experience, another. In any case, in these opening pages Calvin goes out of his way to construe the interplay between "the knowledge of God and of ourselves" as fundamentally reciprocal, as if to insist that what is in fact circular should not be severed and flattened out into a straight line.

Six Kinds of Knowledge

This epistemological reciprocity follows largely from Calvin's premise that humanity and God are intimately — even ontologically — related in the first place. Indeed, for Calvin, human life is none other than life in God: "For quite clearly," he writes in the *Institutio*'s opening paragraph, "the mighty gifts with which we are endowed are hardly from ourselves; indeed, our very being is nothing but subsistence in the one God" (1.1.1). Given this scenario, any accurate, discerning "knowledge of God" must take account of this intimate relationship between God and humanity, and at the same time, any accurate, discerning "knowledge of ourselves" must take account of this "subsistence in God," this radical creaturely dependence on the Creator for every gift, from this morning's breakfast to "our very being." Just as, say, "knowledge of a sailboat" scarcely deserves the name unless it includes at least some rudimentary knowledge of the wind, the force the boat is in every respect designed to ride across the water, so human self-knowledge is a dull and confounded thing, in Calvin's view, unless it includes some knowledge of God, and therefore of human life as life in God lived by the grace of God.

As we will see in the next chapter, for Calvin, a principal, seminal problem for humankind — not our only problem, to be sure, but a devastating one — is precisely this kind of dullness and confusion, this ignorance and forgetfulness of the fact that every good thing in human life, including that life itself, is a loving gift from God's own hand.[5] Were human beings to see this clearly, believe it, and act accordingly, we would spontaneously respond to God with lives of *pietas*, that is, with lives of filial gratitude, love, reverence, and willingness to serve. But instead, Calvin contends, humanity falls into lives of *impietas* disposed in the opposite direction: too faithless to believe, too dull to notice, too ignorant to care, and too forgetful to follow the restorative way of life God sets before us every day.

And if faithlessness, dullness, ignorance, and forgetfulness are fundamental problems, what are the corresponding fundamental remedies? Trust, vigilance, learning, and remembering — and in each case,

---

5. For Calvin, the whole human being is overwhelmed by sin's "miserable ruin," including the faculty of the understanding but also including, just as decisively and disastrously, the faculty of the will, a subject Calvin turns to in earnest in the *Institutio*'s book II. Indeed, in Calvin's overall *ordo docendi* (order of teaching), he largely focuses on the understanding first, and then the will — and in this book, I do the same. For Calvin's discussion of the fallen will, see below, chapters 5 and 7.

65

please note, the remedy points to an ongoing practical program. That is, trust points to formative practices of leaning and relying on God; vigilance points to formative practices of mindfulness and attention; learning points to formative practices of study; and remembering points to formative practices of mnemonic discipline. Taken together, these practices sketch the contours of a remedial, Spirit-led, edifying *paideia* aimed at restoring practitioners to the true and sound humanity for which they were born. From this angle, we may describe Calvin's whole theological and reforming program as an attempt to retrain disciples to believe, see, learn, and recall that they actually live in God by the grace of God — a regimen only possible by the generous power of the Holy Spirit, and culminating in human lives of genuine *pietas*, "that reverence joined with love of God which the knowledge of his benefits induces" (1.1.1).

Thus for Calvin, all theological knowledge — both the knowledge of God we gain via self-knowledge and the self-knowledge we gain via knowledge of God — properly has this practical telos, this governing goal: whole human lives of genuine *pietas*, which is to say, whole human lives of vibrant, graceful relationship with God. Commenting on Titus 3:10, Calvin puts the point plainly: "In doctrine, therefore, we should always have regard to usefulness, so that everything that does not contribute to piety shall be held in no estimation."[6] Indeed, in Calvin's view, *pietas* is what doctrine is for.

When it comes to this opening epistemological pair, then, Calvin first orients "the knowledge of God and of ourselves" toward each other in an ongoing, interdependent spiral, and ultimately orients the spiral itself toward the cultivation of *pietas*. On one side of this spiral, he argues, human self-knowledge involves attending to the manifold, personal, concrete gifts of God in one's own life, so that "by these benefits shed like dew from heaven upon us, we are led as by rivulets to the spring itself" (*ICR* 1.1.1). Thus Calvin appropriates and reframes the classical call to "know thyself," entwining it inseparably with the contemplation and knowledge of God. That is, according to Calvin, truly

---

6. *Calvin's Commentaries* (Grand Rapids: Baker, 1981), 21:340. Cf. his comment on 1 Tim. 6:3: "when there is no progress, and no edification in the doctrine itself, there is already a departure from the ordinance of Christ . . . for the 'doctrine' will not be consistent with 'piety' if it does not instruct us in the fear and worship of God, if it does not edify our faith, if it does not train us to patience, humility, and all the duties of that love which we owe to our fellow men." See 21:153-54.

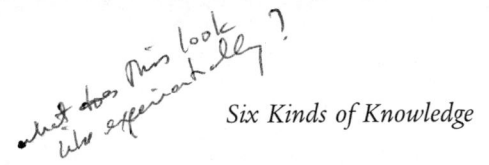

knowing oneself means knowing God's benefits, and truly knowing God's benefits means knowing God as our gracious benefactor, our loving parent. This knowledge provokes us to filial gratitude, love, reverence, and willingness to serve. In this way, genuine self-knowledge leads to the knowledge of God that makes for true *pietas*.

And in turn, on the other side of the spiral, Calvin argues that genuine knowledge of God leads to greater self-knowledge, and this movement, too, makes for true *pietas*. The more we contemplate God's majesty and mercy, for example, the more convinced we become of both our own "poverty" and the "miserable ruin" into which humanity has disastrously fallen. But again, on both counts, the new insight is by no means for its own sake. Even and especially any emphasis on human incapacity and "depravity" plays a fundamentally formational role in Calvin's work, and so is aimed at training and shaping disciples in particular ways. In one sense, then, its role is rhetorical or pedagogical: in effect, Calvin contends that a vivid portrait of human destitution is the crucial corollary — the companion image in a diptych, we might say — to the equally vivid portrait of divine plenitude and grace. In Calvin's view, every good thing really *does* come from God, and seeing this clearly means seeing not only God's abundant generosity but also our own sheer desolation without it. Calvin puts it this way: "Indeed, our very poverty better discloses the infinitude of benefits reposing in God" (1.1.1).

And in another sense, the intended formational function here is to fashion disciples capable of ongoing humble recourse to God. Properly proclaimed and received, insight into human weakness "especially compels us to look upward," Calvin writes, both to "seek thence what we lack" — presumably via practices of prayer — and thereby to "learn humility." In this way, even the worst of our lives may be transformed into occasions for progress along the epistemological spiral of knowing God and ourselves: "from the feeling of our own ignorance, vanity, poverty, infirmity, and — what is more — depravity and corruption, we recognize that the true light of wisdom, sound virtue, full abundance of every good, and purity of righteousness rest in the Lord alone. To this extent we are prompted by our own ills to contemplate the good things of God" (1.1.1).

We may assess the posture Calvin recommends here by contrasting it with other stances "our own ills" might in fact prompt us to take up: anxiety, depression, frustration, despair, and so on. Against these

67

alternatives, Calvin calls his readers to recast both personal and communal "ills" not as humiliating, debilitating measures of defeat, but rather as opportunities to contemplate anew the goodness of God and humbly recall our own perpetual reliance upon it. If this paints a picture of God as replete with goodness and humanity as intrinsically bereft of it, for Calvin this is no insult to humanity, but rather only a candid recognition that whatever goodness human beings do possess is "hardly from ourselves." Every good thing — every virtue, every pleasure, every act of kindness or justice or insight or discipline — is in fact already a gift from God, Calvin contends, truly human only insofar as it is truly divine in origin, and therefore by no means a cause for human boasting or triumphant pride. On the contrary, every good thing human beings possess is always and only a cause for humble gratitude, for filial devotion — in a word, for *pietas*. To point out that the moon is lifeless and lightless on its own is not to deny the moonlight. Rather, it is to see the moonlight more clearly, and thereby to properly orient our appreciation not only toward the moon but also and ultimately toward the unseen sun.

Thus according to Calvin's model, any theological critique of human failings should take place not as an end in itself, much less as a blunt instrument of attack on ourselves or others, but rather as a humbling call to restoration. It should take place for the sake of returning human beings to their own genuine humanity, to genuine humility and renewed contemplation of God's gifts and graciousness — and for Calvin, such contemplation properly leads to *pietas*. In Calvin's view, any and all critique of human "depravity" should ultimately serve the formation of human beings to truly grateful, humble, loving human lives.

A clear and present danger lurks here, however, like a snake in the theological grass. Christian criticism of human failings can and does all too easily collapse into an inhumane, dehumanizing assault, since Christian churches — like all other human communities — are riddled with both self-assertive pride and self-destructive shame. Formation to humility is always at risk of devolving into mere humiliation. But here in the opening pages of the *Institutio*, Calvin effectively offers a key critical principle for helping to guard against such collapse, and helping to recognize it when it happens. The principle is this: any theological critique of human failings should in practice function to form disciples toward *pietas*, that is, toward grateful, humble, vibrant filial love for

God and grateful, humble, vibrant neighborly love for the world, as God commands. If a given critique is delivered or received or in any case actually functions on the ground in any other way, it is itself open to strong theological criticism. Thus, according to Calvin's model, critiques of human "depravity" should always and only be pronounced and appropriated all the way along as attempts to be "prompted by our own ills to contemplate the good things of God." In this sense, such critique should be undertaken in the service of both divine and human dignity. The extent to which things have been otherwise in Protestant Christian communities and elsewhere is itself a sure sign of ongoing Christian "depravity," indeed one of "our own ills" with which Christians must reckon today, and so is an eloquent witness, wherever and whenever it occurs, to Protestantism's own ongoing need for repentance and reformation (1.1.1).[7]

Indeed, repentance and reformation are central to Calvin's whole approach to theological knowledge. Like human knowledge of God, Calvin argues, human self-knowledge is worthwhile only insofar as it is formative toward lives of *pietas*, and this formation involves reformation and repentance. That is, because of humanity's estrangement from God, any return to God involves a "change of mind" that is also a change of heart, and finally a change of life.[8] "For what man in all the world," Calvin writes, "would not gladly remain as he is — what man does not remain as he is — so long as he does not know himself, that is, while content with his own gifts, and either ignorant or unmindful of his own misery." Properly deployed, human self-knowledge — and so the knowledge of God that both makes genuine self-knowledge possible and follows from it in turn — is by no means for the sake of "remaining as one is." On the contrary, it is always for the sake of reforming how one is — which is to say, it is always for the sake of sanctification. And for Calvin,

---

7. Whether Calvin himself, the so-called Calvinists who claim him, or indeed the wider sphere of Protestantism that has wittingly or unwittingly been influenced by him has wisely applied Calvin's critical principle to their own theological critiques of human "depravity" is a serious and open question, one to which I will return in part III.

8. In New Testament Greek, one crucial term typically translated as "repentance" is *metanoia*, literally "change of mind" — though in the ancient world, "mind" meant something more essential to the human person than it tends to mean in North American English today (the phrase "change of heart" today captures something of the ancient word's sense of a truly pivotal, consequential transformation). See, e.g., Matt. 3:2 and 4:17.

most fundamentally, this sanctifying reform means the Holy Spirit's restoration of humanity's primal, vital, ongoing relationship to God. "Accordingly, the knowledge of ourselves not only arouses us to seek God, but also, as it were, leads us by the hand to find him" (1.1.1).

Thus from both vantage points in this first epistemological pair, the knowledge of God and the knowledge of ourselves, Calvin has in mind what might be called "relational-pragmatic" knowledge. Both kinds of knowledge are first of all embedded in the divine-human relationship, and both are carried out with a particular practical end in view: the pedagogical, formational, sanctifying, spiral-shaped course toward more fully realizing that divine-human relationship, and so more fully realizing "true and sound" human being through lives of genuine *pietas*. Thus for Calvin, relational-pragmatic knowledge of God and ourselves is, when done well, a fundamentally humanizing kind of knowledge. And accordingly, it may be contrasted against another kind of knowledge, a dehumanizing kind of knowledge, neither grounded in the divine-human relationship nor carried out for the sake of serving a life of *pietas*. For my purposes here, I will call this latter sort of knowledge "abstract-speculative." Thus by beginning the *Institutio* with an account of "the knowledge of God and of ourselves" that casts both as relational-pragmatic ways of knowing, Calvin points to a second, quite different epistemological pair.

Intimacy and Speculation

"Now, the knowledge of God, as I understand it," Calvin writes, "is that by which we not only conceive that there is a God but also grasp what befits us and is proper to his glory, in fine, what is to our advantage to know of him. Indeed, we shall not say that, properly speaking, God is known where there is no religion or piety" (1.2.1). For Calvin, there is a knowledge of God that "befits us" and is "to our advantage to know," and in contrast, these formulations suggest, there are other kinds of alleged knowledge of God that do not and are not. As the author of the second creation story in Genesis famously puts it, it is quite possible (and quite attractive!) for human beings to attempt to know too much, to know in the wrong way, or for the wrong reasons, or on the wrong footing. Not all knowledge "befits us" or is "to our advantage." According to Calvin, the proper corollary and consequence of human knowl-

70

edge of God is "religion or piety" — indeed, he goes so far as to say that unless it leads to *religio* or *pietas,* alleged knowledge of God is counterfeit. Humanity is meant to know God, but not in a distant, untethered, abstract sense. Rather, Calvin insists, we are meant to know God in an intimate, relational, tangible sense, a knowing that issues in a practical life of *pietas* and is carried out for the sake of that life at every turn.

Indeed, as we have seen, for Calvin *pietas* is "induced" by the "knowledge of God's benefits," that is, the "sense of the powers of God," the relational-pragmatic knowledge of the manifold blessings by which God protects, provides, and cares for us, and for all creation besides. Such knowledge of God — that is, personal knowledge of God's ongoing, enveloping, sustaining gifts, and thus a recognition of God as our loving parent and "the fountain of every good" — is the knowledge that "befits us" as God's children. This is the knowledge of God that is "to our advantage," since it clarifies and grounds us in our actual relationship with God, and so draws us further into the grateful, devoted life of *pietas.* To put the point briefly, for Calvin, God is a God of tangible love toward humankind, and seeks to be known by us as such. Any human attempt to pursue knowledge of God apart from this relationship — say, by inquiring after abstractions such as "What is the divine essence?" — is at best a waste of time, what Calvin calls "merely toying with frigid speculations" (1.2.2).[9]

The adjective — *frigidis* — is telling. It is as if a precocious, philosophically inclined adolescent, presented with a wonderful meal prepared for him by his mother and father, turns not toward his parents in a spirit of grateful love and delight, but rather away from them, asking as a kind of aside a question manifestly beyond his ken: "An excellent meal, yes — but I wonder, What is the *essence* of my parents?" To be sure, there is a certain obliviousness in the question, an ill-mannered disregard for the gifts on the dining room table; and there is something both presumptuous and pathetic about it, too, insofar as it attempts to secure knowledge that for the boy is utterly out of reach. But Calvin's leading concern about this kind of speculation is not that it is impolite or futile (though it is both), but rather that it is "frigid," cold, inert.

It is not a "warm" question. It does not lead the child into a livelier, more vibrant, more warmhearted relationship with his parents. In this sense, it is profoundly counterproductive. It fails to advance, and

---

9. Battles translates this as "idle" speculations, but Calvin's term is *frigidis.*

in fact does what it can to undermine, the actually warm, loving, generous event unfolding in the room. In Calvin's terms, it fails to serve the child's life of *pietas* vis-à-vis his parents, but rather distracts him from it, obscures it, cools it off, and so rather awkwardly passes up an opportunity for familial joy and good pleasure. To return to a distinction we drew in part I, the boy's question pursues not *knowledge of* his mother and father so much as *knowledge about* them. For their part, both parents dearly want to be known by their son, but not via cool, detached speculation — which is to say, not via abstract-speculative knowledge. Rather, they want to be known by him precisely as his mother and father who love him, and who demonstrate their love through concrete acts of kindness as tangible as supper.

Put another way, unless the child receives the meal with genuine filial love, gratitude, reverence, and good will (that is, with true *pietas*), he does not receive it as it actually is, and in that sense does not receive it at all. In truth, the meal is a caring gift from his parents, prepared and presented for the sake of his own well-being and gladness. But he does not receive it as such. Thus he falls out of touch with his actual situation, and so he is doubly lost. He misses the gift, and he misses his parents' graciousness. To be sure, he may physically eat and drink what is set before him, but by doing so on the wrong footing — that is, apart from a spirit and posture of *pietas* — he not only acts disrespectfully, but he also squanders the opportunity for fellowship with his mother and father, which is to say, he squanders the opportunity to know them in and through the meal. And he squanders it, please note, precisely by pursuing abstract-speculative knowledge about them. He abandons the kind of knowledge that "befits" both him and the occasion (relational-pragmatic knowledge) by seeking after a kind of knowledge that is, given the circumstances, entirely unfit.

God gives gracefully; humanity receives gratefully.[10] For Calvin, this is the fundamental pattern at the heart of the divine-human relationship as God intends it, and its choreography of perpetual giving and receiving encompasses the whole of human life. At every turn, Calvin insists, human beings find themselves in this basic situation of be-

---

10. For an exploration of this basic theme in Calvin's work, see Brian Gerrish, *Grace and Gratitude: The Eucharist in John Calvin's Theology* (Minneapolis: Fortress, 1993), and Gerrish, "Calvin's Eucharistic Piety," in *Calvin Studies Society Papers 1995, 1997* (Grand Rapids: Calvin Studies Society, CRC Product Services, 1998), pp. 52-65.

ing in debt to God's graceful generosity, and thus a situation in which filial *pietas* is the most becoming, appropriate human posture and reply. Precisely because human life is enveloped and infused with divine gifts, and indeed is itself a divine gift continuously "subsisting in God," nothing less than the "whole life of Christians ought to be a sort of practice of piety" (1.1.1; 3.19.2). No aspect or compartment of human affairs is left out: "the Christian must surely be so disposed and minded that he feels within himself it is with God he has to deal throughout his life" — and this God with whom humanity always has to do is none other than "the Author of every good" (3.12.2; 1.2.2).[11] Thus, even if we were somehow intellectually capable of detached speculation vis-à-vis God, we would never have occasion to take it up, since detachment from God is not an actual possibility for us. In truth, we live in God. Even our capacity for detached, abstract speculation (a perfectly appropriate exercise applied in other contexts) is already an ongoing, intimate divine blessing, and so when it comes to knowing God, the very attempt at abstract-speculative knowledge is itself a confused deformation, a mixed-up misuse of God's good gifts.

Calvin titles the *Institutio*'s second chapter this way: "What It Is to Know God, and to What Purpose the Knowledge of Him Tends." It is in this chapter that Calvin coordinates *pietas* and knowledge of God, in effect arguing that one is not found without the other. But he does not say, "Unless you are pious, you will not know God," as if piety is a precondition of such knowledge. On the contrary, he argues the opposite: knowing God leads ineluctably to piety, because for human beings, truly knowing God means knowing God's manifold benefits, "sensing" them, recognizing God as "the Author of every good" — and this induces piety in the human knower.

To return to the analogy of the dinner table, the boy truly "knows" his parents in that particular scenario only if he senses or experiences the meal as their gift to him, and so simultaneously recognizes and experiences them as his benefactors, that is, as his loving par-

---

11. Cf. 1.17.2: "Therefore no one will weigh God's providence properly and profitably but him who considers that his business is with his Maker and the Framer of the universe, and with becoming humility submits himself to fear and reverence." See also, as John McNeill notes, Calvin's 1540 letter written in the throes of deciding whether or not to return to ministry in Geneva: "I am well aware that it is with God that I have to do [*mihi esse negotium cum Deo*]." See *Letters of John Calvin*, ed. Jules Bonnet (New York: B. Franklin, 1973), 1:281.

ents. Thus he knows them. And if he truly does so, this knowledge will induce in him — not as a separate, analytical second step, but rather as a kind of aspect or extension or echo of the original recognition — a posture of filial gratitude, love, and devotion. If this posture does not emerge, if he is instead indifferent or distracted or ungrateful or rude, we may rightly dispute the claim that he actually knows his parents, at least in this instance. This is what Calvin means when he writes, "Indeed, we shall not say that, properly speaking, God is known where there is no religion or piety." In other words: what does not lead to *pietas* is not genuine knowledge of God, since by definition, genuinely knowing God, the fountain of every blessing, induces *pietas*. And likewise, this is what Calvin means in the title of the second chapter of the *Institutio*. That is, for John Calvin, "the purpose to which the knowledge of God tends" is *religio*, the full-blown practical life of *pietas*.[12] If alleged knowledge of God does not lead in this direction, it is no knowledge of God at all.

To sum up, genuine knowledge of God, in Calvin's view, is always relational — that is, it is always grounded in the ongoing divine-human relationship. And further, it is always pragmatic — it always serves to advance and deepen that relationship, and in particular, on the human side it serves to advance and deepen lives of *pietas*. Calvin puts it this way: "we are called to a knowledge of God — not that knowledge which, content with empty speculation, merely flits in the brain, but that which will be sound and fruitful if we duly perceive it, and if it takes root in the heart." For Calvin, genuine theology is "sound and fruitful," and for this very reason, abstract, speculative, "bold curiosity" about God is ruled out. In the face of such mysteries as the divine "essence," Calvin counsels his readers that "we ought more to adore than meticulously to search out" (1.5.9).

---

12. Again, it is worth noting here that for Calvin, *religio* did not mean what "religion" typically means in modern English usage today, but rather meant something closer to "spirituality" or "piety" or "inclination toward worship," and may even have carried a connotative echo of the spiritual and liturgical devotion ideally evident in monastic life. See above, pp. 55-56. Accordingly, Calvin does not distinguish sharply between *religio* and *pietas* in the *Institutio*: the terms are often coupled, used synonymously, or otherwise coordinated. If anything, Calvin seems to regard the typical relationship between the two as a seed-to-plant relationship, as when he writes that from piety "religion is born." But this idea is by no means systematically developed in the text. See Calvin, *ICR* 1.2.1.

Accordingly, Calvin argues that disciples contemplating God should stay close to home, attending especially to God's local wonders, that is, those "works whereby he renders himself near and familiar to [them], and in some manner communicates himself." In this sense, human beings should not so much "investigate" or "penetrate" or "meticulously search out" divine knowledge as humbly feel, watch, and listen for God in and through the nearness and familiarity of their own lives and neighborhoods. And if they thereby encounter things too marvelous to fully grasp, they should receive these, too, but as occasions "to adore," not to analyze. At such moments the most "fitting" way to "search for God" is the one that "may so hold our mental powers suspended in wonderment as at the same time to stir us deeply." Thus humanity's relational-pragmatic knowledge of God will at times take the form of adoration, wonder, and awe, and for Calvin, of course, these dispositions are practically made manifest in and through the church's signature disciplines of worship and devotion (1.5.9).

But on the whole, whether mundane or sublime, human knowledge of God will take the ongoing form of a pedagogical path. "What help is it to know a God with whom we have nothing to do?" Calvin writes. "Rather, our knowledge should serve first to teach us fear and reverence; secondly, with it as our guide and teacher, we should learn to seek every good from him, and, having received it, to credit it to his account" (1.2.2). For Calvin, theological knowledge is practical knowledge, useful knowledge, knowledge that "teaches" and "guides" human beings on and along a particular way of life. What way of life? The church's paideutic way of life, an immersive, formative education wherein disciples "learn to seek every good from [God] and, having received it, to credit it to his account" — which is to say, a practical path of prayer and praise, continuously seeking every good from God and thanking God for every good.

As Calvin understands them, then, doctrines such as the intrinsic poverty of humanity and the gracious, overflowing plenitude of God are not just ideas to be thought. Properly understood, theological knowledge should "teach" and "guide" disciples into an immersive practical program, into prayer and into praise and so on, and thereby into whole human lives. In Calvin's view, disciplines of scriptural study, daily prayer, worship, psalm singing, and the Lord's Supper are nothing if not relational-pragmatic practices of knowing God, and so ultimately of living a life of vibrant, graceful intimacy with God. For Calvin, this is what theological knowledge is for. It is not for abstractly "toying with frigid speculations." It is for tangibly and beautifully and practically living life in God.

Creator and Redeemer

Finally, a third epistemological pair at the outset of the *Institutio*, again quite different from the two pairs just discussed, is "the knowledge of God the Creator" and the "the knowledge of God the Redeemer in Christ." For the former, Calvin has in mind the sort of thing Paul proclaims in Romans 1: "Ever since the creation of the world [God's] eternal power and divine nature, invisible though they are, have been understood and seen through the things he has made" (Rom. 1:20). That is, as Calvin puts it, "upon [God's] individual works he has engraved unmistakable marks of his glory . . . insignia whereby he shows his glory to us, whenever and wherever we cast our gaze." By attending to these ubiquitous marks, human beings can come to know God the Creator: "this skillful ordering of the universe is for us a sort of mirror in which we can contemplate God, who is otherwise invisible." In principle, at least, every human being can behold God in this mirror, and so the "knowledge of God the Creator" is available to all. And yet, as we will see in the next chapter, Calvin contends that because humanity has fallen into the "miserable ruin" of sin, none actually do behold and know God in creation. Without the Holy Spirit's remedial gifts of Scripture and faith, though every corner of the universe shimmers with divine glory, every human being continually, obliviously looks away (1.5.1).

And what is worse, even and especially those who sincerely pursue right relationship with God are nevertheless cut off: "after man's rebellion, our eyes — wherever they turn — encounter God's curse." That is, in the wake of our original and continual fall away from God, our "conscience presses us" such that even though "God wills to manifest his fatherly favor to us in many ways, yet we cannot by contemplating the universe infer that he is Father." A sense of guilt clouds our vision; anxieties "overwhelm our souls with despair." And so *pietas*, itself induced by a lively personal sense of God's parental love and favor, becomes inconceivable for even the most exemplary disciples, since they recognize in their alienation from God "just cause for his disowning [them] and not regarding or recognizing [them] as his children" (2.6.1).

Six Kinds of Knowledge

And so a second kind of knowledge is necessary: "the knowledge of God the Redeemer," in which disciples "embrace the grace of reconciliation offered to [them] in Christ" (1.2.1). By way of this second kind of knowledge, human beings come to know Jesus Christ as the "Mediator" between humanity and God, the reconciler in and through whom it becomes "possible for them truly to taste God's mercy, and thus be persuaded that he [is] their Father" (2.6.4). For those to whom the Holy Spirit grants eyes to see, God's creative and providential works declare the knowledge of God the Creator; but for Calvin, only the face of Christ reveals God the Redeemer, that is, the one who reconciles sinners with God, and thereby secures their salvation.

Put differently, by contemplating creation in ways illumined by the Holy Spirit, human beings may come to know God the Creator as their loving benefactor, and themselves as beloved beneficiaries. But even this very knowledge, coupled with a candid admission of their manifold ingratitude and idolatry — that is, their manifold sin — only sharpens their sense of shame and estrangement from God because it sets their sin in direct, disheartening contrast to divine parenthood, mercy, and kindness. It is as if a thief, already feeling some guilt after having robbed and injured an elderly woman on the street, comes to find out that the woman is his own loving mother. She has always cared kindly and generously for him, and now he has returned her grace with disgrace. Shame compounds shame. The more clearly and candidly he examines what he has done, the more convinced he becomes that he no longer deserves to be called her son.[13] In the same way, for Calvin, the reality of sin makes even "the whole knowledge of God the Creator . . . useless unless faith also follow[s], setting forth for us God our Father in Christ" (2.6.1).

Indeed, by contemplating Christ in ways illumined by the Holy Spirit, we may come to know God the Redeemer as our merciful advocate. In Christ, Calvin insists, God's "face shines, full of grace and gentleness, even upon us poor and unworthy sinners" (2.7.8). And so by coming to know God the Redeemer in Christ, we come to know God the Creator as our loving parent, and ourselves as God's children, even

---

13. Indeed, the basic correspondence between Calvin's argument and Luke 15 (the so-called parable of the prodigal son) is striking, and in turn, reading Calvin through the parable helps clarify the fundamentally relational character of his whole theological approach.

in view and in spite of human sin. Christ redeems humanity. He is our reconciling Mediator, the "door whereby we enter into salvation" (2.6.1). To a significant degree, according to Calvin, this rescue is due to Christ's atoning death on the cross, that is, the extent to which, by dying, he plays the role of "propitiator" on behalf of humankind. But as we will see in chapter 7, Calvin's account of redemption is much broader than the cross alone, and in fact, for Calvin, the governing theme of Christ's redemptive work is not his atoning death, but rather his saving incorporation or "engrafting" of disciples into his own body. To be redeemed by Christ, as Calvin understands it, is to live in Christ, and so to live as Christ's body. Humanity's redemption means a return to life in God.

"Return" is the operative word. For Calvin, Christ's mediating, saving work is no ad hoc solution to sin on God's part, no secondary strategy improvised in the face of human rebellion. On the contrary, since "life was in Christ from the beginning, and all the world fell away from it, it is necessary to return to that source" (2.6.1). Thus humanity's restoration means being restored to the original life in Christ — that is, the life in God — for which human beings are made "from the beginning." And so for Calvin, just as in the case of the knowledge of God the Creator, the knowledge of God the Redeemer is finally less a *knowledge about* Jesus Christ and more an intimate, relational *knowledge of* him, a homecoming "return" to him and ultimately a "mystical union" with him, "so that Christ, having been made ours, makes us sharers with him in the gifts with which he has been endowed" (3.11.10).

Accordingly, a crucial theme in Calvin's christological writing is incorporation, that is, the way in which disciples are "engrafted" into Christ's own body such that they may enjoy Christ's own benefits: his righteousness, for example, but also his faith, his obedience — and preeminently, his sonship. In Calvin's view, only those "engrafted into the body of the only-begotten Son are considered to have the place and rank of children" (2.6.1). And only those who consciously "have the place and rank of children" may live out lives of *pietas*, that is, lives of filial love and devotion and willingness to serve. We will examine the theme of incorporation in more detail in chapter 7, when we turn to Calvin's Christology in earnest.

For now, however, we note that as Calvin conceives them, both sides of this third epistemological pair — the knowledge of God the Creator and the knowledge of God the Redeemer in Christ — are

78

relational-pragmatic forms of knowledge, determined by God's relationship with humanity and dedicated to developing that relationship at every turn. The universe is resplendent, Calvin insists, with signs of the Creator's "power," "goodness," "wisdom," and above all "fatherly kindness" (1.5.8), and in Jesus Christ this kindness is secured for "even us poor and unworthy sinners." Engrafted into the Son of God as members of his own body, estranged men and women know themselves as children of God once again — and precisely as God's children, they can see and experience the universe as the radiant site and sign of "fatherly kindness" that it actually is. In this way, as God's children, they may love and revere their heavenly Father, that is, they may live lives not of general or abstract or merely dutiful devotion, but rather of *filial* devotion, warm and tangible, intellectual and embodied, responsive and responsible, grateful and graceful, indeed "that reverence joined with love of God which the knowledge of his benefits induces" (1.2.1). Thus for Calvin, both the knowledge of God the Creator and the knowledge of God the Redeemer properly and ultimately lead disciples into whole human lives of genuine *pietas*.

And precisely as such, both kinds of knowledge in this third epistemological pair properly and ultimately lead disciples into whole human lives of practical formation. For if ubiquitous "marks" of divine glory make the universe "a sort of mirror in which we can contemplate God," and if human beings nevertheless see neither the marks nor the mirror, or if they interpret them merely as signs of God's "curse" — then nothing less than a remedial, paideutic program will do, a disciplinary education whereby disciples may be trained to experience the world in new ways. As we will see in chapter 6, this is exactly the function Calvin envisions for Scripture in Christian life. He compares Scripture to "spectacles" through which we may see anew both the created order and the course of history, thereby coming to know God the Creator more vividly as "the fountain of every good."

Likewise, if knowing God the Redeemer in Christ culminates less in *knowledge about* him and more in *knowledge of* him, that is, in being brought into fellowship with him, incorporated into his body, and therefore made participant in his life and sonship — then nothing less than a restorative, paideutic program will do, a disciplinary education whereby disciples are formed in communion with Christ to live as members of his body. This education is cognitive, of course, insofar as it involves a revised self-understanding, an account of God's work, key legal and moral ideas about discipleship, and so on. But it is also emotional, sensory, somatic, and thoroughly relational — in short, it is a fully human education — insofar as it involves, for example, discerning God's voice in Scripture, singing and speaking prayers of praise and supplication to God, communing with Christ in the Lord's Supper, immersive training in virtue ("patience, humility, and the duties of love," as Calvin puts it), and so on, such that each disciple is "so disposed and minded that he feels within himself it is with God he has to deal throughout his life."[14]

Thus in three related, interlocking ways, three epistemological pairs frame and structure the *Institutio* as a work of doctrine serving Calvin's reformed program of practical formation. With the first pair — "the knowledge of God and of ourselves" — Calvin effectively casts theological knowledge itself as a practical, sapiential spiral, an ongoing pilgrimage in which disciples move from disciplines of "scrutinizing oneself" to disciplines of "contemplating God" and back again, all for the sake of formation to genuine *pietas*. Accordingly, by way of the contrastive second pair — relational-pragmatic knowledge of God and abstract-speculative knowledge of God — Calvin situates theological knowledge squarely within the benefits and bounds of the divine-human relationship, and insists that it edify that relationship at every turn. But strong relationships, as everyone knows, require practices of trust, mindfulness, learning, and remembrance, to say nothing of love and reverence, gratitude and devotion.

Finally, with the third pair — the knowledge of God the Creator and the knowledge of God the Redeemer in Christ — Calvin orients theological knowledge toward, on one hand, the glorious grace of God clear in creation, and on the other, the merciful grace of God clear in Christ. With the Holy Spirit's help, disciples may come to know both of these gracious benefits, or rather both aspects of God's one creative, saving grace. And with such knowledge "as our guide and teacher," Calvin writes, "we should learn to seek every good from him, and, having received it, to credit it to his account" (1.2.2).

These two key gestures — "seeking" every good from God and "crediting" God with every good — mark out the primary practical contours of Christian life for Calvin, the life of *pietas*, the fully human life that all theological knowledge should finally and manifestly serve.

14. *Calvin's Commentaries*, 21:154; ICR 3.7.2.

"Seeking" every good from God means that Christian disciples continually orient themselves toward God as their gracious benefactor, paradigmatically through practices of prayerful petition, supplication, lament, and so on. But at the same time, by extension, disciples cultivate this stance throughout their lives in every respect, a kind of existential posture "facing God," we might say, in a fundamental bearing of receptivity and appeal in all times and places. Indeed, nearly the whole range of human activity falls under one or another form of seeking goods, whether the object of pursuit is a good meal, a good livelihood, a good deed, or an opportunity for good pleasure. And in Calvin's view, living a life of *pietas* means orienting all this activity ultimately toward God as the fountain of every good, and so in this sense living one's whole life as a humble, hopeful, expectant plea, "seeking every good from him."

On the other hand, for Calvin, "crediting" God with every good means interpreting every genuine benefit in our lives as in fact a divine gift, and so as a fresh provocation to *pietas*. Accordingly, it means revering and praising and thanking God for these gifts — during Sunday worship, to be sure, but also at table grace before and after every meal, or upon rising in the morning, or upon retiring at night, or indeed at a thousand other junctures in daily life when genuine blessings come into view. Human affairs are shot through with explicit and implicit attributions of credit — taking credit and giving credit, claiming credit and sharing credit — and as Calvin understands it, living a life of *pietas* means ascribing credit ultimately to God for "every good," thereby recognizing every good meal, every good livelihood, every good deed, every good pleasure as nothing less than a gracious gift from God's own hand.

Who lives this way? Who lives a whole human life as a humble act of prayer and a grateful, gracious act of praise? For Calvin, the one who lives this way is the one who knows God as her benefactor and herself as God's beneficiary. That is, she knows God as her loving parent and herself as God's beloved child. By way of the Holy Spirit's illumination, she does not merely *know about* God. She knows God. Not with an abstract knowledge, or the detached knowledge of surveillance, or the presumptuous knowledge that claims too much, but rather with familiar knowledge, a child's knowledge, the knowledge of intimacy, trust, and affection. In a word, she knows God with a loving knowledge, just as a toddler knows her parents, not independent of them but rather entirely, wholeheartedly dependent on them, both ensconced in her relationship with them and determined by the goal of developing that relationship, delighting in it, reveling in it. Thus the child of God knows God. And thus the child's knowledge of God takes shape in her life as reliance and reverence, day in and day out.

And in Jesus Christ, she knows God as having brought her under the divine wing, incorporating her into his standing as God's begotten, engrafting her into his own body via a "mystical union" beyond her ken. Knowing him and following him, disciples come to know themselves as sinners forgiven in Christ. In communion with him, they are beloved by God despite their sin, and indeed precisely in the face of it. Thus in Christ, they know God as their merciful guardian. Despite their failings, God communes with them, returns them to filial fellowship, and so embraces and enrolls them, precisely as sinners, in God's great school of sanctification.

Accordingly, guided and provoked by this knowledge, they seek every good from God and credit God with every good, from this morning's breakfast to their own very being. For Calvin, this is the practical life of *pietas,* the life toward which disciples are persistently trained in and through Christian formation. It is a life punctuated by practices of prayer and praise, but this punctuation is not for its own sake, as if "spiritual disciplines" are somehow ends in themselves. On the contrary, such disciplines are properly exercised for the sake of life as a whole, that is, for the sake of cultivating a continual posture of prayer and praise, a whole manner of being, a whole way of life.

Who lives this way? For Calvin, the genuine Christian lives this way — or rather, the genuine Christian disciple (Latin *discipulus,* "student") learns to live this way by living along and within a Christian paideutic program. Thus disciples may be formed to true piety *(formarentur ad veram pietatem).*[15] And insofar as such formation involves human knowledge, Christian doctrine finds its proper place in Christian life — that is, its proper setting, purpose, and limit.

---

15. Calvin, *ICR,* "Prefatory Address to King Francis I of France," p. 9.

CHAPTER 5

Radiance and Oblivion

To know God, Calvin argues, is to love God. More precisely: the knowledge of God that Calvin has in mind — a relational-pragmatic knowledge of God as parent and benefactor — induces in the knower the love and reverence that constitute genuine *pietas*. But for Calvin, this knowledge and love take place within a scenario best understood by way of a fundamental, interconnected cluster of theological themes: creation, providence, and sin. With this crucial doctrinal trio, Calvin sketches the basic reality of what God gracefully provides for the world, and the daily reality of what humanity disgracefully does with that inheritance.

Alongside the doctrine of predestination (which we will explore in chapter 8), the doctrine of humanity's thoroughgoing "depravity" is the idea for which Calvin is perhaps best known today — and to be sure, many passages in the *Institutio* would seem to justify that reputation quite nicely. Calvin leaves no doubt, for example, that he understands that we human beings have so corrupted ourselves in the "miserable ruin" of sin that, left to our own devices, we are utterly incapable of effecting our own salvation, so much so that our attempts in that direction only deepen the trouble. Indeed, since the great theological controversies of his day turned largely on questions of whether human beings could to some extent "merit" salvation by their own work, Calvin's preoccupation with the subject is hardly surprising. Against all concepts of human merit before God, Calvin sets out to build a bulwark of theological emphasis on humanity's moral "corruption" and "depravity."

But this particular polemic context only makes more striking the fact that Calvin's basic, organizing figure for human sin in book 1 of the *Institutio* is not "depravity" per se. To be sure, the word does appear occasionally in book 1, and throughout his work Calvin can be bluntly candid about the "hypocrisy," "lust," "haughtiness," "wickedness," "vanity" — the list goes on — characteristic of human life this side of Eden. In his view, humanity's fall into sin is without question a fall into moral ruin, a "depravation of a nature previously good and pure."[1] But another major concept frames, specifies, and organizes his portrait of human sin in the *Institutio*'s opening book, and the familiar emphasis among Calvinists on "depravity" may well cause some interpreters to overlook it. That is, the governing indictment of fallen humanity in book 1 is that humans are "dull," "blind," "forgetful," "ungrateful," "insensible," "dim" — in a word, oblivious.

Oblivious to what? At least three things: most broadly, oblivious to the glory of God in creation; more specifically, oblivious to the "sense of divinity [*divinitatis sensum*]" in our own minds and bodies; and most decisively, oblivious to the ongoing parental kindness and generosity of God in our own lives, day in and day out. For Calvin, the whole world without remainder is actually radiant with the majesty, presence, and grace of God, and yet, mired in sin, human beings are too dull, too blind, too senseless to see it and feel it and live according to it. Like fish who have forgotten the water around and within them, we fail to notice the One in whom we live and move.

Again and again Calvin returns to this fundamental theme. Oblivion, not "depravity," is Calvin's organizing figure in book 1 for what has gone wrong in human life, the crisis from which human beings require salvation. The crisis is moral in character, to be sure, and in that sense oblivion may be understood as a particular species of "depravity" — which term, at least as typically used in modern English, is most closely associated with corruption, wickedness, perversion, evil, and so on. But oblivion, as Calvin deploys the concept, has both a moral dimension (e.g., being oblivious to a clear and present benefactor) and an amoral one (e.g., being oblivious to a secret), and in that sense embraces both human insolence and human finitude, brute contempt and mere ignorance.

---

1. John Calvin, *Institutes of the Christian Religion*, ed. John T. McNeill (Philadelphia: Westminster, 1960), 2.1.5 (hereafter cited as *ICR*; section references cited in parentheses in the text).

Moreover, unlike "depravity," oblivion has to do particularly with sense and sensibility, awareness and experience, perception and insight, and so finally with relational propriety and decorum — the sphere of *pietas* and *impietas*. Indeed, oblivion amounts to piety's reversal: being disastrously unaware of and unresponsive to one's own actual situation, including and especially one's relationship with God. Accordingly, in book 1 Calvin contends that humanity has taken leave of its senses, and that God's saving work is to help it come back to them anew. Again, the depravity of fallen human nature is a topic by no means absent from book 1, and in book 2 Calvin gives it center stage — though even there the theme of human insensibility still plays a significant part. In book 1, however, the fundamental contrast that structures Calvin's overall case is between splendor and stupor, the tragic disconnection between, on one side, the radiance of God in creation and, on the other, the self-absorbed oblivion of humanity.

Calvin takes theological cues here from Paul, and in particular from the opening argument in the Epistle to the Romans. Indeed, book 1 can be read largely as a reflection, elaboration, and development of the apostle's claim that "since the creation of the world [God's] eternal power and divine nature, invisible though they are, have been understood and seen through the things he has made. So they are without excuse; for though they knew God, they did not honor him as God or give thanks to him, but they became futile in their thinking, and their senseless minds were darkened" (Rom. 1:20-21). For Paul, then, while human sin takes many forms, a kind of root form of it, the basic mistake from which the others follow (from "degrading passions" to "envy, murder, strife," and so on), is what he calls an inexcusable, "futile," "senseless" disregard for how God's power and nature can be "understood and seen through the things he has made."[2] And this disregard is evident, please note, above all through a conspicuous lack of doxology and gratitude: "they did not honor him as God or give thanks to him." Thus Paul pictures a radiant creation in the first place, and an oblivious humanity in the second place — and in book 1 of the *Institutio*, Calvin picks up and develops these themes in his own distinctive way.

---

2. Paul's case that this kind of oblivion is the basic disaster from which the other forms of sin follow comes clear as the passage unfolds: see, e.g., the "Therefore" in v. 24, the "For this reason" in v. 26, and the "And since" in v. 28.

Creation

In Calvin's view, the universe is a marvelous, "dazzling theater" where divine glory is perpetually, ubiquitously on display: "in God's individual works — but especially in them as a whole — God's powers are actually represented as in a painting," he writes. "Thereby the whole of mankind is invited and attracted to recognition of him, and from this to true and complete happiness" (*ICR* 1.5.10).[3] Immersed in this brilliant work of theatrical or painterly divine art, human beings "cannot open their eyes without being compelled to see [God] . . . whenever and wherever [they] cast [their] gaze" (1.5.1). In this way, Calvin contends, God the Creator may be recognized and in that sense known, and such knowledge "ought not only to arouse us to the worship of God, but also to awaken and encourage us to the hope of the future life" (1.5.10).

Indeed, explaining this latter point, Calvin goes so far as to argue that even the apparent obscurity of divine mercy and justice in the visible world should function in its own way as an encouraging sign. For since divine promises are trustworthy, even today's "inchoate and incomplete" glimpses must "presage even greater things, the manifestation and full exhibition of which are deferred to another life" (1.5.10). Thus Calvin rather daringly suggests that through the eyes of faith, even the trials and setbacks of human life may be occasions for Christian hope and anticipation.[4] In this way, "whithersoever you turn," whether up to a starry sky or down to a stray shard of justice in human affairs, "evidences" abound "that serve to illuminate and affirm the divine majesty." For the "true spectator," Calvin maintains, such evidence "can easily be observed with the eyes and pointed out with the finger" (1.5.8, 9).

---

3. For Calvin's frequent figure of the heavens and the earth as a "theater" (*theatrum*) of divine glory, see, e.g., 1.5.8; 1.6.2; 1.14.20; 2.6.1; 3.9.2; and elsewhere.

4. This position is daring not least because of the dangers that attend it, including the risks that it be understood (1) to encourage quietism with respect to affliction, and/or (2) to discourage expressions of grief and lament in times of hardship, promoting instead a relentless Christian optimism. On the other hand, however, alongside these risks sit the clear pastoral advantages of Calvin's position, since it potentially allows for hopeful, empowering interpretations of otherwise debilitating circumstances. But to appropriate this position today, the pastoral risks, too, constantly must be borne in mind, along with counterbalancing ideas to safeguard against misunderstanding and misuse. In part III, I will turn to these matters in earnest.

Nor need the disciple restrict her survey to the world outside her; she may also turn to her own mind and body. "There is within the human mind," Calvin writes, "and indeed by natural instinct, a sense of divinity [*divinitatis sensum*]." Again following Paul in Romans, Calvin argues that God, to "prevent anyone from taking refuge in the pretense of ignorance," implants in every human being "a certain understanding of his divine majesty," in effect a universal "seed of religion" according to which "men one and all perceive that there is a God and that he is their Maker" (1.3.1). Even the "reprobate," who may or may not explicitly deny belief in God, nevertheless exhibit this religious "seed" indirectly or despite themselves, impulsively fearing God in guilt, for example, or seeking God in distress (1.3.2).

But for Calvin, this inward awareness is not only cognitive; it is also physical and palpable: "For each one undoubtedly feels within the heavenly grace that quickens him." Accordingly, all are capable of "finding God in [their] body and soul a hundred times," not least in "such exquisite workmanship in their individual members, from mouth and eyes even to their very toenails." In Calvin's view, each and every human being, right down to his or her toes, is a "rare example of God's power, goodness, and wisdom, and contains within himself enough miracles to occupy our minds, if only we are not irked at paying attention to them." Even "infants," he insists, "while they nurse at their mothers' breasts, have tongues so eloquent to preach [God's] glory that there is no need at all of other orators" (1.5.3-4).

The key theme running through all this is that God's majesty and love for the world, and in particular for humanity, are in no way obscure. On the contrary, they are abundantly, intimately, radiantly obvious. They are clear and present everywhere, "shining forth" within us and without us. And for Calvin, as clear as they are in God's original creation of the world, they are no less clear in God's ongoing governance of it: "we see the presence of divine power shining as much in the continuing state of the universe as in its inception." That is, when it comes to God, the title "Creator" effectively entails the titles "Governor" and "Preserver," too, since God not only makes but also "sustains, nourishes, and cares for everything he has made, even to the least sparrow" (1.16.1; cf. Matt. 10:29).

Providence

To imagine that God originally created but does not now uphold, direct, and look after the universe would be, Calvin maintains, both "cold and barren," and those who do so "are far from that earnest feeling of grace which [Paul] commends, because they do not at all taste God's special care, by which alone his fatherly favor is known" (1.16.1). In other words, to affirm a robust doctrine of divine creation without an equally robust doctrine of divine providence is, in effect, to cut off the very source of *pietas*. For as we have seen, in Calvin's view, *pietas* is nothing less than the love and reverence "induced" by the manifold ways in which disciples "taste God's special care" here and now, the ongoing nurture "by which alone his fatherly favor is known."

The point is crucial to Calvin's whole theological approach. Knowing God's "fatherly favor" — that is, "sensing," "feeling," "tasting" divine blessing and benefits — is the event that gives rise to *pietas*, and so forms the continual basis of Christian life itself. A key intellectual condition of this kind of knowing is a lively conception of God's creative and providential power, since any claim that God has provided this or that particular benefit, or indeed that God provides every benefit everywhere, presupposes that God is a beneficent provider who actually does provide. Indeed, for Calvin, the doctrine of divine providence (that is, divine provide-ence) is a clarifying development of this presupposition.

Thus in Calvin's view, if Christian life does not include a robust doctrine of divine providence, it will be "cold and barren" for at least three related reasons: first, because a God who does not continually, tangibly provide benefits is no active, present, loving parent, but instead an idle monarch shut away in heaven; second, because if today's good things are not actually gifts of God, then the grounds for daily prayer, praise, thanksgiving, and indeed *pietas* itself are effectively pulled out from beneath the church's feet; and third, because, accordingly, the everyday world is thereby drained of its color and character as an unfolding divine gift being given here and now. Indeed, without a robust doctrine of divine providence, what is "given" in the sense of being a gift becomes merely "given" in the sense of being the case. The world flattens out, appearing not as an ongoing divine work of art but rather as a hodgepodge of things and thoughts and chance. And for Calvin, this flattened-out version of the world is not only less lovely than the alternative, it is also less accurate, less true to how things really are. For in truth, the world in all its variety is an unfolding divine gift, an ongoing symphony in which "nothing takes place by chance": "not one drop of rain falls without God's sure command" (1.16.4, 5).

But here someone may well object: Doesn't this view make God responsible not only for every drop of rain, but also for every drop of sin, suffering, and evil? Calvin addresses this objection at length in the *Institutio*, and the main outlines of his response feature four interrelated ideas. First, Calvin argues that in the case of sin, God works providentially in and through the sinner's act, in effect making use of it for divine purposes. Judas's betrayal of Jesus is a paradigmatic example of this kind of two-tiered intent: while Judas's motives were presumably condemnable, God makes use of the betrayal as part of salvation history. On one level, then, culpability for the act thus remains with the sinner, even as, on another level, God works in and through the same act, "bending" or "directing" it toward quite different ends. Echoing Genesis, Calvin puts it this way: "[God] knows right well how to use evil instruments to do good" (2.3.6; 1.17.5).[5]

Second, Calvin argues that God works providentially in and through suffering as a kind of pedagogue, "either to instruct his own people in patience, or to correct their wicked affections and tame their lust, or to subjugate them to self-denial, or to arouse them from sluggishness; [or] again, to bring low the proud," and so on (1.17.1).[6] Third, Calvin suggests that "our miseries" may at times function as occasions for God's glory to shine in subsequent rescues and remedies: here Calvin turns to the Gospel of John's story of Jesus healing a man born blind, in which Jesus declares, "Neither this man nor his parents sinned; he was born blind so that God's works might be revealed in him" (John 9:3).[7]

---

5. See Gen. 50:20, where Joseph says to his brothers: "Even though you intended to do harm to me, God intended it for good, in order to preserve a numerous people, as he is doing today."

6. The doctrine that God uses suffering pedagogically is a difficult, dangerous teaching attended by both profound pastoral advantages and equally profound pastoral risks. In part III below, I treat these advantages and risks in more detail.

7. Calvin even goes so far as to suggest that God gave Adam "a mediocre and even transitory will" — that is, a will that lacked sufficient perseverance to resist the fall into sin — so that "from man's Fall [God] might gather occasion for his own glory," since sin is a precondition of divine salvation. The suggestion is tentative, however, since only a

And fourth, decisively framing and limiting all three of the ideas just described, Calvin repeatedly emphasizes that divine providence — particularly when it comes to sin, suffering, and evil — is finally beyond human understanding. He typically writes of God's "hidden providence" in these cases, and of the consequent need for disciples to "cherish moderation" and "sobriety" in their reflection upon it, eschewing presumptuous speculation. After all, Calvin contends, "it would not even be useful for us to know what God himself, to test our moderation of faith, on purpose willed to be hidden" (1.14.1). Rather, in Calvin's view, what is useful is a stance that modestly receives everything, whether ray of sun or drop of rain, as a divine gift, part and parcel of the Creator's unfolding, immersive, providential work of art.

To interpret and experience the world this way — something each human being is capable of doing in principle, according to Calvin, but which, mired in sin, everyone in one way or another rejects or neglects — is to live constantly and consciously awash in God. Inwardly, the disciple feels "the heavenly grace that quickens him" and "finds God in his body and soul a hundred times." Outwardly, the disciple beholds "unmistakable marks" of divine glory wherever she turns. And with respect to the daily events of their lives, rain or shine, such disciples interpret each good as a divine gift, enduring each trial as divine pedagogy or an occasion for divine glory, and so experiencing whatever they encounter — pleasurable or challenging, delightful or demanding — as part of a divine program of formative education, a *paideia*, a way of discipleship. Accordingly, they gratefully love, revere, and listen to God as the one who both "nourishes and educates" them, and in so doing they live out whole human lives of genuine *pietas* (1.14.22). Indeed, as Calvin portrays it, we could hardly do otherwise, since "so many burning lamps shine for us in the workmanship of the universe to show forth the glory of its Author" that "they bathe us wholly in their radiance" (1.5.14).

---

few sentences earlier Calvin insists that "the reason [God] did not sustain man by the virtue of perseverance lies hidden in his plan; sobriety is the better part of wisdom." We may note in passing, however, how even Calvin's own "sobriety" on this point lasts only a few lines before he, too, cannot resist hazarding a suggestion! See Calvin, *ICR* 1.15.8.

Oblivion

And yet — we do otherwise. In fact, according to Calvin, we all do otherwise, every one of us without exception. We take the world for granted. We interpret it — now anxiously, now offhandedly — in terms of chance. We grasp the goods in our lives as our own achievements or entitlements or dumb luck, but by no means as divine gifts. Likewise, we suffer hardship as mere adversity, or in any case as merely unfortunate, but by no means as formative education. In this way, actually bathed in divine radiance, we fall into oblivion, that is, into "ingratitude," idolatry, and *impietas*. Surrounded by a "brightness which is borne in upon the eyes of all," we fall into shadows, into sin, into the fault that means our fall away from the relationship with God for which we were born (1.6.1).

And what precisely is this fault? Calvin calls it "the fault of dullness," along with a range of similar names: "weak vision," "blindness," "insensibility," "forgetfulness" (1.5.15; 1.6.1; 1.4.1; 1.6.2; 1.6.3). This dullness is no innocent naïveté, no mere lack of capacity or information, but rather is constituted "partly by ignorance, partly by malice": "the blindness under which [human beings] labor," Calvin writes, "is almost always mixed with proud vanity and obstinacy" (1.4 title; 1.4.1). Though every human mind includes a "sense of divinity," we invariably smother, corrupt, suppress, or otherwise ignore it. Though the universe fairly shimmers with divine glory, we invariably fail to see it, or, having glimpsed it, we forget it — or rather, we confound and distort it into any number of "artificial religions" (1.6.3). Oblivious, vain, forgetful, and obstinate as we are, Calvin writes, "no real piety remains in the world" (1.4.1). Plenty of alleged piety remains, of course, in Christian quarters as much as anywhere else, but it is counterfeit, an idolatrous parody of *pietas* devised by human beings "so as to seem to approach the God from whom they flee" (1.4.4).

From this angle, then, the sin of human beings amounts to what Calvin calls a "struggle against their own senses," that is, a struggle against their own natural awareness of God (1.4.2). Though God palpably indwells and surrounds and cares for humans; though a basic human vocation is "to contemplate God's works, since [humanity] has been placed in this most glorious theater to be a spectator of them"; though the universe itself is nothing less than "a living likeness" of its creator — despite all this, left to their own devices, human beings remain dismally oblivious, becoming over time only "more and more hardened in their insensibility" (1.6.2; 1.5.1; 1.5.6; 1.6.2). In a key passage, Calvin puts it this way:

> But although the Lord represents both himself and his everlasting Kingdom in the mirror of his works with very great clarity, such is our stupidity that we grow increasingly dull toward so manifest testimonies, and they flow away without profiting us. For with regard to the most beautiful structure and order of the universe, how many of us are there who, when we lift up our eyes to heaven or cast them about through the various regions of earth, recall our minds to a remembrance of the Creator, and do not rather, disregarding the Author, sit idly in contemplation of his works? In fact, with regard to those events which daily take place outside the ordinary course of nature, how many of us do not reckon that men are whirled and twisted about by blindly indiscriminate fortune, rather than governed by God's providence? (1.5.11)

Beholding the universe, we disregard the Author; beholding events, we disregard the Governor. In both cases, the basic point is the same, and it sums up the fundamental, organizing figure for human sin in book 1 of the *Institutio:* a dull, oblivious disregard for the radiant gifts of God around and within us.

And not only in book 1. As we will see, in book 2 human insensibility and "dullness of wit" remain important themes in Calvin's portrait of sin, but there the overall emphasis and organizing focus shift to infidelity, disobedience, "depravation of a nature previously good and pure," and so on (2.1.1; 2.1.5).[8] The fundamental reason for this shift is clear in the title of book 2, "The Knowledge of God the Redeemer," for such things as human infidelity, disobedience, and the "depravation of human nature" are precisely the disasters from which Jesus Christ offers salvation, as we will see in chapter 7. And yet even in book 2 and beyond in the *Institutio,* humanity's oblivion persists as a prominent, sometimes leading figure for sin in Calvin's thought.[9]

---

8. See also, e.g., 2.1.4-5: "Unfaithfulness, then, was the root of the Fall. But thereafter ambition and pride, together with ungratefulness, arose . . . [so that] in place of wisdom, virtue, holiness, truth, and justice, with which adornments he had been clad, there came forth the most filthy plagues, blindness, impotence, impurity, vanity, and injustice."

9. A representative, by no means exhaustive, sampling follows: 2.1.9: "the mind is

Radiance and Oblivion

As well it might, given his anthropology. In broad terms, Calvin contends that according to God's original design, a human being "consists of a soul and a body," and that the soul "consists of two faculties, understanding and will" (1.15.2, 7). Between these latter two elements, Calvin is quite clear about which one is meant to be in charge: "the understanding is, as it were, the leader and governor of the soul," he writes, and accordingly, "the will is always mindful of the bidding of the understanding, and in its own desires awaits the judgment of the understanding" (1.15.7). The implication of this anthropological architecture, of course, is a kind of principle: as the understanding goes, so goes the soul, and so goes the person. In humankind's fall into sin, then, whatever malformation is peculiar to the understanding would presumably play a key role in the overall catastrophe, and so would be a particularly fitting, synecdochic figure for it. In other words, in the thoroughgoing catastrophe of human sin, the distinctive ruin of the understanding, that "leader and governor of the soul," may aptly stand for the whole.

And what specific malformation, in Calvin's view, afflicts the fallen human being's faculty of understanding? Oblivion. Our "mind, because of its dullness, cannot hold to the right path," he writes, "but wanders through various errors and stumbles repeatedly." Accordingly, "dullness and ingratitude" overtake us, and since "all our senses have become perverted, we wickedly defraud God of his glory." Unable to see and sense and savor the world as we should, we wander and stagger, "groping in the darkness." Indeed, Calvin continues, so malformed is the human understanding that it cannot even "discern which things it ought to exert itself to know." Consequently, we foolishly misdirect our powers of attention, sensation, and analysis. "For this reason, in investigating empty and worthless things, [the understanding] torments it-

given over to blindness and the heart to depravity"; 2.2.21: a man who thinks he knows more than God has revealed to him in Scripture is "all the more blind because he does not recognize his own blindness"; 2.2.12: "Indeed, man's mind, because of its dullness, cannot hold to the right path"; 2.6.1: "Dullness and ingratitude follow, for our minds, as they have been blinded, do not perceive what is true. And as all our senses have become perverted, we wickedly defraud God of his glory"; 3.24.12: "The supreme Judge, then, makes way for his predestination when he leaves in blindness those whom he has once condemned and deprived of participation in his light"; 3.24.16: God makes "even kings and magistrates sharers in the heavenly doctrine though because of their blindness they should rage against it"; and so on.

93

self in absurd curiosity, while it carelessly pays little or no attention to matters that it should particularly understand" (2.2.12).

In this way, first by establishing the faculty of understanding as the "governor of the soul," and then by laying the crucial "fault of dullness" at its doorstep, Calvin effectively conceives humanity's fall into sin as, we might say, a headfirst fall. He conceives it as a dive into a dull, vain, self-absorbed oblivion — not headfirst in any strict corporeal or sequential sense, of course, but rather in a structural, anthropological sense, a kind of logical and theological priority if not a chronological one. To be sure, for Calvin, the "miserable ruin" of sin involves the thoroughgoing malformation of human being. Nothing less than "the whole man is overwhelmed — as by a deluge — from head to foot, so that no part is immune from sin" (2.1.9). But at the same time, Calvin's anthropological sketch points to the idea that the ruinous flood does indeed envelop us *"from head to foot"*: that is, from the faculty of understanding, the soul's "leader and governor" now ruined by "the fault of dullness," all the way down to the body's pilgrim feet, and so to our wayward "wandering through various errors and stumbling repeatedly." Thus even Calvin's anthropological framework supports the idea that oblivion is a fundamental, organizing figure for human sin in the *Institutio*, particularly in book 1. And in this respect Calvin parallels Paul in Romans, where the apostle maintains that sin's foundational form is an inexcusable, "senseless" oblivion to how God's power and nature can be "understood and seen through the things he has made."[10]

Moreover, again paralleling Paul, Calvin contends that sin is by no means strictly reducible to oblivion, but rather proliferates from it with a dreadful, dazzling variety. Accordingly, in Calvin's view, pride, malice, hypocrisy, and a whole range of other vices play their crucial part in humanity's original and ongoing malformation, and in the end, the fallen human will is no less a ruin than the fallen human mind.[11]

---

10. See Rom. 1, especially vv. 20-21, and see above, n. 2.

11. In fact, Calvin goes so far as to declare that "the power of sin" has its "chief seat" in the will (2.2.27) — a claim at first glance appearing to contradict his anthropological portrait, according to which "the will is always mindful of the bidding of the understanding, and in its own desires awaits the judgment of the understanding" (1.15.7). However, in 1.15.7 Calvin has in view the human being "as created," that is, unspoiled by sin, whereas in 2.2.27 his subject is the human being already devastated. Thus the two passages may be reconciled this way: while humanity originally fell headlong, that is, via

Radiance and Oblivion

But for Calvin, an original and radical dimension of humanity's fall has to do with sensibility and right relationship; with understanding and decorum; with neither noticing nor remembering God's loving, parental care, and so failing to respond fittingly and beautifully, as God's children, in and through lives of *pietas*. And appropriately enough, if humanity's fall originally and radically has to do with sensibility, right relationship, understanding, and decorum, God's saving remedy will, too — which brings us to Calvin's account of Holy Scripture and the Holy Spirit, the subject of the next chapter.

But first, to sum up Calvin's case thus far: created as God's children, we are made for *pietas,* that is, for whole human lives of filial love, knowledge, reverence, and intimacy with God. In keeping with this calling, God graciously provides a universe — including our own bodies, minds, and histories — that is itself a marvel, shining from every corner with clear marks of divine presence and power, majesty and mercy. Despite this splendor, however, we are dimly, disastrously oblivious, ignorantly or vainly but in any case recklessly unaware of our actual situation.

We sit and feast at a great banquet table — and ignore the host. We receive gift upon gift — and coolly, casually open each box as if it were already our own property. We misread the world as merely the world and not as a divine work of art, a luminous mirror of both God and the kingdom of God. We misread events as mere events, haphazard and arbitrary, and not as radiant manifestations of God's nourishment and care for every creature in creation, "even to the least sparrow." Dull, insensible, forgetful, vain — in short, oblivious in this way, we fall into *impietas.* We take ourselves and the world for granted. We eat, and grasp, and worry, and die.

---

the dullness of the understanding, in the resulting wreckage the "power of sin" settled, as it were, with its "chief seat" in the will. According to this view, then, part of sin's devastation is how it disorders even the way in which the soul's faculties function in relation to each other: now the understanding, blinded by its own blind abandon, has forfeited its proper role as "leader and governor of the soul," and now the will, equally malformed and dysfunctional, desires and chooses exactly what it should neither desire nor choose. Indeed, as he spells out this anthropological disarray, Calvin may well have in mind Rom. 7:19-25, and in particular, the disorder summed up in v. 19: "For I do not do the good that I want, but the evil I do not want is what I do."

CHAPTER 6

Seeing through Scripture

Part of what makes it clear that "dullness" is Calvin's organizing figure for humanity's fall into sin in book 1 of the *Institutio* is the saving remedy that, according to Calvin, God provides — since, after all, the divine rescue presumably will fit the predicament, the key the lock, the cure the disease. And the rescue, key, and cure God initially provides humanity, Calvin contends, is Christian Scripture. Precisely and expressly to "disperse our dullness" so that humanity "might not sink into oblivion," God provides "the light of his Word" to illuminate the divine will and character more clearly.[1] In his opening discussion of Scripture in the *Institutio,* Calvin compares the Bible to spectacles: "Just as old or bleary-eyed men and those with weak vision, if you thrust before them a most beautiful volume, even if they recognize it to be some sort of writing, yet can scarcely construe two words, but with the aid of spectacles will begin to read distinctly; so Scripture, gathering up the otherwise confused knowledge of God in our minds, having dispersed our dullness, clearly shows us the true God" (*ICR* 1.6.1).[2] Thus Calvin casts Christian Scripture as a clarifying instrument that "clearly shows us the true God" — even more clearly, that is, than does the shimmering, radiant universe itself.

And yet we may ask this question, examining this famous figure

---

1. John Calvin, *Institutes of the Christian Religion,* ed. John T. McNeill (Philadelphia: Westminster, 1960), 1.6.1 (hereafter cited as *ICR;* section references cited in parentheses in the text).

2. See also 1.14.1 and Calvin, *Commentaries on Genesis* (Grand Rapids: Baker, 1981), p. 62.

more closely: If "Scripture" corresponds to "spectacles," what corresponds to the "most beautiful volume" thrust before a group of bleary-eyed readers, the lovely book that the spectacles help them to read? At first glance, an obvious answer is that the "beautiful volume" corresponds to "the true God." But the broad choreography of Calvin's case thus far in the *Institutio* — that creation is a theater resplendent with divine glory, and that humanity is nevertheless oblivious to it — indicates that the "beautiful volume" may also correspond to creation as God's own handiwork, that divine masterpiece in which God is "in a certain manner, manifest."[3] This reading of the "spectacles" simile is consistent not only with Paul's claim in Romans that God's power and nature can be "understood and seen through the things he has made," but also with how Calvin repeatedly instructs disciples "to contemplate [God] in his works," and that such contemplation should "occupy our whole life" (1.5.9; 1.14.2; Rom. 1:20).

Thus in Calvin's view, the role of the Bible in Christian life is not only to disclose "the true God" within its own pages, but also to act as a kind of clarifying lens through which disciples may come to see God all around and within them, and indeed to recognize themselves and the whole world as "living likenesses" of God (1.5.6). Seeing through Scripture, we might say, disciples may learn to see creation more accurately and vividly as the graceful work of God, from the starry sky above to the most mundane details of daily life below. Likewise, listening through Scripture, disciples may learn to develop "ears to hear" creation more perceptively as a divine symphony, thereby retraining and retuning their aural attention and insight. And so on.

From this angle, a whole program of scriptural, paideutic education opens up, in effect a scriptural rehabilitation of human sensibility. Learning to see through the "spectacles" of biblical texts, disciples learn to see the world; learning to see the world, we learn "to see God," Calvin writes, "who everywhere gives signs of his presence."[4] And learning to see God, we learn to see, hear, experience, and know — in short, to "sense" in every way we can — our actual situation as children of God, and so as beneficiaries of God's continual love and care. And the more this actual situation comes clear to us — that is, the more we wholeheartedly take it to be our actual situation — the more deeply we

---

3. Calvin, *Commentaries on Genesis*, p. 59.
4. Calvin, *Commentaries on Genesis*, p. 60.

97

are drawn into lives of genuine *pietas,* revering, loving, and serving God at every turn.

Scripture and the Spirit

All this can and does take place, Calvin contends — but only as the Holy Spirit wills it and enables it in and with human beings. For Calvin, the Spirit's accompaniment and persuasive power are the indispensable conditions of all growth and progress along this formative course of learning, not least with respect to understanding the Bible itself. On one hand, then, Calvin insists that if we "turn aside from the Word," we "may strive with strenuous haste, yet, since we have got off the track, we shall never reach the goal" (1.5.3). And yet, on the other hand, Calvin argues that human dullness and confusion are so thoroughgoing that, left to our own devices, even if we earnestly turn *toward* biblical texts, we can only mistake and mistrust them, unless God the Spirit guides and illumines our judgment. Merely reading the Bible will not do. The Spirit must be present with and in the reader, "sealing" Scripture with an "inward testimony" so that "it seriously affects us" (1.7.5). In other words, the "same Spirit" who "has spoken through the mouths of the prophets must penetrate into our hearts to persuade us that they faithfully proclaimed what had been divinely commanded." Absent this inward, Spirited persuasion, even the Bible's most diligent readers can only remain skeptical and confused, for unless God "illumines their minds, they ever waver among many doubts!" (1.7.4).

Thus in Calvin's view, the Holy Spirit is both the "Author" of Scripture and the necessary companion in our interpretation of it, illuminating our minds and persuading our hearts "both to read and to hearken" to biblical texts "as if there the living words of God were heard" (1.9.2; 1.7.1). In this way, Calvin contends that the whole career of Scripture in Christian life — from ancient authorship to present-day reading, preaching, and hearing — is suffused by the Holy Spirit's guidance and illumination.[5] "But nothing is accomplished," Calvin writes,

---

5. Indeed, in view of this Spirit saturation, the whole debate over whether Calvin conceives Scripture as "inerrant" is, I argue, fundamentally out of place. It is no accident that the very category of "inerrancy" does not arise as such for Calvin in his discussion of Scripture; his emphasis rests instead on the consummate reliability of Scripture as an instrument through which the Holy Spirit dispels the church's oblivion vis-à-vis God,

"if the Spirit, as our inner teacher, does not show our minds the way . . . [and] by a wonderful and singular power, forms our ears to hear and our minds to understand" (2.2.20).[6]

Indeed, for Calvin, Scripture and Spirit are so intimately joined "by a kind of mutual bond" that they are, from the human point of view, inseparably linked: "the Word is the instrument by which the Lord dispenses the illumination of his Spirit to believers" (1.9.3). Accordingly, if the Bible is God's "special gift" to the church for dispersing human dullness and oblivion, the paideutic program Calvin has in mind here is as pneumatological as it is biblical (1.6.1). In their ongoing training and formation, as disciples learn to see through Scripture and so learn to see the world as a "living likeness" of God, the Holy Spirit serves as their indispensable guide and teacher all the way along.

Thus Calvin sketches a twofold *paideia,* a school nested within a school, the Bible nested within the cosmos. In the broadest frame, as we have seen, for Calvin the universe itself is a grand divine curriculum, a "dazzling theater" (1.5.8) in which human beings would come to know God by contemplating divine works of majesty and mercy — if only our sensibilities were sound. Remarking on creation in his commentary on Genesis, Calvin puts it this way: "We know God, who is himself invisible, only through his works. . . . This is the reason why the Lord, that he may invite us to the knowledge of himself, places the fabric of heaven and earth before our eyes, rendering himself, in a certain manner, manifest in them. . . . Therefore, as soon as the name of God sounds in our ears, or the thought of him occurs to our minds, let us also clothe him with this most beautiful ornament; finally, let the world become our school if we desire rightly to know God."[7] The Creator wills to be

---

like a new pair of spectacles, the better to perceive God's benevolent love for us. When it comes to this particular task, Calvin maintains, the church may and should wholeheartedly trust Scripture and the Spirit — but this need not entail, and Calvin does not go on to say, that in order for the Spirit to accomplish this task Scripture's entire library must be devoid of errors or contradictions. For an example of recent discussions on Calvin and scriptural inerrancy, see Robert L. Reymond, "Calvin's Doctrine of Holy Scripture," in *A Theological Guide to Calvin's Institutes,* ed. David W. Hall and Peter A. Lillback (Phillipsburg, N.J.: P&R Publishing, 2008), pp. 44-64.

6. See also 3.1.4: "Paul shows the Spirit to be the inner teacher by whose effort the promise of salvation penetrates into our minds, a promise that would otherwise only strike the air or beat upon our ears"; and 3.2.33: "without the illumination of the Holy Spirit, the Word can do nothing."

7. Calvin, *Commentaries on Genesis,* pp. 59-60.

Rereading the Institutio

known by creatures, and so sets them in a cosmic "school" wherein they may come to know the invisible God "magnificently arrayed in the incomparable vesture of the heavens and the earth."[8] That is, in the grandeur of land and sea and sky, in the marvels of mind and body, in the great and small events of history and daily life — in all these and more, God is continually "rendering himself, in a certain manner, manifest." Thus Calvin goes on to describe "the world as a mirror in which we ought to behold God."[9]

"We ought to" — but we do not. We either ignore this cosmic curriculum entirely or study it foolishly, confounding ourselves into a thousand forms of idolatry — and so, "we are not at all sufficiently instructed by this bare and simple testimony which the creatures render splendidly to the glory of God" (1.5.15). Delinquent and oblivious, we neglect to "let the world become our school." Instead, we drop out, and since there is no place else to go, we wander the school halls in a dull, self-absorbed stupor, forgetting even where we are and why. What we need, then, is a fresh orientation, a means of reenrollment, a field guide, a manual, a pair of "spectacles" — and a teacher to show us the way.

And so God provides Holy Scripture and the Holy Spirit, a compact curriculum on one hand and an indwelling instructor on the other. To characterize the "special gift" of Scripture, Calvin uses terms strikingly reminiscent of his portrait of creation. He calls Scripture "the very school of God's children," for example, and "a mirror in which [God's] living likeness glows" (1.6.4; 1.14.1). That is, describing the Bible, Calvin recapitulates key terms he used to describe the universe: "school," "mirror," "living likeness" of God, and so on. In this way, Calvin portrays Scripture as a school within a school, a likeness within a likeness, a reflection within a reflection. Like Jan van Eck's convex mirror in his *Arnolfini Portrait* or M. C. Escher's iconic glass sphere, the Bible is at once a constituent part of a larger work of art and a reflected encapsulation of it, a summary model of the whole.[10]

Indeed, according to this view, the biblical canon is itself a little

---

8. Calvin, *Commentaries on Genesis*, p. 60.
9. Calvin, *Commentaries on Genesis*, p. 62.
10. See Jan van Eck's *Arnolfini Portrait* (1434), National Gallery, London, and M. C. Escher's *Hand with Reflecting Sphere* (lithograph, 1935). Moreover, the frame of van Eck's mirror is decorated with a circle of scenes from Christ's passion, making it even more fitting as a figure for "seeing through Scripture."

cosmos, a microcosm through which "God, to instruct the church, not merely uses mute teachers" — that is, the universe and everything in it — "but also opens his own most hallowed lips" (1.6.1). In Scripture, then, disciples may find a clarified, amplified version of what creation already testifies about God the Creator that they are too insensible to notice on their own. And so for their part, Christian disciples, their eyes and ears trained by looking and listening for God in the microcosm of Scripture, may thereby come to see and hear God more clearly in the macrocosm, too — that is, in the vast school and mirror of creation, the "dazzling theater" all around and within them.

In this way, Scripture may genuinely function for disciples as a pair of "spectacles," a clarifying instrument through which everything else may be more vividly, accurately seen. Or again, returning to the aural metaphor, Scripture may genuinely function for them as a "herald," as Calvin puts it, "who excites [their] attention, in order that [they] may perceive [themselves] to be placed in this scene" both "for the purpose of beholding the glory of God" and "to enjoy all the riches which are here exhibited."[11] In a brief comment on Psalm 29 in the *Institutio*, Calvin writes that the psalmist, after marveling at "God's awesome voice" audible in "thunder, winds, rains, whirlwinds," and so on, "finally adds at the end that his praises are sung in the sanctuary because the unbelievers are deaf to all the voices of God that resound in the air" (1.6.4).

The claim is striking: the reason that God's praises are sung in sanctuaries and not also everywhere else, Calvin maintains, is that those without the benefit of the Holy Spirit's instruction — preeminently, instruction in and through Scripture — are still too dull to hear "all the voices of God" resounding in the world at large. It is as if a sanctuary functions as a kind of studio and stage in the midst of creation, a place where what should be audible anywhere ("all the voices of God") is amplified, and what should be happening everywhere (humanity's praise of God) is manifest, by the Spirit's gift. Again, Calvin's case conjures up the image of a microcosm within a macrocosm, this time a temple within a temple: God's voice perpetually fills the temple of creation but goes unrecognized and therefore unheeded by human beings; but in the microcosmic temples of the church, God's Word is amplified and clarified. That is, in the smaller sanctuaries God's voice may be discerned more clearly in the "school" and "mirror" of Scrip-

---

11. Calvin, *Commentaries on Genesis*, p. 62.

ture, the sermons of well-trained preachers, the psalm singing of the whole congregation, and so on. But the smaller sanctuary should by no means eclipse the cosmic one; rather, it should point toward it, disclose it, and train disciples so that their whole lives may be lived out as liturgies writ large.

As we have seen, early critics of Reformed worship spaces found them reminiscent of schoolhouses, what with their fixed seating, whitewashed walls, and liturgies dominated by Scripture reading and frequent, lengthy, expository preaching. In a sense, the critique fits, since in Calvin's view, Christian life is nothing if not a paideutic path of discipleship grounded first of all in the Christian Bible, "the very school of God's children" — and accordingly, worship should be designed and carried out largely (though not exclusively) as an exercise in formative education. That is, for Calvin, churches should be houses of prayer and praise, but precisely as such, they should also be sites of rigorous intellectual and sensory formation: maximally free of perceived distractions — hence the unadorned walls, fixed seating, absence of musical instruments, and so on — and maximally geared toward discerning God's word in Scripture, and so toward learning to see, hear, and experience the world in scriptural terms.

Like the Israelites in the desert, and like countless monastics in the early church, in their own way Calvin and his colleagues sought a new Sinai: a stark, clear, uncluttered place where they could engage anew with the Holy Spirit and Holy Writ. Thus even the clean, spare architectural and aesthetic style of early Reformed worship spaces may be understood not only as a matter of polemic iconoclasm or sectarian taste, but also as a kind of return to the desert without leaving the city. For Calvin, a Christian sanctuary should indeed function as a schoolhouse, a place of concentration, focus, and learning — and ultimately a place where the catechism and especially the Bible may be engaged and internalized such that they form how disciples experience and live in the wider world.[12]

Moreover, viewed from a slightly different angle, the relatively un-

---

12. The idea that Christian liturgy — and so-called ritual action in general — functions as a kind of "focusing lens" for human practitioners in their intellectual, moral, and other formation is well represented in modern ritual studies. Cf., e.g., Jonathan Z. Smith, "The Bare Facts of Ritual," in *Imagining Religion: From Babylon to Jonestown* (Chicago: University of Chicago Press, 1982), pp. 53-65, especially p. 54 — "A sacred place is a place of clarification (a focusing lens)" — and p. 63.

adorned simplicity of early Reformed worship spaces may also reflect Calvin's emphasis on divine accommodation to humanity's sensory and intellectual limits.[13] That is, though creation may be filled with "all the voices of God that resound in the air," human beings nevertheless require remedial training to make those voices out. The Christian Bible, read and expounded in a relatively serene, simple setting, provides a kind of basic, streamlined, beginner's laboratory for this training. Calvin believed the constraints on human competence were due partly to humanity's ongoing dullness, oblivion, vanity, and so on, but they were also due to human finitude on one side and the boundless glory of God on the other. The "dazzling theater" of creation is just that — "dazzling" — even and especially to the most perceptive, Spirit-led human observers. And so, since even a rehabilitated human sensibility cannot but be overwhelmed by divine glory, God accommodates us by communicating through relatively simple, accessible forms, in church architecture and liturgy no less than in Scripture.

In the opening paragraph of his commentary on Genesis, after contending that "the measure of our capacity is too contracted" to comprehend the divine wisdom displayed in creation, Calvin insists that we disciples should nevertheless contemplate God's works as best we can, precisely as humble children totally immersed in divine creativity and care:

> We see, indeed, the world with our eyes, we tread the earth with our feet, we touch innumerable kinds of God's works with our hands, we inhale a sweet and pleasant fragrance from herbs and flowers, we enjoy boundless benefits; but in those very things of which we attain some knowledge, there dwells such an immensity of divine power, goodness, and wisdom, as absorbs all our senses. Therefore, let men be satisfied if they obtain only a moderate taste of them, suited to their capacity. And it becomes us so to press towards this mark during our whole life, that (even in extreme old age) we shall not repent of the progress we have made, if only we have advanced ever so little in our course.[14]

---

13. On Calvin's doctrine of accommodation, which frames and pervades his work, see Ford Lewis Battles, "God Was Accommodating Himself to Human Capacity," in *Interpreting John Calvin*, ed. Robert Benedetto (Grand Rapids: Baker, 1996).

14. Calvin, *Commentaries on Genesis*, pp. 57-58.

"During our whole life," Calvin contends, we should modestly but firmly press toward a deeper, more daily awareness of God by way of the manifold divine works before our eyes, under our feet, and at our fingertips. And to assist us along this course, God provides the book of Genesis, the fundamental "intention" of which is "to render God, as it were, visible to us in his works."[15] Those works surround and pervade us, but we lose sight of them, forget them, ignore them, and Scripture makes God visible to us in them again. In the *Institutio* Calvin puts the same point this way: human beings should attentively "contemplate God's works" in creation, since they have been "placed in this most glorious theater to be a spectator of them," but they can do so properly only if they "prick up [their] ears to the Word, the better to profit" (1.6.2). Seeing through Scripture, they may come to see the "glorious theater" of creation more clearly. Attempting to see without Scripture, they can only grope in the void, like "bleary-eyed" men and women who have lost their eyeglasses.

Thus for Calvin, we are in fact awash in God, surrounded and pervaded not only by divine "works" but also by "divine power, goodness, and wisdom" that "absorbs all our senses" — provided our senses are properly formed, attuned, and alert. Whether due to our sinful oblivion or simply our creaturely limits, divine glory will always exceed our sensory grasp, making us at best capable of "only a moderate taste" of God's gifts and greatness. And for this very reason, God accommodates us with the gifts of Scripture, the Holy Spirit's guidance and illumination, and, as we will see in the next chapter, Jesus Christ.

In Calvin's view, then, the proper role of the Christian Bible, the chief purpose for which it is divinely given and illuminated, is not only to render God intelligible between its covers. It is also and ultimately "to render God, as it were, visible to us in his works" — that is, to render God intelligible to us in and through God's ongoing creative, providential activity around and within us. For Calvin, this means rehabilitating and restoring "all our senses" so that, insofar as the Holy Spirit wills and enables it, we become ever more keenly aware of how we "enjoy boundless benefits" from God's own hand. And in turn, this awareness draws us ever more deeply into a life of *pietas:* that "reverence joined with love of God which the knowledge of his benefits induces."[16]

15. Calvin, *Commentaries on Genesis*, p. 58.
16. Calvin, *Commentaries on Genesis*, p. 57; Calvin, *ICR* 1.2.1.

To be sure, Scripture properly serves any number of purposes: it functions as the medium through which the Holy Spirit conveys wisdom and sound doctrine, moves and persuades human hearts and minds, marks out appropriate boundaries for theological reflection, convicts, reassures, inspires, and so on. But ultimately all these purposes properly serve Scripture's principal, governing purpose for the Christian church: by way of the Bible, the Holy Spirit "clearly shows us the true God." In Calvin's view, this ultimately means not only gaining information *about* God, but also coming to know God in a way analogous to a child's knowledge of his mother or father, an intellectual and also quite personal, relational, sensory awareness of "divine power, goodness, and wisdom." That is, the Bible not only shows us information on the subject of God; it "shows us the true God." It is a place of divine encounter with humanity, a privileged site — and for the church, *the* privileged site — where God "opens his own most hallowed lips" and directly addresses human beings (1.6.1).

But as Calvin conceives it, this privileged status should by no means turn the church away from creation as itself a venue for encountering and coming to know God. On the contrary, the role of Scripture is to correct and clarify the vision of the church precisely so disciples may "see God," as Calvin puts it, "who everywhere gives signs of his presence."[17] Guided and illumined by the Holy Spirit, disciples learn to look into Scripture for the sake of looking through it, that is, for the sake of using it as a corrective, clarifying lens.

Scripture in the *Institutio*

Not surprisingly, this is precisely how Scripture functions in the *Institutio* itself. Throughout the text, Calvin consistently sees and reasons and works through Scripture. Indeed, a modern reader of the *Institutio* may be struck by how each page is peppered with chapter-and-verse biblical references, including a barrage of quotation marks and bracketed citations. But what may be more striking is that in Calvin's day, copies of the *Institutio* contained virtually none of these formal,

---

17. Calvin, *Commentaries on Genesis*, p. 60. See also Calvin, *ICR* 3.20.40, where Calvin maintains that God is "not confined to any particular region but is diffused through all things."

graphic references. The scriptural allusions, paraphrases, and quotations were all there in the text, of course, but they were typically embedded more or less seamlessly into the prose on the page, without quotation marks or bracketed citations to set them off. Calvin did provide scriptural citations in the *Institutes,* but in the original editions they appear off to one side, in the margins, juxtaposed alongside whole blocks of text with no indication of the particular phrase or sentence to which they refer. Moreover, the citations Calvin provides number fewer than half of those that appear in modern editions today.[18]

The fact that Calvin's readership then was more biblically literate than it is today accounts for part of this, but by the same token, the practice reveals something important about the way Calvin thinks about Scripture — or rather, the way he thinks through it, continually making his case via scriptural terms, images, and patterns of thought. His references to Scripture are frequently paraphrased, suggesting that, at least occasionally, he incorporated scriptural phrases and sentences from memory as he wrote. Calvin typically preached extemporaneously, without notes, after intensive preparation and study.[19] Indeed, Calvin's theological work as a whole gives the clear impression of a mind thoroughly formed in and through a life of engagement with biblical texts. And so we may say, theologically speaking, that in the *Institutio* Calvin sees through Scripture at every turn: thinking with it, pointing toward it, elaborating on it, and so on.

For example, shortly after his discussion of the Bible's role and authority in Christian life, Calvin turns to the stories of creation in the book of Genesis, arguing that these stories are meant to work against "the slowness and dullness of our wit" by helping us "to know [God] more intimately, lest we always waver in doubt." Such knowledge is "especially useful," since "once the beginning of the universe is known, God's eternity may shine forth more clearly, and we may be more rapt in wonder at it." Thus for Calvin, in the first place the purpose of the

---

18. See Richard Muller, *The Unaccommodated Calvin* (New York: Oxford University Press, 2000), pp. 140-42. Muller persuasively argues that the relatively low, selective number of Calvin's explicit scriptural references in the *Institutio*, along with their marginal formatting, indicates that they function for Calvin not so much as "citations" in the sense of identifying particular texts — much less as proof-texting appeals to scriptural authority — but rather more as intertextual signposts, guiding the reader into the Bible and its commentaries for further study.

19. Muller, *The Unaccommodated Calvin,* p. 144.

Seeing through Scripture

creation stories in Genesis is to clarify the character of the universe as a divine work of art, and therefore as a marvel and mirror of divine virtuosity. In this way, Scripture helps us see the world for what it really is, and so makes us "more rapt in wonder" not only at the cosmic masterpiece itself, but also and ultimately at the excellence of the Artist (1.14.1).

Moreover, Calvin continues, even the divine achievement of creation "not in a moment but in six days" is significant scriptural testimony, since it poignantly discloses God's "fatherly love": "For if he had put [Adam] in an earth as yet sterile and empty, if he had given him life before light, he would have seemed to provide insufficiently for his welfare" (1.14.2). The phrase "would have seemed" is telling. For Calvin, God loves humanity in any case, regardless of how the precise sequence of creation unfolds, but to convey that love more clearly, God composes creation according to how it might "seem" to human beings.

Which human beings? No doubt Calvin has in mind "our first parents," as he puts it, but also and crucially the subsequent readers of the opening pages of Genesis, for there the Holy Spirit reveals what no "Adam" or "Eve" was around to see: namely, how God "willed to commend his providence and fatherly solicitude toward us in that, before he fashioned man, he prepared everything he foresaw would be useful and salutary for him" (1.14.22).[20] Like a host setting the table before the guests arrive, God "shows his wonderful goodness toward us" — shows it, that is, not only to the first guests who eventually appear at the front door, but also and especially to all who are made privy to the host's preparatory work (1.14.2). In this way, Calvin contends, God the Spirit sets out to instruct us, Scripture's readers, we of "slow and dull wit" who require this education.

For Calvin, then, creation's inaugural choreography is itself a kind of living Scripture, a rhetoric of works, an edifying testimony and demonstration of divine love meant to persuade, assure, and form humanity toward a particular way of experiencing the world. And in Genesis, this rhetoric of works is described and illuminated in a rhetoric of words, the better to disclose both the true character of the universe (gift and bright mirror of God) and the true character of God (strong and loving Parent). For in truth, Calvin maintains, the world is a place divinely arranged for humanity "quite like a spacious and splendid

---

20. For "our first parents," see Calvin, *Commentaries on Genesis*, p. 161.

house, provided and filled with the most exquisite and at the same time most abundant furnishings" (1.14.20). In short, the world is a home, built and prepared and provided by a skillful, gracious host, and in that sense is a vivid, tangible, panoramic sign of divine power and care. Christian Scripture, for its part, allows us to see and experience this sign more clearly here and now, around and within us.

Nor should such experience of the world be only an occasional pastime. Rather, Calvin maintains, when it comes to God's work in creation, we should "occupy our whole life in contemplating it" (1.14.2): "There is no doubt that the Lord would have us uninterruptedly occupied in this holy meditation; that, while we contemplate in all creatures, as in mirrors, those immense riches of his wisdom, justice, goodness, and power, we should not merely run over them cursorily, and, so to speak, with a fleeting glance; but we should ponder them at length, turn them over in our minds seriously and faithfully, and recollect them repeatedly" (1.14.21). Calvin reportedly ended each day with just this kind of contemplation in prayer, thankfully reflecting on the events of that particular day and God's work in and through them. He presumably understood his proposed cycle of daily prayer to be an exercise with similar potential to shape the daily posture and mindfulness of Christian disciples. As we have seen, these dedicated times of prayer are best conceived as punctuations, reminders, and refreshments within a larger, "uninterrupted" mode of "holy meditation" on God's works, an ongoing task properly encompassing "our whole life."

Finally, then, we may ask this question: If Holy Scripture is akin to "spectacles" that enable disciples to more fruitfully engage God and contemplate creation as a gift and mirror of God, to what end should such engagement and contemplation be directed? Here Calvin returns once again to the *Institutio*'s governing theme: any "holy meditation" on God's power and grace shining forth in the world should "bestir [us] to trust, invoke, praise, and love [God]," a string of relational terms Calvin sums up with the idea that "we are indeed [God's] children, whom he has received into his faithful protection to nourish and educate." Accordingly, precisely as God's trusting, loving children, we are continually "to petition him for whatever we desire; and we are to recognize as a blessing from him, and thankfully to acknowledge, every benefit that falls to our share" (1.14.22).[21] We recall that Calvin evokes this pair of

---

21. For a discussion of this twofold formulation, see above, pp. 49, 80-82.

fundamental gestures — petition and thanksgiving — in the *Institutio*'s opening definition of *pietas* (1.2.2). Thus for Calvin, reading the Bible properly culminates in practices of prayer and praise — which is to say, reading is properly carried out for the sake of those practices. Seeing through Scripture with the Holy Spirit's guidance and persuasion, disciples learn to see the world as radiant with God's grace and glory. Contemplating such radiance, they learn to live out prayerful, doxological lives.

In this way, if Calvin opens his discussion of Scripture in book 1 of the *Institutio* (in chapter 6) by comparing the Bible to "spectacles," he closes that discussion (in chapter 14) with this call to "contemplate in all creatures, as in mirrors, those immense riches of [God's] wisdom, justice, goodness, and power." Scripture's spectacles, it turns out, are not only for reading the creed or the catechism or indeed the Bible itself correctly, but also and ultimately for more clearly seeing the whole world and one's whole life within it. Indeed, understood from this angle, the principal purpose of Scripture in Calvin's view is to lead disciples into a more discerning engagement with God and with the world as a divine gift and mirror of God, precisely so that they might take "pious delight in the works of God open and manifest in this most beautiful theater" (1.14.20). For only the foolish, rash, and presumptuous "strive to go forth outside the world," Calvin insists. "As if in the vast circle of heaven and earth enough things do not present themselves to engross all our senses with their incomprehensible brightness!" (1.14.1).

In this sense, then, Calvin's theological approach is profoundly "worldly," and the disciplinary *paideia* he has in mind — the immersive program of Scripture reading, worship, psalm singing, prayer, and so on — amounts to a return to God and therefore a return to the world. That is, from an isolated, withdrawn, desensitized exile of "dullness" and oblivion, disciples come home to a renovated sense of creation as God's marvelous gift and mirror, and of God as a gracious, strong, and loving parent. Whether read and heard at home gathered around the hearth or in church gathered around the pulpit, Scripture serves not only as a "school" but also as a kind of hospital in which the Holy Spirit regenerates human sensibilities, restoring sight to the oblivious, acuity to the dull, interpretive wisdom to the foolish, and so on.

For human beings mired in the "miserable ruin" of sin, God's word in the Bible is "a more direct and more certain mark whereby he is to be recognized" than is the cosmos itself, and so for the schoolhouse of the Christian church, the Bible must always serve as the privileged text at the center of Christian *paideia* (1.6.1). But that formative program itself is geared toward making disciples who can contemplate not only God's word in Scripture but also God's work and life in the world. For Calvin, the Bible is not merely the church's spectacle, a special sacred site set off from ordinary things; it is also and crucially the church's "spectacles," a clarifying instrument for seeing ordinary things more clearly, and thereby living into the world more deeply, wisely, and realistically.

Thus in Calvin's view, Scripture's place of privilege in Christian life is quite clear, but it is a pedagogical privilege, not a categorical one. That is, the Bible is by no means supposed to eclipse the world as a venue for encountering and knowing God, as if its pages constitute the only place on earth where God can be met or known. On the contrary, Calvin argues that God's word in Scripture, so far from eclipsing the world, is actually a luminous window through which disciples can see the world as it truly is: a "dazzling theater" of divine glory. In this way, while Scripture itself is a remedial "mirror in which [God's] living likeness glows," at the same time it serves as a training ground for learning to see God's likeness in the larger mirror of creation (1.14.1; 1.5.6). Thus the Bible, "the very school of God's children," is precisely what helps us "let the world become our school" (1.6.4).[22] Immersed in Scripture's compact curriculum, disciples are formed both to be "mindful that wherever [they] cast [their] eyes, all things they meet are works of God, and at the same time to ponder with pious meditation to what end God created them" (1.14.20).

None of this happens, of course, without the Holy Spirit's guidance and illumination. Nor does it happen, in Calvin's view, without a robust disciplinary regimen across several registers of social life. As we have seen, twice-weekly corporate worship attendance was mandatory in Geneva, preaching services occurred daily, and more intensive lectures on Scripture were often held in the afternoons. Reformed sermons were lengthy expositions of biblical texts, but Calvin's prayers, too, including the daily prayer cycle and Day of Prayer service on Wednesdays, were drenched in scriptural language and images. Likewise, morning and evening domestic worship properly included pas-

---

22. For "let the world become our school," see Calvin, *Commentaries on Genesis*, p. 60.

sages of Scripture read aloud, and psalm singing dominated Reformed devotion both at home and at church — to say nothing of the songs laborers may have sung or hummed "in the houses and in the fields," as Calvin hoped. Thus in the *Institutio,* Calvin can write in passing, "And in our daily reading of Scripture . . ." (3.2.4).

Indeed, a scriptural reformation of human sensibility would require an ambitious practical program of formative education and exercise — which is exactly what Calvin envisions for disciples in Geneva. Ideally, at least, they were to wake up in the morning to Scripture, retire in the evening to Scripture, and hear the words of Scripture throughout the day in prayer, worship, song, and conversation. Over time, then, and always by way of the Spirit's sanctifying pedagogy, disciples learn to see through Scripture, to hear through Scripture — in short, to experience the world through Scripture, and so at last to regard and engage the world as it is, a graceful gift and bright mirror of God. In this way, according to Calvin, disciples begin to come to their senses. The numbness of oblivion begins to give way to the vivid, quickening sensations of life.

CHAPTER 7

God with Us

Though heaven and earth shimmer with divine glory, human beings are absorbed in their own oblivion. Seeing through the "spectacles" of Scripture, however, disciples may be taught and led and formed by the Holy Spirit to see God, themselves, and the wider world in a clear, revealing light. Creation may thus begin to appear as it actually is, a gracious gift and bright mirror of God. Likewise, the details of a disciple's own life may thus begin to appear as they actually are, objects and events shot through with divine generosity, wisdom, presence, and power. And all this, Calvin warns, in itself can only come across as devastatingly bad news.

Us without God

For once we begin to see clearly, what emerges initially and above all is the dreadful realization that our vision has been so very dim, that we have thoroughly taken leave of our senses, and thus have disastrously taken leave of our proper relationship with God. That is, what comes into view is precisely the "miserable ruin" of our own previous and ongoing sin, our own ingratitude, our own self-absorption or cowardice or folly, our own dull disregard for God's gracious gifts and, above all, for God. In this way, Calvin contends, as long as disciples have nothing more than knowledge of God the Creator, even and especially the most sincere among them cannot contemplate creation without an overwhelming sense of shame. For "after man's rebellion, our eyes — wherever they turn — encounter God's curse," and such an appalling panorama "must overwhelm our souls with despair."[1]

The dilemma here is not that disciples fail to perceive God's manifold gifts to humankind, or indeed to them personally. The dilemma is that perceiving them can only compound their sense of disgrace and distance from God, since "conscience presses us within and shows in our sin just cause for [God's] disowning us and not regarding or recognizing us as his sons" (*ICR* 2.6.1). That is, so far as we can see, with our own filial *impietas* we have forfeited our status as God's children once and for all. Callously and foolishly, we have done all we can to cast that status aside. Like the younger son in the famous parable, we meet even God's apparently warm, welcoming, merciful embrace with only disbelief and denial: "Father, I have sinned against heaven and before you; I am no longer worthy to be called your son" (Luke 15:21).

In other words, given our previous and ongoing sin, we cannot and will not believe we have any legitimate claim to being God's children — nor should we, since God "does not recognize as his handiwork men defiled and corrupted by sin" (2.6.1). Originally, God made humanity in the divine image, but our ruin has left us "so corrupted that whatever remains is frightful deformity" (1.15.4). Sin's self-inflicted wounds, we might say, have spiritually and practically distorted our humanity beyond recognition. And so in Calvin's view, there can be no question of simple amnesty for human sinners, or some arbitrarily declared blank slate; nor can human sinners by themselves somehow erase the damage they have done and continue to do. On God's side, humanity's *impietas* is in itself intolerable, indelible, and disastrous; on humanity's side, even and especially for those who have been awakened to their actual situation, "conscience presses within," overwhelming them with despair (2.6.1).

Thus Calvin contends that from our vantage point, if all we possess is knowledge of God the Creator, we can only find ourselves to be irreconcilably estranged from God — and this is among the first things we see when we begin to come to our senses. The great mirror of creation, and with it "the whole knowledge of God the Creator that we have discussed," is thus practically "useless" for us, Calvin writes, since

---

1. John Calvin, *Institutes of the Christian Religion*, ed. John T. McNeill (Philadelphia: Westminster, 1960), 2.6.1 (hereafter cited as *ICR*; section references cited in parentheses in the text).

the most radiant reflections of divine grace only compound the sense of shame and regret through which "our conscience presses us." Creation's "many burning lamps" do shine with divine glory, but for us, racked with guilt, their light is all too bright and revealing, like the bleak, blinding glare in an interrogation room (1.5.14).

For in truth, we have squandered our inheritance, our father's property, as the parable in Luke 15 puts it, and there is no retrieving or remaking or otherwise restoring it. It is gone, and we are to blame. Accordingly, we are mortified, in every sense of the word, and so we shrink from the lamplight. We are overcome with a sense of dishonor and desolation. We find ourselves "no longer worthy" to be called God's children. On the contrary, we find ourselves clearly alienated from God, even cut off from God, and so in that sense without God — and since no reconciliation appears possible, we fall back into "dullness and ingratitude." If genuine *pietas* follows from a lively sense of God's "fatherly favor," only a fresh round of *impietas* can follow from a numbing sense of guilt and shame (2.6.1; 1.16.1).

The point is crucial. As we have seen, for Calvin, a disciple's whole life is properly a life of *pietas*, of filial love and reverence for God, not abstractly but precisely as "induced" by relational-pragmatic knowledge of God's good gifts (1.2.1). And for each disciple, this kind of life presupposes that God is in fact her benefactor, her loving parent, and so that she is in fact a beloved child of God. Without this linchpin presupposition, the whole life of *pietas* — for Calvin, the whole Christian life — is impossible. For if I do not understand myself as God's child, and God as my active, loving parent, how can I take up a stance vis-à-vis God of filial devotion, trust, and love?

And yet for Calvin, on its own, being made aware of the "miserable ruin" of our own sin radically calls just this presupposition into question. By all appearances, it removes the linchpin, the basic idea underlying the life of *pietas*. That is, sin's ruin apparently cancels any claim to be God's beloved son or daughter, so that we, too, can only say, "I have sinned; I am no longer worthy to be called your child." In this sense, then, our ruin amounts to a kind of exile. A pall of shame falls across the world around us, and our "eyes — wherever they turn — encounter God's curse." Shrouded and obscured in this way, even the goods and pleasures in our life function only as reminders of our own disgraceful, oblivious response to God's grace.

Thus in Calvin's view, the "miserable ruin" of human sin involves a twofold devastation: one formational, the other perspectival. First, sin's oblivion takes place as a practical corruption or malformation of human life, an ungrateful, self-absorbed version of humanity, in effect reversing the grateful, loving life of *pietas,* the fully human form of life God intends for us. So severe is this reversal, Calvin contends, that it renders us little more than shadows of ourselves, and so does real damage to our relationship with God, a bond that ought to be made of mutual love and knowledge, intimacy and recognition.

When Calvin writes that God "does not recognize as his handiwork men defiled and corrupted by sin," he means not that God no longer knows who we are, but rather that who we have become is profoundly and practically at odds with the creatures God originally made us to be. For Calvin, a human being's status as a son or daughter of God is not an intangible, disembodied idea, a mere title divorced from the form his or her life actually and practically takes. On the contrary, being a son or daughter of God is a tangible, embodied, lived form of life in and with God, and forfeiting its constitutive contours means forfeiting one's own true identity, in effect attempting to take up a deeply distorted position against oneself and apart from God. In this way, the "miserable ruin" of sin is a formational crisis for humanity. Accordingly, it manifests as a miserable *ruin*.

But the crisis is also perspectival: it manifests as a *miserable* ruin. For insofar as a disciple focuses exclusively on her own sin, her new awareness sets in motion a vicious, paralyzing cycle of guilt, anxiety, shame, and despair. To be sure, for Calvin, both the damage wrought by sin and humanity's responsibility for it are quite real, but so is divine mercy. And if God elects to rescue a given person from the oblivion of *impietas,* to "snatch [her] from death," as Calvin puts it, nothing can stand in the way, including the severity of that person's sin, whatever it may be (3.3.21). And yet human beings, mortified and consumed by their own disgrace, cannot by their own lights distinguish divine mercy from divine condemnation. Like Adam in Eden, newly ashamed after eating the illicit fruit, our own assessment of our sin sends us scrambling to flee God in fear, stammering denials and blame, thus compounding the very rupture we should be seeking to repair (Gen. 2:25; 3:8ff.).

In other words, trapped in a downward spiral of indignity and shame, even our perspective on our own "miserable ruin" takes part in that ruin itself, making us all the more miserable. As we glimpse our own "dullness," that dullness dims our vision. Summing up these points near the outset of book 2, Calvin puts the problem this way: "The natural order was that the frame of the universe should be the school in which we were to learn piety [*pietas*], and from it pass over to eternal life and perfect felicity. But after man's rebellion . . . even if God wills to manifest his fatherly favor to us in many ways, yet we cannot by contemplating the universe infer that he is Father. Rather, conscience presses us within, and shows in our sin just cause for his disowning us and not regarding or recognizing us as his sons" (2.6.1). Made to behold God's glory in creation and thereby learn piety, we instead fall away from both God and our true vocation. And moreover, this fall renders us so alienated that "even if God wills to manifest his fatherly favor," such gifts appear to us not as signs that "he is Father," but rather the reverse: "our eyes," Calvin writes in the same passage, "wherever they turn — encounter God's curse." Creation's school remains in session, it turns out, but the curriculum has been turned entirely on its head.

Thus we human beings are trapped in a double bind. On one hand, we have forsaken our own full humanity by living out lives of *impietas*, effectively withdrawing from the relationship with God for which we are made. In this sense, we attempt to live "without God," and accordingly, we therefore gravely require some way to reconcile and reunite with God, some avenue of rapprochement, some path that includes both divine forgiveness and our own restoration to fully human life in God. And on the other hand, even if we have been awakened to this disaster, our perspective on it is so distorted with shame that even God's graceful gifts can only come across as aspects of "God's curse." In this sense, too, we are apparently "without God." Though in fact we may be awash in divine mercy and care, from our perspective we remain convinced that we are alone, and we therefore require some compelling form of persuasion, some way to be assured that despite our miserable ruin, God's forgiving, "fatherly favor" is meant for us.

In short, in Calvin's view, we require a reunion with God on one hand and a divine sermon on the other. We need to be both reconciled and reassured. We need a return to the life in God for which we were born, and so to the trust and hope and confidence in God that make for full humanity. Even and especially as embodied human beings, as vulnerable creatures, as flesh, we need a tangible, practical return to divine intimacy and a compelling, encouraging divine word to dispel our despair once and for all.

God with Us

The Mediator

And so God's Word becomes flesh. Twice-over "without God," we are both malformed and miserable, and so God comes to us precisely as *Immanuel*, "God with us," the fully divine, fully human being Jesus Christ (cf. 2.12.1). In this way God meets us where we are, graciously accommodating our particular needs with a mother's strength and a father's tender care. We need reconciliation with God, and so Christ comes as "the Mediator" between God and human beings (2.6.1). We need restoration to a practical, immersive, embodied intimacy with God, and so Christ comes as a fully divine, fully human body in whom we may intimately, vicariously, actually participate, such that, as Paul puts it, "it is no longer I who live, but it is Christ who lives in me" (Gal. 2:20). We need reassurance, an encouraging word, a divine sermon to persuade us once and for all that our guilt and shame, indelible and justified as they may seem, are nevertheless mercifully set aside — and so Christ comes as God's Word incarnate, our "Redeemer," the one in whom God's "face shines, full of grace and gentleness, even upon us poor and unworthy sinners" (2.7.8).

And most fundamentally, above and below and alongside all these other needs, we need to recover again our original place as children of God, the position and posture in which fully human life — the life of *pietas* — is possible. Accordingly, Christ comes not as "Redeemer," but rather "as Redeemer in the person of [God's] only-begotten Son," thereby "setting forth for us God our Father." Because of this status, through him, with him, and in him, disciples may "truly taste God's mercy, and thus be persuaded that he [is] their Father" (2.6.4). For Christ is "the Mediator" between God and humanity, not merely on good terms with both sides, but himself the Son of God, himself fully divine and fully human.

Like any excellent mediator, then, Christ carries out this work in two directions. First, Christ the Mediator embodies, clarifies, and proclaims to humanity — in both word and act — God's "grace and gentleness, even upon us poor and unworthy sinners." In this respect, precisely as God's Son, Christ is what Calvin calls "the image of the invisible God" (2.6.4; cf. Col. 1:15). In creation God shines indirectly, in the great mirror of divine "handiwork"; in Holy Scripture, God speaks directly, "opening his own most hallowed lips"; but in Jesus Christ, God comes to humanity in the flesh, indeed as flesh, and so as *Immanuel*,

"God with us." Contemplating him, disciples may — should the Holy Spirit assist them — truly contemplate God's "fatherly kindness." Hearing him and reflecting on his life, they may truly hear and reflect on God's comforting, challenging, inspiring good news (1.5.8). Thus Christ represents and acts on behalf of God — indeed as God incarnate — vis-à-vis human beings.

And second, facing the other direction, Christ the Mediator represents and acts on behalf of human beings — indeed as humanity incarnate, the genuine, humble, righteous, beautiful human being — vis-à-vis God. In this respect, precisely as the Son of Humanity, Christ reconciles them to God once and for all. Calvin's Christology is perhaps best known today for its emphasis on Christ's atoning death on the cross, that is, the extent to which by dying, Christ offers God an "expiatory sacrifice" on behalf of humankind. But in the *Institutio*, Calvin situates Christ's atoning death within a much larger program of redemptive work, including a three-part "office" of "prophet, king, and priest" (2.15.1).

Christ's atoning death, Calvin contends, takes place as one aspect of his "priestly office." By dying "in the place of the sinner," he "sets forth" a sacrificial expiation whereby he "sanctifies us and obtains for us that grace from which the uncleanness of our transgressions and vices debars us" (2.16.5; 2.15.6). That is, to the extent that "our eyes — wherever they turn — encounter God's curse," in his passion and death Christ bears that curse for us (2.16.6). To the extent that we are disgraced by our sin, racked with shame about our ingratitude and contempt for God's gifts, Christ protects and assures us by accepting our guilt as his own and absorbing its dreadful consequences (2.16.5).

In Calvin's view, this way of thinking is in keeping with ancient ideas about sin, guilt, and priesthood detailed "under the law" in the book of Leviticus, among other places, and in particular in Isaiah: "The Lord has laid on him the iniquity of us all" (2.15.6; 2.16.6; Isa. 53:6). And accordingly, the pastoral, kerygmatic function of Christ's atoning death is precisely to calm the "conscience" that "presses us within": "because trembling consciences find repose only in sacrifice and cleansing by which sins are expiated," Christ's death provides a consummate consolation: "We must, above all, remember this substitution, lest we tremble and remain anxious throughout life" (2.16.5). That is, Calvin argues that Christ's death was carried out so that "when he discharged all satisfaction through his sacrifice, we might cease to be afraid of God's wrath" (2.16.6). In this sense, as an enacted divine sermon, his death proclaims the familiar angelic cry, "Do not be afraid!"

But as important as the doctrine of Christ's expiatory sacrifice is for Calvin, it exhausts neither his account of Christ's death nor his discussion of Christ's "priestly office" — to say nothing of his wider "prophet, king, priest" triptych of christological redemption. In fact, in the *Institutio*, Calvin's overall portrait of human salvation in Christ is a diverse amalgam of atonement images, composed from a variety of angles, like a serial description of the many sides of a precious gem. Thus according to Calvin, while Christ's death does function as both an expiation and a divine word of comfort, it accomplishes other indispensable work as well. For example, in his direct treatment of the reference to Christ's death in the Apostles' Creed, Calvin catalogues two major effects of that death, both of which are distinguishable from the "expiation" doctrine just described.

The "first fruit that his death brought to us," Calvin writes, is that by it God destroys both death and "him who had the power of death, that is, the devil," thereby delivering "all those who through fear of death were subjected to a lifelong bondage [Heb. 2:14-15]." That is, Christ dies in order to conquer death — "not to be engulfed in its abyss, but rather to engulf it" — and thereby to deliver us both from death and from the "fear of death," instilling in us a bold sense of hope, courage, and equanimity. And the "second effect of Christ's death," Calvin continues, is this: "by our participation in it, his death mortifies our earthly members . . . it kills the old man in us that he may not flourish and bear fruit" (2.16.7). In Calvin's view, Christ's death is not restricted to him alone; disciples, too, may take part in it spiritually and practically, "united with him in a death like his," as Paul puts it, so that "our old self was crucified with him so that the body of sin might be destroyed, and we might no longer be enslaved to sin" (Rom. 6:5-6).

For Calvin, this liberating "mortification of the flesh" — "flesh" here functioning, as it sometimes does in the New Testament, as a figure for humanity's inclination toward sin — does not take place in disciples' lives abstractly or abruptly, like some magical bolt from the blue. Rather, "the life of a Christian man is a continual effort and exercise in the mortification of the flesh, till it is utterly slain, and God's Spirit reigns in us" (3.3.20). That is, the process of "dying to sin" takes place over time, in and through the tangible, everyday, Spirit-led paideutic exercises of Christian life, and particularly in and through reformed versions of classic ascetic disciplines: "self denial," which Calvin calls "the sum of the Christian life"; "bearing the cross"; and so on.[2] By way of such practices, and so ultimately by way of the power of the Holy Spirit, disciples are "united with [Christ] in a death like his," participating in him as a practical way of life that is also a way of death — that is, the death of "the body of sin" so that a new body may rise with and in Christ and the Holy Spirit.

In this way, Calvin provides his version of a theme often associated with Christian asceticism generally and monasticism in particular, namely, that the "mortification of the flesh" requires "continual effort and exercise" in Christian life. But in Calvin's view, of course, such effort and exercise are the bailiwick of the whole church, bar none, and so in this sense, each disciple is properly enrolled in the Spirit's program of retraining and reforming her body and mind toward new forms, skills, and capacities, like an athlete whose "old self" is remade into something new. The Spirit does the sculpting, and both the "mortification of the flesh" and the "vivification of the spirit" take place "by participation in Christ," that is, through being "engrafted into the life and death of Christ," but disciples are by no means passive in the process (3.3.8, 9, 20). They strive and exercise their bodies and minds, not on their own, but precisely as they live in and through Christ and the Holy Spirit. Practically disciplined in this way, a disciple may be gradually formed — "through continual and sometimes even slow advances" — into the ideal Christian man or woman: not the cloistered or consecrated cleric, but rather, as we saw in chapter 1, "the devout householder, clear and free of all greed, ambition, and other lusts of the flesh" (3.3.8; 4.13.16).

Even in his account of Christ's death, then, the theme of participation in Christ figures significantly in Calvin's case; across his wider

---

2. See Calvin, *ICR* 3.7 ("The Sum of the Christian Life: The Denial of Ourselves") and 3.8 ("Bearing the Cross, a Part of Self-Denial"). For "mortification," see, e.g., 3.7.7, 3.3.8, and 2.16.13: "the mortification of our flesh depends upon participation in his cross." As we will explore in part III, Calvin's ascetic ideas about human participation in Christ's death are difficult and at times perilous, and in any case are permanently vulnerable to misuse (by Calvin himself as well as by others), particularly insofar as they may be taken to encourage or exalt human suffering. A key safeguard here is what might be called a "retrospective" interpretive rule: the proviso that while already-existing afflictions may be retrospectively interpreted as a form of communion with Christ's passion and death, further affliction is by no means to be prospectively pursued or prolonged.

christological account, the theme serves as a kind of touchstone. In his full portrait of Christ's "priestly office," for example, Calvin argues that "Christ plays the priestly role, not only to render the Father favorable and propitious toward us by an eternal law of reconciliation, but also to receive us as his companions in this great office" (2.15.6). That is, Christ plays the role of priest so that, in him and through him, humanity might participate in a vicarious, ecclesiastically inclusive mode of priesthood.

"For we who are defiled in ourselves," Calvin explains, "yet are priests in him, offer ourselves and our all to God, and freely enter the heavenly sanctuary." Precisely as the consummate priest, Christ enters the "heavenly sanctuary" on the congregation's behalf, but not in such a way as to leave the congregation behind, alone in the nave, so to say. Rather, the whole congregation enters the "heavenly sanctuary" in him and with him, "as his companions in this great office." And consequently, this incorporation into Christ's priesthood, like the constituent incorporation into his death, involves an active, practical participation in a whole range of priestly duties and disciplines, from worship generally to prayer in particular. Here Calvin's principal emphasis is not so much on Christ taking our place on the cross, but rather on Christ enabling us to take his place with him and in him, incorporating us into his body, receiving us into his priestly life and work, and so inaugurating that "kingdom of priests" foretold, Calvin insists, in Scripture (2.15.6; cf. Rev. 1:5-6).

Likewise, with respect to Christ's redemptive "kingship," Calvin maintains that "Christ fulfills the combined duties of king and pastor," spiritually protecting, defending, and nourishing the church at every turn. Accordingly, again following Paul, Calvin calls Christ the "Head of the church, . . . which is Christ's body" (2.15.5; cf. Eph. 1:22-23). That is, for Calvin, the church is gathered up by and in Christ as its king and deliverer, the Son of David, and disciples find "restoration in the Head alone" since "salvation flows from the Head to the whole body" (2.6.2, 3).

The organic, corporeal imagery here is striking, since typically a king resides far above and therefore apart from his subjects. For Christ and the church, however, while disciples are "sheltered under the King's protection," this shelter is so intimate as to involve communion with the Protector, even a share in his own body. Indeed, the very reason "Christ stands in our midst" is "to lead us little by little to a firm union with God" (2.15.5). Prefigured in David, Christ is the king and shepherd who gathers his scattered sheep to himself, not only defending them against the wolves who would threaten them, but also seeking out the last and the lost, carrying them home on his shoulders.

Even the church's faith is sound and sure only insofar as it participates in Christ's faith: "although faith rests in God," Calvin writes, "it will gradually disappear unless he who retains it in perfect firmness intercedes as Mediator. Otherwise, God's majesty is too lofty to be attained by mortal men" (2.6.4). The true church, according to Calvin, is graciously granted not only faith *in* Christ, but also participation in the faith *of* Christ, the "perfect" faith of *Immanuel*, "God with us." And for Calvin, a disciple's participation in Christ is not merely an idea to be thought, or a state of affairs to be glimpsed only here and there. Rather, that "union" is a reality to be clearly and consistently realized in and through tangible, ongoing formative disciplines, preeminently by taking part in "the communion of prayer" and "the Sacred Supper" (3.11.10; 4.17.45; 4.17 title).

Finally, with respect to Christ's "prophetic office," Calvin calls the Son of God "the fullness and culmination of all revelations," the consummate "herald and witness of the Father's grace," and so a "teacher" in whose doctrine "all parts of perfect wisdom are contained." As such, "he is distinguished from other teachers with a similar office." But here again, Christ does not carry out this office strictly on his own, but rather gathers and incorporates the church into his life and work: "he received anointing, not only for himself that he might carry out the office of teaching, but for his whole body [i.e., the church], that the power of the Spirit might be present in the continuing preaching of the gospel." As in his priesthood, Christ's prophetic "anointing was diffused from the Head to the members, as Joel had foretold: 'Your sons shall prophesy and your daughters . . . shall see visions,' etc." (2.15.1, 2; cf. Joel 2:28).

Thus the theme of christological incorporation once again frames Calvin's account: Christ is the ultimate prophet, the one whose "perfect doctrine . . . has made an end to all prophecies," but at the same time, precisely because the church is Christ's body, the proclamation of that prophecy continues in and through Christian preaching. And further, insofar as that preaching serves as the means by which Christ gathers disciples to himself in the first place, his prophetic office is itself a type of incorporating work, a pedagogy oriented toward engrafting human beings into his body, the church. That is, through the paideutic disciplines of preaching and listening, reading and reflecting, singing psalms and studying doctrine, disciples are drawn ever more deeply by the Holy Spirit into Christ's presence, life, and prophetic work (2.15.2).

Thus for Calvin, in all three modes of Christ's redemptive work ("prophet, king, and priest"), the phenomenon of "participation" in Christ — of disciples being incorporated or "engrafted" into his body — plays a basic, constitutive role.[3] In and through Christ, disciples are priests permitted into "the heavenly sanctuary," members of the divine monarch's own body, and prophets learning and proclaiming — in both word and deed — the divine prophet's message.[4] Likewise, in and through Christ, disciples die to sin by continually partaking in Christ's death and rise to new life by partaking in his resurrection. And again, in and through Christ, disciples enter "the Heavenly Kingdom" by participating in his ascension, or rather, by his participating in disciples' flesh: "Since he entered heaven in our flesh, as if in our name, it follows . . . that in a sense we already 'sit with God in the heavenly places in him,' so that we do not await heaven with a bare hope, but in our Head already possess it" (2.16.16; cf. Eph. 2:6).

Indeed, the idea of Christ acting "in our name" — that is, in certain respects his actions count as ours — is operative in at least one other key christological theme in the *Institutio*: Christ's redemptive obedience. To the question, "How has Christ abolished sin, banished the separation between us and God, and acquired righteousness to render God favorable and kindly toward us?" Calvin responds that "we can in general reply that he has achieved this for us by the whole course of his obedience." As he so often does, Calvin trades here on Paul: "'As by one man's disobedience many were made sinners, so by one man's obedience we are made righteous' [Rom. 5:19, paraphrase]." That is, just as the catastrophe of sin follows from Adam's disobedience, so the glory of redemption follows from Christ's obedience to God throughout his life, from the manger to the cross, whereby he "acquires righteousness

---

3. For a recent discussion of this theme in Calvin's work, see J. Todd Billings, *Calvin, Participation, and the Gift: The Activity of Believers in Union with Christ* (Oxford: Oxford University Press, 2007).

4. Cf. Calvin, *ICR* 2.7.1: "For all have been endowed with priestly and kingly [and we may add, prophetic] honor, so that, trusting in their Mediator, they may freely dare to come forth into God's presence."

Rereading the Institutio

to render God favorable and kindly." And how is this favor imparted to human beings? Through their participation in Christ, a "partaking" enabled by the Holy Spirit: "You see that our righteousness is not in us but in Christ, that we possess it only because we are partakers in Christ; indeed, with him we possess all its riches." Christ is obedient, we might say, "in our name" and for our sake, and so "the obedience of Christ is reckoned to us as if it were our own" (3.11.23).

For Calvin, our participation in Christ is always strictly vicarious: we are "reckoned" fully righteous, or prophetic, or royal, and so on, but apart from Christ we are no such thing. Accordingly, though Calvin frequently uses the language of "union" to describe the ideal relationship between disciples and Christ, it is more "communion" he has in mind, an intimacy in which the distinction between the parties is preserved all the way along. Indeed, one might argue that once this distinction is lost or obscured, intimacy itself is lost or obscured with it, two collapsing into one, companionship into solitude — and for Calvin, everything hangs on our intimate companionship with Christ. Thus Calvin envisions a relationship between disciples and Christ in which there is distinction but no separation; as we will see, Calvin deploys this "distinction without separation" formula in his account of the sacraments. Parsing Paul's famous line about radical intimacy with Christ, "it is no longer I who live, but it is Christ who lives in me" (Gal. 2:20), we may put the point this way: for Calvin, intimacy with Christ means that on the disciple's side, her speciously independent "I" no longer lives, even as her identity remains distinct and intact ("Christ lives in me"). After all, the very idea of "participation" would seem to require just this kind of distinction, a preservation of difference and therefore of intimacy.

In fact, in a key passage in book 3 of the *Institutio*, Calvin characterizes the relationship between disciples and Christ as a "mystical union," but he does so as part of a larger polemic against what he takes to be the "gross mingling of Christ with believers" implied by any doctrine of "essential righteousness" (3.11.10).[5] That is, even as Calvin contends that the "spiritual bond" between disciples and Christ is so intimate as to be "mystical," he underlines that this intimacy entails no "mixture," no change of essence, no loss of identity on either side.[6] Or,

---

5. Calvin's particular opponent here is Lutheran theologian Andreas Osiander.
6. Thus for Calvin, the term "mystical" *(mystica)* indicates no ontological absorption into God, much less a feat of exceptional holiness or intimacy with God achieved by

to turn the coin over: even as he rejects the view that Christ's indwelling presence actually renders us "really righteous" and not only vicariously so, Calvin nevertheless insists on our "union with Christ":

> that joining together of Head and members, that indwelling of Christ in our hearts — in short, that mystical union [*mystica unio*] — are accorded by us the highest degree of importance, so that Christ, having been made ours, makes us sharers with him in the gifts with which he has been endowed. We do not, therefore, contemplate him outside ourselves from afar in order that his righteousness may be imputed to us, but [rather] because we put on Christ and are engrafted into his body — in short, because he deigns to make us one with him. (3.11.10)

"For this reason," we have "fellowship of righteousness" with Christ. Our justification before God consists in Christ's righteousness being vicariously imputed to us — but not "from afar." Rather, it is imputed both from within, insofar as Christ dwells "in our hearts," and from immediately nearby, insofar as by God's grace "we put on Christ and are engrafted into his body," which is to say, by God's grace we live in God. We do not live *as* God. We remain who we are; our distinction from God is intact. But now our separation from God is overcome. We may and do act as if we are without God, but in Jesus Christ, God is *Immanuel*, "God with us." In that sense we are reconciled. Even though we turn away from God, even though we are "poor and unworthy sinners," Christ graciously makes us "sharers with him," participants in him, "engrafted into his body" — in short, "one with him" (3.11.10).

To be sure, as Calvin conceives it, aspects of Christ's redemptive work do not directly involve our participation — indeed, Christ's role as an "expiatory sacrifice" is a prominent example, since the emphasis there is on Christ "taking our place" in the sense of acting instead of us and without us.[7] Here Christ does indeed act as our *substitute*. But Cal-

---

an ascetic virtuoso. Rather, the term signals that the "union" between disciples and Christ (1) is fundamentally a divine act, and so (2) is marvelous, mysterious, and finally incomprehensible. Moreover, the fact that Calvin positions "mystical union" at the heart of his case (granting it "the highest degree of importance") means that he intends it to apply to all disciples, not merely to an elite class.

7. One might argue that even here the logic of vicarious participation is in play, since Calvin contends that Christ offers his sacrifice on humanity's behalf, and its bene-

vin's account of Christ's redemptive work is much broader than this idea alone, and across this broad range the theme of participation in Christ functions as a clear, consistent refrain. In these cases, Calvin's emphasis is less on Christ "taking our place" and more on Christ taking us up into his place, that is, into a life with and in him, so that his actions are also vicariously our own. Here Christ acts as our *Head* and *companion*. He acts for us and with us. He represents humanity, but at the same time lives in intimate "mystical union" with humanity, precisely as "God with us," and so acts in such a way as to assume and include us in his action, his body, himself.

In other words, according to Calvin, Christ's priesthood, kingship, prophecy, and indeed obedience and "acquired righteousness" are all redemptive for humanity precisely insofar as disciples share or "partake" or "participate" in him, engrafted into his body, and therefore are incorporated into his standing and sonship. Even Calvin's emphasis on Christ's "expiatory sacrifice" is itself a motif framed and determined by this larger theme, for in Calvin's view, unless disciples participate in Christ, the benefits of expiation do not flow to them. "We know," Calvin writes, "that he benefits only those whose 'Head' he is, for whom he is 'the first-born among brethren,' and who, finally, 'have put on him.' This union alone ensures that, as far as we are concerned, he has not unprofitably come with the name of Savior" (3.1.3).[8]

In short, for Calvin, Christ redeems us only insofar as we live in him, and in that sense live in God. In ourselves alone, we are "defiled,"

---

fits, in turn, flow to human beings. But in the *Institutio*, Calvin does not develop his account of Christ's "expiatory sacrifice" with reference to our participation in it — perhaps as part and parcel of his polemic against the "papists" who claim to "sacrifice [Christ] anew," as Calvin puts it, in the Roman Mass (2.15.6). In any case, when it comes to Christ's expiatory work, in key respects Calvin moves in a direction contrary to the idea of participation. For example, Calvin is quite clear that in and through the cross, Christ liberates us by "transferring our condemnation to himself and by taking our guilt upon himself" (2.16.5); that is, in death, Christ takes on "our guilt" in such a way as to render us free of it. But this "transfer" model puts the accent on what we might call the "nonparticipation" of disciples in Christ, since in this scenario, the condemnation and guilt disciples no longer bear are now borne by Christ alone: "He offered as a sacrifice the flesh he received from us, that he might wipe out our guilt by his act of expiation" (2.12.3).

8. See also 3.1.1, the opening words of book 3: "as long as Christ remains outside of us, and we are separated from him, all that he has suffered and done for the salvation of the human race remains useless and of no value to us."

but in him we are priests. In ourselves alone, we are seditious, but in him we are royal subjects, saved because "salvation flows from the Head to the whole body." In ourselves alone, we are insensible and confused, but in him we are prophetic "heralds and witnesses," again because the prophet's "anointing was diffused from the Head to the members." In ourselves alone, we are disobedient, but in him we receive the benefits of genuine obedience, since "the obedience of Christ is reckoned to us as if it were our own." In ourselves alone, our corruption, our sedition, our oblivion, our waywardness — in short, our sin — provides "just cause" for God to disown us; but in Christ we are sons and daughters of God. And so for Calvin, finally and preeminently, in themselves alone, at best human beings can only discern and dread "God's curse," but in Christ, it becomes possible for disciples "truly to taste God's mercy, and thus be persuaded that he [is] their Father" (2.6.4).

The resonance here with Calvin's descriptions of *pietas* is unmistakable: for Calvin, *pietas* is our life-encompassing, loving, reverent, fundamentally filial response to God's "fatherly favor." And Jesus Christ, in Calvin's view, is the one through whom we can "truly taste" that favor here and now. Engrafted into God's only-begotten Son, we vicariously share in his standing, and in that sense are restored as sons and daughters of God: for only those "engrafted into the body of the only-begotten Son are considered to have the place and rank of children" (2.6.1). Indeed, apart from Christ, though all of creation is radiant with God's "fatherly kindness," that cosmic mirror is "useless" to us, since all we see in it is further cause for our own shame (1.5.8; 2.6.1). And accordingly, apart from Christ, the fully human life of *pietas* is for us inconceivable, precisely because as far as we can tell, our sin has rendered us "no longer worthy," as the parable puts it, to be called God's children (Luke 15:21).

Indeed, in book 1 of the *Institutio*, in the same section where Calvin first defines *pietas*, he writes, "In this ruin of mankind no one now experiences God either as Father or as Author of salvation, or favorable in any way, until Christ the Mediator comes forward to reconcile him to us" (1.2.1). Christ enables disciples to "experience God as Father." He delivers and demonstrates the divine sermon, the good news that God's "face shines, full of grace and gentleness, even upon us poor and unworthy sinners" (2.7.8). And since experiencing God as a strong, gentle, graceful parent is the essential condition of genuine *pietas*, and since *pietas* is nothing less than "the beginning, the middle, and the end of Christian life," the redemptive work of Jesus Christ is ultimately to make genuine *pietas* possible for human beings.[9] In this way, he secures their salvation. That is, Christ's wide and varied labor in and for human beings — as prophet, priest, king, servant, healer, and so on — is finally for the sake of this twofold, governing task: reconciling sinners to God as children of God, and thereby restoring sinners to fully human life, the life of *pietas*, loving and revering God on earth and in heaven.

In Christ's Image

For Calvin, humanity's fall into sin's "miserable ruin" means that "no real piety remains in the world" (1.4.1). But this is also to say, bearing in mind Calvin's view of the constitutive role *pietas* plays in genuine human life, that "no real humanity remains in the world," and so Christ comes to restore us to that real humanity. On one hand, this restoration is strictly vicarious: that is, in ourselves malformed and inept, we are graciously, externally covered or clothed in Christ's humanity, his righteousness and obedience. In this way, Christ at once restores our identity as God's children and persuades us that this restoration is bona fide and unshakable. He achieves the reconciliation with God we require and delivers the divine sermon we need to hear. In this way, he allows disciples to "experience God as Father," and so secures for them the basic condition of genuine *pietas*, of genuine humanity.

But on the other hand, as Calvin understands it, this restoration is not only vicarious, it is also transformational. It involves not only the "justification" of disciples hidden in and under Christ, but also their continual "sanctification," their gradual, actual reformation by the Holy Spirit toward full humanity in God, and so ultimately toward a righteousness and obedience of their own. "By partaking in him," Calvin writes, we disciples receive this "double grace" (3.11.1). First, *Immanuel* is "God with us" in the sense of standing for us and among us, sheltering and vicariously vindicating or "justifying" us by way of his righteousness and obedience. In this respect, Calvin is quite clear that God saves not the righteous, but sinners: justification is always *iusti-*

---

9. Calvin, "Commentary on 1 Timothy 4:8," in *Calvin's Commentaries* (Grand Rapids: Baker, 1981), 21:109.

ficatio impii (e.g., 3.3.10-11). But at the same time, second, Immanuel is also "God with us" in the sense of challenging and empowering us to follow him as his disciples, that is, as students enrolled in his practical course of study, edifying and "sanctifying" us by his leadership, example, and ongoing companionship. God does not save human beings because of this "regeneration"; rather, for whomever God wills to save, God also wills this regeneration (e.g., 3.3.21). The Holy Spirit acts in them and upon them, reforming and restoring them to their full humanity — which is to say, conforming them to Christ even as they live in Christ.

For "in the beginning," Calvin argues, God created humanity in and through Christ, and formed humanity after Christ's image. That is, humanity's original integrity in Eden — Adam's "full possession of right understanding," his poised "affections," his "senses tempered in right order," and the fact that "he truly referred his excellence to exceptional gifts bestowed upon him by his Maker" (1.15.3) — was an integrity modeled on Christ in the first place. "Even then," Calvin writes, "Christ was the image of God," the archetype of "whatever excellence was engraved upon Adam" (2.12.6). And moreover, even then, before humanity's fall into sin, Christ played the role of "Mediator" between creature and creator; "Even if man had remained free from all stain, his condition would have been too lowly for him to reach God without a Mediator" (2.12.1).[10] And so in that long-lost garden of delight, through Christ the Mediator, Adam was "joined to God," an arrangement Calvin calls "the true and highest perfection of dignity"; thus humanity in Eden "mounted up even to God and eternal bliss" (2.12.6; 1.15.8). Indeed, for Calvin, "life was in Christ from the beginning," and so before the disastrous oblivion of sin, human life was nothing less than life in God: "it was the spiritual life of Adam to remain united and bound to his Maker" (2.6.1; 2.1.5).[11]

In Calvin's view, then, when we fall away from this spiritual life, we fall away from this original "life in Christ," and so from our proper con-

---

10. Calvin does not develop this idea at length in the *Institutio*, but a glimpse of what he might have in mind is discernible in 3.2.1: "For, since God dwells in inaccessible light [1 Tim. 6:16], Christ must become our intermediary. Hence, he calls himself the light of the world."

11. Here Calvin explicitly leans on John's prologue, and particularly on John 1:3-4: "All things came into being through him, and without him not one thing came into being. What has come into being in him was life, and the life was the light of all people."

formity to Christ as creatures formed in his image. And for just this reason, it is only fitting for Christ to come and redeem us as "the Second Adam," the one who "restores us to true and complete integrity" (1.15.4). For after all, who better to reform us than the one in whose image we were first formed? Rebuilding a ruin, what better tool is there than the original blueprint, and what better craftsman than the original builder? Thus for Calvin, Christ's redemptive work is no ad hoc solution improvised by God in the face of human rebellion; rather, it is a faithful continuation and development of God's creative work "in the beginning." It is the divine refusal, we might say, to take our pathetic, self-destructive "No" for an answer. In sin, humanity falls away from God — and in particular, from Christ. And so in redemption, God accommodates this fall, rescuing and restoring humanity to its proper, original, immersive relationship with God — and in particular, with Christ.

In other words, Calvin maintains that "in the beginning," human life was life in Christ, and therefore was formed in and through and after him, "the image of God" — and accordingly, regenerated human life is, too. Put briefly, since "life was in Christ from the beginning, and all the world fell away from it, it is necessary to return to that source" (2.6.1; cf. John 1:3-4). In this way, "the end of regeneration is that Christ should reform us to God's image," for "Christ is the most perfect image of God; if we are conformed to it, we are so restored that with true piety, righteousness, purity, and intelligence we bear God's image" (1.15.4).

Modeled on Christ, this regeneration applies to the whole human person, not merely to some special "spiritual" faculty, and to her whole human life, not some "spiritual" province within it. A human being's sanctification, as Calvin understands it, is a kind of homecoming to the fully human integrity created in Eden: a sound mind, heart, and sensorium, all put to use for the sake of a sound life. In and across this "whole excellence," the divine image may again shine in human beings, including the human body, since originally, "although the primary seat of the divine image was in the mind and heart, or in the soul and its powers, yet there was no part of man, not even the body itself, in which some sparks did not glow" (1.15.3).

Restoring this image, then, requires an immersive, holistic approach, and so Christ's sanctifying work forms and reforms our mind, heart, soul, and strength: "through his Holy Spirit, [Christ] dwells in us and by his power the lusts of the flesh are each day more and more mortified; we are indeed sanctified, that is, consecrated to the Lord in true purity of life, with our hearts formed to obedience to the law" (3.14.9). Insofar as we partake in Christ's death, "our old man is crucified by his power, and the body of sin perishes." Likewise, partaking in his resurrection, "we are raised up into newness of life," and what we might call the body of regeneration thrives: a reformed and reforming mind, heart, and sensorium, the better to serve a loving, humble, doxological life — in a word, a life of *pietas* (3.3.9; cf. Rom. 6:5-11).

Thus for Calvin, in and through the sanctifying work of Jesus Christ and the Holy Spirit, human beings are remade "little by little," stepping forward with "continual and sometimes even slow advances." Over a lifelong pilgrimage, they repent, which is to say, they undergo a "turning of life to God," a transformative conversion that is also a return. "I interpret repentance as regeneration," Calvin declares, "whose sole end is to restore in us the image of God," which is to say, to restore us to the intimate participation in God for which we were born (3.3.9).[12] As in the garden of old, we may be "joined to God" by Christ the Mediator, thereby enjoying what is for us "the true and highest perfection of dignity," and so "mount up even to God and eternal bliss" (2.12.6; 1.15.8). Thus we may at last return to true "human happiness, whose perfection it is to be united with God," and whose pursuit is nothing less than "the principal use of [human] understanding," "the chief activity of the soul," and the surest sign that we are "endowed with reason" (1.15.6). For Calvin, this union, this happiness, this life in God — this is what human beings are for.

Flesh and Faith

Finally, on the church's side of this bond, how does this union take place? God freely, graciously chooses to save whomsoever God wills, Calvin insists, on no other basis than the divine good pleasure. The Spirit

---

12. Calvin explicitly links humanity's *imago Dei* to our "participation" in God in 2.2.1: "when [Adam] had been advanced to the highest degree of honor, Scripture attributed nothing else to him than that he had been created in the image of God [Gen. 1:27], thus suggesting that man was blessed, not because of his own good actions, but by participation in God." For Calvin, the height of human nobility is our having been created in the divine image, which Calvin here glosses as "participation in God." And if being created in the divine image is itself a form of "participation in God," then restoring that image involves restoring that participation.

stirs within anyone God elects to "snatch from death," illuminating her mind and leading her to Christ, who, with the Spirit, justifies and sanctifies her, incorporating her into his own body, and so leading her "little by little to a firm union with God" (3.3.21; 2.15.5). She neither deserves nor initiates this rescue, but at the same time, she does not simply receive it passively, dormant and inert. Rather, she comes alive. She plays her role. She acts, not by her own lights and efforts alone, but rather as awakened, guided, and empowered by the Holy Spirit and Jesus Christ. Everything she does in this respect is itself a gift from God, but her activity is no less "hers" for that, just as in the Lord's Prayer "the bread that we petition God to give us is also called 'ours,'" when in fact it actually "becomes ours by God's loving-kindness and free gift" (2.5.14).[13]

But more precisely, what is her role here? Granted that at every turn, the initiative and vitality are always divine: How do we human beings participate in our own rescue, this "mystical union" with Christ? On one hand, we participate in the flesh — that is, our flesh is a key medium, we might say, through which we may by God's grace "cleave firmly and undividedly" to Christ, God's "Word made flesh." Indeed, according to Calvin, "it was necessary for the Son of God to become for us 'Immanuel, that is, God with us,' and in such a way that his divinity and our human nature might by mutual connection grow together" (2.12.1).

In other words, as *Immanuel*, God is "a body from our body, flesh from our flesh, bones from our bones, that he might be one with us" (2.12.2). In this sense, our union with God depends on the unity of Christ's two natures, human and divine: we cling to the first — or rather, he clings to us by way of the first — and we thereby commune with the second. God comes to us in Christ as an incarnate, embodied human being, and exactly as such, "he is near us, indeed touches us, for he is our flesh" (2.12.1). When it comes to the church's side of the "mystical union" with Christ, then, "God with us" means "God with us in the flesh." Through him, intimacy with God is possible for human beings. "Christ shared in flesh and blood," and therefore is "comrade and partner in the same nature with us" (2.13.2). As we will see in chapter 9, this intimate, embodied, "mutual connection" is sacramentally — that is, practically and paradigmatically — realized in "the Sacred Supper."

But on the other hand, "flesh alone does not make the bond of

---

13. See, e.g., Matt. 6:11: "Give us this day our daily bread."

brotherhood" with the Mediator, since "faith intervenes, to engraft us spiritually into the body of Christ" (2.13.2). That is, while flesh may be a key medium of Christ's graceful, accommodating, intimate bond with human beings, by itself it is insufficient. Our union with Christ is immersive, and so includes more than the human body (though not less!). In broad strokes, as we have seen, Calvin maintains that a human being "consists of a soul and a body," and that the human soul "consists of two faculties, understanding and will" (1.15.2, 7). Accordingly, a disciple's union with Christ must involve the whole range of these registers, not only "flesh and blood" but also "mind and heart" (1.15.3), not only the human body but also the human intellect, emotions, volition, and so on.

For Calvin, "faith" cuts across these capacities: it is a "kind of knowledge" that ultimately "takes root in the depth of the heart" (3.2.14; 3.2.36). In this sense, it is "more of the heart than of the brain, and more of the disposition than of the understanding" (3.2.8). Faith has to do with a person's overall posture and orientation, her basic stance and bearing. It is intellectual, to be sure: "Faith rests not on ignorance, but on knowledge" (3.2.2). But faith's knowledge is not common knowledge: "this kind of knowledge is far more lofty than all understanding," and yet "it understands more than if it perceived anything human by its own capacity." Faith is intellectual and reasonable, then, but at the same time stretches out from and beyond intellect and reason. It "does not comprehend what it feels." It is "persuaded of what it does not grasp." It "consists in assurance rather than in comprehension" (3.2.14). Indeed, according to Calvin, at its core, faith has to do with being deeply, existentially persuaded. It has to do with trust, with "full assurance," and so with a fundamental "confidence" in something and someone (3.2.15).

Confidence in what? In "divine benevolence and salvation." Confidence in whom? In Christ, and through him, in the triune God. Calvin defines faith this way: "a firm and certain knowledge of God's benevolence toward us, founded upon the truth of the freely given promise in Christ, both revealed to our minds and sealed upon our hearts through the Holy Spirit" (3.2.7).

As such, faith is utterly impossible for human beings to generate on their own. Like our daily bread, we can only receive it as God's gracious gift and as what Calvin calls the Holy Spirit's "principal work" in us and for us. That is, by endowing disciples with faith, the Spirit illuminates their minds and hearts and persuades them to trust in Christ's "freely given promise" that God is "benevolent toward [them]," in other words, that even now, God is their loving, merciful parent, and that they are God's children. Trusting in Christ and his gospel promise, they trust God; in this sense, "through [Christ] we believe in God" (3.2.1; cf. 1 Pet. 1:21). And by trusting God in this way — intellectually persuaded in a mode that both includes and exceeds the heights of their intellects, and emotionally persuaded in a mode rooted in the depths of their hearts — disciples are "engrafted spiritually into the body of Christ." They surrender themselves into God's care. They trust God. They lean on God. They hand themselves over. Enlivened and guided by the Holy Spirit, they receive the gift of faith in Christ, and so are received into Christ himself, living in him and therefore in God.

Indeed, for Calvin, faith finally is less a mode of grasping or obtaining and more a mode of receiving and being received, a whole posture and "disposition" of trust and receptivity. In this sense faith is a form of openness and emptiness: "We compare faith to a kind of vessel; for unless we come empty and with the mouth of our soul open to seek Christ's grace, we are not capable of receiving him." By itself, faith "does not possess the power of justifying," but only takes part in justification "insofar as it receives Christ." In fact, Calvin goes so far as to say that in itself, the "vessel" of faith is of "no worth": if it helps by "bringing Christ" to us, it does so "just as an earthen pot crammed with money makes a man rich." In Calvin's view, then, faith is ultimately a way of welcome opened up in us by the Holy Spirit, a receptive disposition by which we "come empty . . . to seek Christ's grace." In other words, for Calvin, faith is not a grasping fist, but rather a humble, open hand. It is not a brilliant lecture, but rather a listening ear. In short, faith is an old pot, and by God's grace alone, it is filled with gold (3.11.7).[14]

14. In this passage Calvin is fencing with Osiander — and along the way, he opens the door to an account of faith as basically kenotic, a mode of "emptying oneself" for the sake of God's indwelling presence. This idea evokes a whole range of biblical images, including the prophetic mode of being "full of the Holy Spirit" (e.g., Luke 4:1; Acts 2:4; see also Acts 6:5: "Stephen, a man full of faith and the Holy Spirit") and Paul's claim that "it is no longer I who live, but it is Christ who lives in me" (Gal. 2:20). Moreover, conceiving faith in this way is very much in keeping with Calvin's portrait of Christian life as first and foremost a life of Spirit-led self-denial. According to this view, to be "faithful" is in fact a kind of *kenosis* (self-emptying), whereas to be "faithless" is a kind of being, as we say, "full of oneself." Cf. 3.12.8: "let us hold it as a brief but general and sure

God with Us

That treasure, of course, is Christ himself, and even the old earthen pot is a divine gift of the Holy Spirit. Once a disciple finds herself in possession of these gifts, the whole world may appear in a new light. Persuaded of God's benevolence toward her, indeed that she is a child of a loving, active divine parent, she may now see creation and her life within it for what they truly are — but this time without being overwhelmed with shame and anguish. By the Holy Spirit's illumination and pedagogy, disciples may come to glimpse something of the "dullness" of their sight, the "miserable ruin" of their sin, and even the sense in which "God's curse" condemns the damage they have done and continue to do. But at the same time, Christ assures them that, under his wing, they are nevertheless accepted and forgiven and loved by God. Thus Christ establishes for them a bulwark against anxiety and despair.

And likewise, Christ assures them that, under his tutelage, "little by little" they will be reformed, regenerated, sanctified, and so one day restored to their fully human dignity. Thus Christ establishes for them a bulwark against shame and hopelessness. At once protected and liberated in this way, disciples may look forward in hope, genuinely humbled and chastened by their sin, and at the same time set free for a life of dignity and "boldness" that "arises only out of a sure confidence in divine benevolence and salvation" (3.2.15). Justified by God's redemptive work, they hear from Christ the words of consolation, "Neither do I condemn you." Sanctified by God's redemptive work, they hear from Christ the challenging, dignifying command, "Go your way, and from now on do not sin again" (John 8:11). By this "double grace," as Calvin puts it, Christians live out their discipleship, always listening twice, we might say, to the Word of God.

In the end, then, by the Holy Spirit's illumination and pedagogy, disciples may indeed come to understand the "miserable ruin" of their sin as "just cause for [God's] disowning [them] and not regarding or recognizing [them] as his sons" (2.6.1). They do not flinch from this assessment, deny it, or seek to diminish it in any way. They see it and confess it. But at the same time, they do not imagine that their miserable ruin outstrips God's mercy, for the Holy Spirit does not leave them

---

rule that prepared to share the fruit of God's mercy is he who has emptied himself, I do not say of righteousness, which exists not, but of a vain and airy semblance of righteousness. For to the extent that a man rests satisfied with himself, he impedes the beneficence of God."

alone in their contrition, or indeed in their ruin. Rather, she leads them to Christ, "clothed with his gospel" (3.2.6) as proclaimed in Scripture, including, of course, the Gospel of Luke, where Christ tells a parable that contains, among other things, a vivid promise of God's merciful, abiding love: "There was a man who had two sons . . ." (Luke 15:11ff.). Seeing through Scripture, then, disciples may learn to see themselves as God's children, welcomed home despite their ruin, and indeed precisely in the face of it. Do not be afraid, Jesus says, again and again. Come home.

To embark on this path of discipleship, a path of continually listening to Christ, learning from him, and "growing together" with him in a "mystical union" over time, is for Calvin to embark on a paideutic program of practical discipline at least roughly equivalent to the one he envisioned for Geneva. For Christ does not come to us abstractly or arbitrarily; rather, he comes "clothed with his gospel," in and through the words of Scripture read at home or in church, or expounded from the pulpit, and so his disciples, if they are to meet him there, engage in a relatively intensive regimen of domestic and liturgical scriptural study. Likewise, for Calvin, Christ comes to us at the table of "the Sacred Supper" — or rather, through that supper we are led to him in heaven, and so his disciples, if they are to meet him there, engage in a regular (and, Calvin recommends, frequent) discipline of the Lord's table. And so on. In daily and weekly prayer and worship, in psalm singing, in everyday decency and dignity, disciples undergo their immersive *paideia,* their "formative education" toward restoring their true humanity, that is, the integrity of the image of God in them, and so their "mystical union" with God in Christ.

If the Bible is "the very school of God's children," Christ is their biblical "schoolmaster," the "teacher" who interprets Scripture for them and with them. And at the same time, since scriptural texts are ultimately corrective "spectacles" through which they see the world, Christ is their cosmic schoolmaster, too (1.6.4; 3.1.4; 4.8.7). He instructs them in what and how to learn from the school of creation, and in particular, draws their attention to important aspects of God's work in the world that they, in their dull disregard, would otherwise overlook. Insofar as Christ's curriculum is kerygmatic and sapiential, it requires disciplines of attending and discerning; insofar as his curriculum calls disciples to a more richly and rigorously doxological life, it requires disciplines of corporate, domestic, and private worship and devotion.

And insofar as Christ's curriculum is moral or ethical in character, it requires disciplines of behavioral accountability — and so the scrutiny and regulation of Geneva's consistory, too, ultimately belong under the theological rubric of "sanctification" in Calvin's reforming project. That is, for Calvin, the practices that constitute the church's *paideia* are properly understood as acts of participation in the transformative, regenerative work initiated and realized by Christ and the Holy Spirit. Living in God, disciples are "little by little" renewed, reformed, remade.

Even so, they are "far removed from perfection," still "entangled in vices" (3.3.14). They are still dull of vision, weak of mind, and small of heart. In short, they still require the reformative work that now defines their life. They have not yet finished the course. They remain in exile. But in Christ, their feet are now set surely on the pilgrim's path of liberation and return. Their true humanity has now come into view and into reach. Once lost and oblivious, they largely remain so, but in Christ, "drawn by the Spirit of God," they are nevertheless "lifted up in mind and heart above our understanding. For the soul, illumined by [Christ], takes on a new keenness, as it were, to contemplate the heavenly mysteries, whose splendor had previously blinded it. And man's understanding, thus beamed by the light of the Holy Spirit, then at last truly begins to taste those things that belong to the kingdom of God, having formerly been quite foolish and dull in tasting them" (3.2.34). With this new keenness, this new sense of taste, this reformed sensibility, they may see, interpret, and respond to heaven and earth as they are. No longer overwhelmed with shame at their estrangement from God, no longer convinced that they have been disowned as children, they now play their part in the divine work of sanctification and communion. Reconciled and assured by Jesus Christ, invigorated and guided by the Holy Spirit, they enroll in the great school of Scripture, and through it, in the wider university of the universe itself. The light of those "many lamps" that shine with God's glory throughout creation is for them no longer a cause for dread and disgrace, but rather for continual contemplation and wonder, praise and good pleasure. And accordingly, disciples receive the whole world as a many-splendored divine gift, and their lives within it as the gracious, tailor-made destiny God has set for them.

Which brings us, of course, to the question of destiny, and so to the doctrine of "predestination," perhaps the most notorious idea of all in Calvin's work.

CHAPTER 8

Doxology and Destiny

Living in Christ, disciples enjoy a "double grace." On one hand, insofar as Christ stands with them and for them, they are justified in God's sight, forgiven and reckoned as righteous. And on the other, insofar as Christ instructs them and shapes them through the Holy Spirit, remaking them "little by little" according to Christ's own image and thereby according to their own genuine humanity, they are sanctified in God's *paideia*. Thus doubly assured that in Christ they are bona fide children of God, neither disowned nor forsaken but rather embraced and welcomed home, disciples live toward lives of true *pietas*, of filial love and reverence and willingness to serve. As the Spirit grants it, they see through Scripture. They trust in God's mercy and care. They strive and support each other as the practical community of the church, the living body of Christ incarnated in its members. Through their reformed and still reforming sensibilities, they experience the world around and within them as a radiant gift and mirror of divine glory, grace, and presence. Immersed in this radiance and drawn by the Spirit into lives of formative discipline and learning, they strengthen their relational, pragmatic knowledge of God and of themselves, the two endlessly interconnected parts of all human wisdom.

In this way, Calvin contends, God saves human beings. Living in Christ, disciples live in God. And with all this in view, we are now in a position to press two questions we have thus far held at bay: First, on what basis does God decide to grant this gift, the gift of salvation? And second, to whom does God grant it? On both counts, Calvin spells out his position by way of his doctrine of predestination.[1]

Humility and Hope

Strictly speaking, "predestination" is itself something of a redundant term, since the very idea of "destiny" already implies a course of events appointed or determined ahead of time: What is the practical difference, after all, between being "destined" for something and being "predestined" for it?[2] For Calvin, however, besides the fact that the Latin word *praedestinationem* figures in the work of Bernard of Clairvaux, for example, and especially in Augustine, the prefix "pre" helps highlight a crucial polemic. To wit: in Calvin's view, God destines the elect for paradise before they carry out any good work whatsoever, thus ruling out the idea that salvation is earned or deserved as a kind of reward. Salvation is not a case of this kind of exchange, Calvin insists. It is no *quid pro quo*. Rather, it is a gracious divine gift, utterly gratuitous, unilaterally initiated by God, and conditioned by neither more nor less than God's good pleasure. Thus Calvin joins the sixteenth-century debate over destiny, the argument about whether the decisive, saving distinction that separates the saved from the damned, the elect from the reprobate, may be attributed even in part to the elect's meritorious work.

---

1. Calvin was by no means the first Christian theologian to do so, nor did he thereby become particularly distinctive in his own day. Augustine, Thomas Aquinas, and others taught versions of so-called double predestination well before Calvin, as did many of his reforming predecessors and contemporaries, including Tyndale, Melanchthon, Zwingli, and Bucer. Indeed, R. Scott Clark has argued that Calvin's reputation today as "the predestinarian theologian par excellence" indicates "more about the success of anti-Calvin Lutheran polemics and the effect of the Enlightenment on historiography than it does about Calvin's exegesis, theology, or preaching." Calvinist fascination with the doctrine in the late sixteenth and seventeenth centuries surely had a good deal to do with it, too, as did Calvin's own polemic writing and public disputation on the subject. But the degree to which the doctrine defines his reputation today is certainly out of all proportion with its actual role in his work. See R. Scott Clark, "Election and Predestination: The Sovereign Expressions of God," in *A Theological Guide to Calvin's Institutes*, ed. David W. Hall and Peter A. Lillback (Phillipsburg, N.J.: P&R Publishing, 2008), pp. 90-122.

2. The word "destiny" derives from the Latin *destinare*, "to make firm; to establish"; thus the term may be etymologically glossed, "a course already and firmly established."

Calvin's answer to this question, in a word, is an emphatic no. For him, a human being's salvation always follows from God's free decision, and that decision is completely unconditioned by human work — and in fact gives rise to that work in the first place. That is, any virtuous feat accomplished by a human being is already a divine gift to her, and so her good work is no ticket into God's good graces but rather is at best an indication that she is already there: already justified by Christ, and now in the midst of being sanctified by him in the Holy Spirit. Indeed, for Calvin, to understand human achievement as in any respect earning or meriting divine deliverance is to mistake an aspect of salvation for its cause. It is as if a disoriented, drowning man desperately reasons that God might deign to save him if only he can demonstrate his worth by clinging mightily to the lifeline in his hands — whereas in fact, God has already provided, and continues to provide, both the lifeline and the man's strength to hold on to it. By clinging to the line, then, the man shows not that he deserves to be rescued but rather that he is being rescued even now, graciously and wonderfully, through no merit of his own. Thus, salvation by no means flows from a person's good works; instead, her good works flow from her salvation, indeed as part and parcel of God's generous, sanctifying rescue.

It is certainly possible, as many of Calvin's readers have done, to understand this position as a kind of logical extension or necessary correlate of his doctrines of divine sovereignty, majesty, providence, sin, justification by grace, and so on. That is, if God is sovereign, eternal, gracious, and providentially active in and through all things without exception, and if sin has rendered humanity utterly lost and debilitated, then human salvation must be divine work, gracefully conceived and decreed *ab aeterno* (from eternity), and so in that sense established "before" or apart from all human labor. And if God freely, eternally determines who will be saved, then God also freely, eternally determines who won't. John Calvin, so this line of interpretation goes, was simply willing to follow this logic out to its predestinarian conclusion without equivocation or compromise.

On the contrary, however, the doctrinal constellation in question here — creation, providence, sin, justification, sanctification, election — is in fact a mutually constituting, interdependent web of ideas in Calvin's work, and so we can just as easily say that his doctrines of creation and divine providence are logical extensions or correlates of his doctrine of election as the other way around. And moreover, in Calvin's actual presentation of predestination in the *Institutio* and elsewhere, while he is explicitly alert to questions of logical and doctrinal consistency, in the main, he makes his case on other grounds: exegetical fidelity, pastoral usefulness, and so on. Calvin thinks that God's grace precedes and engenders all human righteousness, and he thinks so primarily because the Bible, on his reading, says so.

And yet at the same time, Calvin thinks the reason the Bible says so is that the Holy Spirit means to educate and edify — that is, to paideutically train — disciples through Scripture's role as both "school" and "spectacles" for the church, all for the sake of particular pastoral, formational ends. In this sense, in Calvin's view, exegetical fidelity and pastoral usefulness are two sides of the same coin: the Bible says what it says so that the church can do what it does, namely, train disciples to develop the skills and capacities necessary for fully human being, which is to say, for fully intimate communion with God in Christ. For Calvin, this kind of training is what doctrine is for: "We have given the first place to the doctrine in which our religion is contained," he writes, "since our salvation begins with it. But it must enter our heart and pass into our daily living, and so transform us into itself that it may not be unfruitful for us."[3] Salvation may "begin" with doctrine, but it ends with formation and fruit, and the doctrine of predestination, as Calvin understands it, is a case in point. Through Holy Scripture, the Holy Spirit instructs disciples about predestination so that the church, as a community of practice formed in part by this teaching, might become more fully human, drawn ever closer to communion with God.

How might the doctrine of predestination function in this way? First and foremost, the doctrine should form disciples toward what Calvin calls "true humility" (*ICR* 3.21.1). That is, the doctrine of predestination is the consummate attack on so-called works righteousness, the idea that human beings may to some extent earn or deserve salvation through works of obedience, charity, and so on. In Calvin's view, this idea gives rise to a thousand forms of pride, since it seems to put human beings in the place of choosing either paradise or perdition — and those who believe they have chosen the former are only too eager

---

3. John Calvin, *Institutes of the Christian Religion*, ed. John T. McNeill (Philadelphia: Westminster, 1960), 3.6.4 (hereafter cited as *ICR*; section references cited in parentheses in the text).

to congratulate themselves, and then look down on those who have chosen differently. According to this view of human destiny, God may indeed invite us and assist us and cajole us and command us, but at the end of the day, the difference-making decision is ours. We carry the baton the final step. In this doctrine of election, human beings take part in the act of electing.

To construe salvation this way, Calvin insists, is finally to construe it as a human work, and so as an occasion — however camouflaged — for human "boasting," as Paul puts it (e.g., 1 Cor. 4:7). That is, if my work has played a necessary part in God's decision to save me, in effect "inducing" God to include me among the elect, then my salvation is, at least in part, attributable to me — an idea that for Calvin "tears humility up by the very roots." On the other hand, Calvin argues, the doctrine of predestination protects and preserves that humility, precisely because it construes salvation unequivocally as divine work, as God's "eternal decree," and so as a form of election in which only God does the electing. God *predestines* human beings, choosing the elect before they choose God, and indeed thereby granting the elect the renewed inclination and capacity to choose God at all. Their salvation and good works, then, so far from being occasions for boasting, are instead occasions for humility, wonder, thanks, and praise. For if my work has played no part whatsoever in God's decision to save me, but rather flows from that decision, then my salvation is, in every respect, attributable to God alone. All boasting about works is ruled out, and all that remains is a continual cause for humble gratitude. Indeed, this is precisely how Calvin introduces his doctrine of predestination in the *Institutio*, namely, as an essential aid to forming disciples toward humility and conscious dependence on God: "neither will anything else suffice to make us humble as we ought to be nor shall we otherwise sincerely feel how much we are obliged to God" (3.21.1).

And for Calvin, these formative effects are not only a matter of intellectual reflection; they also take place on the ground and in the flesh, in and through the nit and grit of everyday, embodied, theological life. Properly understood, the doctrine of predestination directs us to conceive our daily work not as a series of opportunities to curry divine favor, but rather as a steady stream of divine gifts flowing in along a predestined path, and so as a series of opportunities to gracefully receive those gifts in and through the Holy Spirit as we move along. This implies a fully active stance on our part, not a passive one: as we travel,

Doxology and Destiny

we may and should energetically pursue acts of justice, kindness, obedience to divine commands, and so on, all the while recognizing these acts as themselves gifts from God. Thus disciples may learn to regard such works not as signs of their own excellence or merit, but rather as signs of God's overwhelming generosity, and at the same time of their own ongoing intimacy and dependence on God as God's own children. In this sense, properly conceived, good works are humbling. They should figure in disciples' lives not as occasions for pride, but always and strictly as occasions for gratitude and joy. Every good work is an undeserved blessing received by the laborer, and an undeserved blessing is no cause for triumph. Here Calvin quotes Augustine, counseling Christians to beware, "lest while you are claiming for yourself that you have found the just way, you perish from the just way. I have come, you say, of my own free choice; I have come of my own will. Why are you puffed up? Do you wish to know that this also has been given to you?" (2.3.10; cf. 1 Cor. 4:7).

Thus, as Calvin conceives it, the doctrine of predestination is designed to help disciples guard against becoming "puffed up," the better to cultivate them as truly humble, grateful, joyful human beings. They may and should accomplish good work throughout their lives, indeed at every opportunity they encounter, but "this also," Calvin maintains, "has been given to you." This also is a gift from God. This also is grounds for your filial love and reverence, your *pietas,* your trust and thanks and praise.

Moreover, even as the doctrine of predestination ideally protects disciples and forms them toward humility and a vibrant sense of "how much [they] are obliged to God," it also protects and forms them toward robust assurance and hope. It strengthens their faith. For if their salvation finally turns on their own decisions, their own resources, their own competence, their own works, then there is "ample reason for men's minds to become dejected," particularly in view of the "miserable ruin" of human sin (3.24.9). On the other hand, if the saving decision is God's alone, and so turns on divine resources, divine competence, and divine work, then disciples may rest assured, for "here is [their] only ground for firmness and confidence" (3.21.1). Then Christian proclamation of salvation may actually resound as good news for them. Then they may genuinely live in faith and consolation, humbly and hopefully relying not on their own fidelity or righteousness or mercy, but on God's. In this sense, Calvin calls the doctrine of predestination "the foundation of our salvation," the purveyor of these "three benefits," these "very sweet fruit": the cultivation of humility, the felt experience of our obligation to God, and the only true, trustworthy "ground for firmness and confidence" in our salvation. Without this kind of doctrinal framework and safeguard, human beings live in pride, ingratitude, and "constant fear" (3.21.1).

For Calvin, then, taking seriously the doctrine of predestination — an idea ostensibly pertaining to a pilgrim's final destination in the hereafter — in fact shifts the felt quality, complexion, and tenor of the whole pilgrimage, including every step along the way here and now. Precisely because her ultimate end is, so to say, "already decided," the whole journey appears in a new light — eschatologically "backlit," we might say — and an entirely different posture, bearing, and style of travel become possible for her. She is no longer blazing a trail, but following one. She is no longer anxiously reaching, earning, trying to make progress by her own merit, but rather receiving and welcoming her life as a continual divine gift, an already established path along which God "nourishes and educates" her every day.

Once the Holy Spirit genuinely persuades a pilgrim that she is predestined for paradise, the felt experience of her daily life undergoes a fundamental, perspectival reversal. She is still a pilgrim in the wilderness, still alert to her surroundings, still looking up ahead as she travels. But now she is no longer lost or in danger of becoming lost. Now she is no longer trying to "get somewhere," no longer moving into and through the landscape, penetrating it as best she can. Instead, it is as if she is on a riverboat moving downstream, and rather than penetrating and moving through the landscape, the landscape is coming to her, moving toward and around her like an unfolding, enveloping, passing gift: her destiny.

The river bends this way and that, but its final destination is not in question, and the current is strong and steady. She need not work to get there, and so her work takes other forms: accepting the gifts that come her way, using them well, strengthening her skills, correcting her habits, living into her full humanity. What she once experienced as an uncertain, anxious wandering, a hodgepodge, a cacophony, she now experiences as a pilgrimage, a poem already written, a symphony, and a formative course of study. That is, she understands herself to be enrolled in God's great school of sanctification, and so understands that her primary task, precisely as a disciple, is to learn. Accordingly, she is active and vigorous, awake and striving, but her basic, underlying mode of being is not acquisitional, not trying to obtain God's gifts by her own good works, but rather receptive, making the most of what God provides, living with confidence into a destiny already appointed and prepared. In other words, precisely because her ultimate destination is established and understood, her governing task as she moves along is by no means to earn or entice or otherwise acquire divine favor, but rather to live in and alongside God in Christ and the Holy Spirit, and so to be continually formed and reformed, strengthened and corrected, renewed and sanctified at every turn.

For after all, if her ultimate destination is "eternally decreed" by God, so is every bend in the river, every turn in her journey, her destiny, her everyday life. According to Calvin, "not one drop of rain falls without God's sure command," and for human beings this means that each daily detail, no matter how apparently arbitrary or mundane, plays its part in the unfolding destiny God has set for them (1.16.5). What Calvin's doctrine of divine providence expresses generally, his doctrine of predestination expresses with particular reference to human salvation: God governs all things, from the grand and fundamental to the finest, most trivial details. Seen in this light, a disciple's entire life may be recast not as an act of achieving and acquiring over against God, but rather as a hospitable act of receiving from God, responding with God, and so living in God. And in the end, for John Calvin, this means living a doxological life.

That is, if a disciple's whole pilgrimage is a predestined, paideutic course of regeneration, and in that sense is a continuous, unfolding divine gift, then the fitting human response to such a gift, or rather, the fitting human style of receiving the gift as it unfolds along the way, is a humble, grateful, doxological style. The cultivation of humility and the praise of God are inseparably linked in the *Institutio*, and at times are virtually synonymous. Lamenting the widespread ignorance of the doctrine of predestination, for example, Calvin pairs and coordinates humility and praise: "How much the ignorance of this principle detracts from God's glory, how much it takes away from true humility, is well known" (3.21.1). Likewise, in book 3 Calvin entitles a chapter, "Boasting about the Merits of Works Destroys Our Praise of God" (3.25). There is a kind of doxological zero-sum game at play in Calvin's work, in which "boasting" over good works in effect takes credit that properly should be given to God — and disciples "should not claim for themselves the slightest part of his praise" (2.3.10). Indeed, whenever they do, they "wrongfully retain the credit for grace that passes through them, as if a wall should say that it gave birth to a sunbeam that it received through a window" (3.12.8).[4] Conversely, then, Calvin insists on the "rule" that "anyone who stands before God to pray, in his humility giving glory completely to God, abandon all thought of his own glory" (3.20.8). In this sense, for Calvin, bona fide humility walks hand in hand with bona fide doxology. The more we boast in ourselves, the less we properly honor, revere, and love God; the more we live out lives of genuine humility, the more God may be genuinely praised.

Thus for Calvin, "works righteousness" always amounts to idolatry, that is, to misdirected glorification. And if God is nothing less than "the fountain of every good," then God is also the proper ultimate addressee for every accolade, every thanksgiving, every hallelujah: "we should learn to seek every good from him, and, having received it, to credit it to his account" (1.2.1, 2). Each day's goods, then, from our breath to our bread to our acts of benevolence, present us with a genuine challenge: for in truth, Calvin maintains, each and every good is a divine gift, and as such, it deserves a graceful reception, that is, a sincerely grateful, fruitful, doxological reception. On our own, of course, oblivious and debilitated, vain and anxious, we can only fail at this. But in and with Christ and the Holy Spirit, we may be formed and trained and given new capacities, new skills, new life.

Little by little, then, enrolled in this paideutic program, we may learn to live gratefully and doxologically, seeking every good from God and praising God for every good. For *every* good, Calvin insists: every provision, every lesson, every companion, every challenge, every kindness, every work of obedience or charity or virtue or charm — in short, every detail of my day-to-day destiny, within me and around me, however trivial or mundane, including the inestimable gift of that destiny as a whole. And so in Calvin's view, an indispensable intellectual condition for this form of thankful, doxological life is the doctrine of predestination — the idea that God has established a comprehensive, immersive, sanctifying destiny for me, and that my task is to receive it and live into it with gratitude and grace. I cannot do this without a vibrant, ongoing communion with the Holy Spirit, but nor does the Spirit grant this life to me without at the same time enlisting my full, formative participation.

---

4. For this image, Calvin borrows, as he so often does, from Bernard of Clairvaux.

Doxology and Destiny

In this way, Calvin frames his discussion of predestination in terms of paideutic formation, and specifically in terms of humility, hope, gratitude, confidence, and doxology. That is, the idea of predestination is supposed to help disciples cultivate particular dispositions of continual confession, thanksgiving, and praise, such that their salvation — including the everyday manifestations and details of the whole course of that salvation, which is to say, their everyday destiny — is received as it truly is: an unfolding divine gift, properly credited to God alone. Calvin's doctrine of predestination, then, is indeed about destiny, but it is also and finally about doxology, and the ways in which the fully human life of *pietas* entails a life of humble thanks and praise without ceasing.

To interpret Calvin's work on predestination apart from this kind of formation — say, as primarily a case of logical or doctrinal rigor, or in terms of exegesis alone — is to miss the heart of what Calvin is trying to say, and more importantly, what he is trying to do. What is he trying to do? He is trying to sketch an intellectual framework meant to serve the formation of a particular kind of human life. Or, more precisely, he is trying to sketch his understanding of the "heavenly doctrine" revealed in Scripture, a doctrine meant to serve the formation of fully human beings in Christ's image: humble, grateful, doxological human beings, living in God, enrolled in the church, pilgrims on the way to paradise. Even in Calvin's day, and certainly in ours, his doctrine of predestination was a matter of great controversy, and much of Calvin's writing on it, in the *Institutio* and elsewhere, is preoccupied with defending it against its critics. But while some of the idea's important details may be gleaned from these largely defensive, polemic campaigns, the heart of the doctrine is formational — and unless the reader begins there, she will miss the main thing amid the clamor of dispute.

Some critics, for example, in Calvin's day as in ours, charge that Calvin's work on predestination allows insufficient room for human freedom to choose the good. Calvin answers, in short, that apart from our fundamental relationship with God, there is no such thing as full humanity, much less fully human freedom to choose the good. For Calvin, we are truly free only when God acts in us and through us and with us, prompting, guiding, and enabling us to choose the good. Just as the "daily bread" mentioned in the Lord's Prayer is primarily a divine gift but is also thereby "ours" in a secondary sense, so are all our goods, all our works, and all our lives (2.5.14). They are all "ours," to be sure, but

147

only in this secondary sense, and as such they belong to the sphere of human freedom. Primarily and preeminently, however, they are divine gifts to us, and as such are concrete events of divine freedom. As Calvin puts it in his famous description of Christian life: "We are not our own ... we are God's" (3.7.1).

This basic idea can be traced throughout Calvin's work, including his doctrine of creation: "For how can the thought of God penetrate your mind," he writes, "without your realizing immediately that, since you are his handiwork, you have been made over and bound to his command by right of creation, that you owe your life to him? — that whatever you undertake, whatever you do, ought to be ascribed to him?" (1.2.2). For Calvin, human beings undertake and do and are responsible accordingly, but at the same time, these very activities are nevertheless properly and ultimately ascribed to God, in whom we live and move. Indeed, even "our very being," as Calvin puts it in the *Institutio*'s opening paragraph, "is nothing but subsistence in the one God" (1.1.1). Quoting Bernard of Clairvaux, Calvin sums up his position this way: "We, I say, are, but in the heart of God. We are, but by his dignifying us, not by our own dignity" (3.2.25). We do not live alone, or on our own power. We live in God — and so our freedom, our good work, our dignity, our salvation can only take place in and by God's grace.

On another flank, Calvin's critics contend that his teaching on predestination renders God not a God of grace but rather a God of cruelty and caprice, saving only a few while consigning many more to destruction. After all, these critics charge, if even the elect are in themselves undeserving, why does God withhold similar mercy from everyone else? Or, to turn the coin over, if God predestines human beings to reprobation, how can this be squared with the divine love proclaimed in the Christian gospel?

Calvin's ostensible answer here is at least fourfold: first, we are in no position to stand in judgment of God; second, disciples should focus on their own salvation, eschewing all speculation — let alone assessment — about who else God may or may not have chosen; third, since God is not obliged to rescue even one person from humanity's self-imposed ruin, that God rescues the elect can only be considered a marvelous act of generosity; and fourth, though we may scarcely comprehend it, God must in some sense be glorified by salvation and reprobation alike (3.21-24).

But running through and behind all these arguments is the basic idea that God actually does withhold mercy, that God actually does predestine particular human beings to perdition. This basic idea may be challenged, and challenged on the very grounds Calvin stakes out in his teaching on predestination. Because Calvin excludes all speculation about the destinies of others, and in particular about the identities of those predestined to destruction, he advances what amounts to a de facto agnosticism about the ranks of the reprobate — certainly about who is or is not among those ranks, but also about whether those ranks include anyone at all. Calvin himself does not take this last step, of course, and in fact explicitly excludes it, but key fundamentals of his case point in this direction in intriguing, theologically promising ways.

Sheep out of Wolves

Like the overwhelming majority of his theological forebears, teachers, and contemporaries, Calvin takes for granted that at the end of all things, God will divide humanity into two classes: the saved and the damned, the elect and the reprobate. And moreover, Calvin is convinced that the latter group is by far the larger one, so that human salvation amounts to God "snatching from death" a small remnant — "scarcely one man in a hundred," he is fond of saying — from a much larger mass of condemnation (1.4.1; 1.5.8; 3.20.14). Calvin draws these conclusions primarily from his reading of Scripture: for him, the many passages in the Bible that seem to suggest universal salvation are in fact properly read otherwise, and the many passages that seem to suggest a much more limited salvation are properly read as proclaiming just that.

But Calvin also argues from experience on this point, following Augustine, among others, by framing the question in terms of Christian preaching: "If the same sermon is preached, say, to a hundred people," Calvin writes, providing a momentary glimpse, perhaps, into his own preaching life, "twenty receive it with the ready obedience of faith, while the rest hold it valueless, or laugh, or hiss, or loathe it" (3.24.12). Indeed, he incredulously declares, if in fact it "pleases God to extend [salvation] to the whole human race, why does he not encourage to repentance the very many whose minds are amenable to obedience?" If so many hear the gospel, why do so few apparently believe, and confess, and genuinely follow? The only compelling answer to these questions, Calvin contends, is that while God openly announces the gospel of repentance and mercy for all to hear, only those whom God has also "supplied with eyes and ears" believe it and fully devote themselves to it. For careful observers of Christian preaching and listening, then, "experience teaches that God wills the repentance of those whom he invites to himself, in such a way that he does not touch the hearts of all" (3.24.15; for "eyes and ears," see 3.22.10).

And so for Calvin, "experience teaches" what Scripture, on his reading, clearly proclaims: God "does not indiscriminately adopt all into the hope of salvation but gives to some what he denies to others" (3.21.1). God grants the gift of salvation to whomsoever God wills, and by all appearances, though many are called, few are chosen. Indeed, "If he willed all to be saved, he would set his Son over them, and would engraft all into his body with the sacred bond of faith" — and since faith in Christ is apparently not universal, neither is salvation (3.22.10).

But for Calvin, apparent Christian "faith" does not flatly and simply guarantee membership among God's elect. Calvin is only too aware that "professed faith" may or may not be sincere, and so may or may not indicate actual incorporation into Christ's body, actually being "clothed with Christ's sanctification" (3.24.8). Considered side by side, then, a member of the elect and a member of the reprobate may be indistinguishable from a human point of view, since both may profess allegedly heartfelt faith and perform evidently good works.[5] In their respective motives, levels of sincerity, and so on, they may differ markedly from each other, but no disciple can definitively assess the depths of another disciple's heart, never mind the true status of her neighbor's relationship with God. Only God can do that.

Each disciple may — and, Calvin argues, each disciple should — regularly scrutinize the depths of her own heart, listen to God's call as it is personally addressed to her, feel God's persuasive Spirit acting within her, trust and cling to Christ with genuine faith, that is, with "a firm and certain knowledge of God's benevolence toward us" — but her expertise is strictly limited to her own case. She is in no position to examine or judge her neighbors in these intimate respects. Again, only God can do that. In this way, Calvin bars one door to Christian judgmentalism: precisely because faith is so deeply personal, he con-

---

5. On the capacity of "profane men" to act in a way that "appears praiseworthy," see Calvin, *ICR* 2.3.4. Generally, Calvin's position is that God may and does work through both the elect and the reprobate to accomplish good works.

Doxology and Destiny

tends, only my own relationship with God is available to my examination and assessment; speculation about my neighbors in this regard is epistemologically specious, presumptuous, rash — and therefore ruled out (3.2.7).

Indeed, Calvin goes so far as to argue that, here and there among the reprobate, something very much like "faith" can be found. The reprobate, too, may earnestly "believe that God is merciful toward them," and so the reprobate, too, may be "affected by almost the same feeling as the elect, so that even in their own judgment they do not in any way differ from the elect." Nor is this necessarily a matter of simple delusion or self-deception on their part, since in some cases God may actually grant the reprobate "the gift of reconciliation," an actual "awareness of his grace," and therefore what seems to be "a beginning in faith." Though they may actually number among the reprobate, they nevertheless "are justly said to believe" (3.2.11). Calvin hastens to add, however, that the alleged faith of the reprobate is only alleged: "Even if it is close to faith, it differs much from it" (3.2.12). And yet it is so "close to faith" — and this is the important point — that those who have it sincerely believe that they are faithful, and that God is merciful to them.

But if even apparently sincere claims to faith may be found among the reprobate, is there then no observable distinguishing mark that clearly separates the elect from the rest of humanity? For Calvin, one key mark does remain: only the faith of the elect endures. That is, God grants the elect bona fide faith, a gift that includes "the living root of faith so that they may endure to the end," since, after all, a person's "call and faith are of little account unless perseverance be added" (3.2.11; 3.24.6). And so while God may grant to the reprobate "a taste" of what may look and feel like true faith, it lacks the "living root," and so is only a counterfeit, "transitory faith." Sooner or later, it passes away. When it comes to the reprobate, then, God may in fact "manifest to them his mercy," granting them "the inward illumination of his Spirit," but only "for the time being," a brief or extended but in any case temporary span after which their awareness of divine mercy withers and finally "vanishes" (3.2.11; 3.14.8). Thus in Calvin's view, even were we somehow to gain a vantage point from which we could definitively survey and assess the sincerity of another person's claim to faith, the mere presence of sincerity is by itself no litmus test for membership among the elect, for their apparent faith, while presently sincere, may or may not last. That is, God may or may not have granted to them the gift of bona fide faith, which includes perseverance. Only time will tell.

In practical terms, then, according to Calvin, I cannot look around and pick out the elect from among the reprobate, for I lack a reliable criterion. I may find someone who offers an eloquent "profession of faith," but for all I know, it may be insincere or delusional. And moreover, even if I could directly assess my neighbor's sincerity, though I may discover convincing evidence of earnestness, my neighbor's apparent faith may or may not be actual faith, and so may or may not persevere. Indeed, as Calvin notes, even and especially my own faith is properly humbled and refined by this teaching, in effect sending me back again and again to the Bible and to the Lord's table so that the "full assurance" of my faith may be made all the more full and assured by God's graceful persuasion through Word and sacrament. In this way, Calvin bars a second door to Christian judgmentalism: with respect to my own faith, I must continually remain humbly dependent on God, lest my "firm and certain knowledge of God's benevolence" cross over into a crass sense of entitlement or triumph, what Calvin calls "the confidence of the flesh" as opposed to the strong, unassuming "assurance of faith" (3.2.11).[6]

Thus when it comes to those who explicitly profess Christian convictions (a group, we should recall, that comprised the vast majority of Calvin's world and readership), Calvin contends that while each disciple may take heart in her own election as the Spirit reveals it to her, she remains agnostic about who else is predestined for paradise and who for perdition. But what should she make of those who profess no

---

6. By its very nature, Calvin contends, faith looks ahead to the future with confidence in God's parental love and mercy unto salvation, and so includes within it the presumption of its own perseverance. But at the same time, Calvin warns, the apparent faith found among the reprobate in its own way looks to the future with confidence, and whether a given person's alleged faith will ultimately prove to be of the bona fide or the transitory variety remains to be seen. "In the meantime," Calvin writes, "believers are taught to examine themselves carefully and humbly, lest the confidence of the flesh creep in and replace assurance of faith" (3.2.11). Calvin's formational point here, then, is not that disciples should anxiously or cynically step aside from their faith in order to call it into question, but rather that they should lean into their faith even as they constantly strengthen and refine it, always looking ahead with bold trust in God's grace, but at the same time learning to carry this trust in a becoming, humble, thankful way. In short, for Calvin, the doctrine of the apparent faith of the reprobate properly functions as a practical check on Christian pride.

Christian faith at all? What of those who dismiss Christianity, or who openly deny or oppose it, or who by acts of inhumanity seem to demonstrate that they live well outside the Spirit's sanctifying custody? In short, if the Shepherd calls his sheep, and if we grant that for the time being those who answer him may well include wolves in sheep's clothing — what about those who appear quite plainly to be wolves, undisguised and ravenous?

Here is the third door to Christian judgmentalism, and Calvin bars it at least twice. First, he bars it with his doctrine that sin is universal and deep-seated among human beings, including among the elect, who remain sinners even as they are, little by little, sanctified and reformed (3.3.10-11). In this sense, the sheep in Christ's fold do not in themselves differ from wolves, and so are in no position to judge them as if from on high: "For no man makes himself a sheep but is made one by heavenly grace" (3.22.10). And second, Calvin bars this third door to judgmentalism with his doctrine that God may and does "make sheep out of wolves," and that God does so in "his own time" (3.23.1; 3.24.11; cf. 3.24.10).

That is, while the elect may have been chosen since before the foundation of the world, they are nevertheless "gathered into Christ's flock by a call not immediately at birth, and not all at the same time, but according as it pleases God to dispense his grace to them." Before this call, the elect "wander scattered in the wilderness common to all," and in their wandering "do not differ at all from others" (3.24.10). Indeed, before this call, the elect may or may not "wallow in the most abominable and execrable sins." Like Rahab, Manasseh, and the thief crucified with Jesus, their lives before their call may include little or no inkling of their election, no hints of their forthcoming conversion — until that conversion actually takes place (3.24.11). Like Saul before he became Paul, they may even wage war against humanity before being abruptly or gradually but in any case decisively turned around and transformed.

In short, by all appearances, they may be wolves. But whenever and wherever God wills it, "God makes sheep out of wolves." In spite of how things may seem, if God has chosen them, then they are destined for conversion and ultimately for paradise — though this drama will unfold only when and how God sees fit. "For God," Calvin writes, "whenever it pleases him, changes the worst men into the best, engrafts the alien, and adopts the stranger into the church" (4.12.9). Potentially, then, the very worst of all sinners, or the supposed outsider, or the complete stranger — each may actually number among "those whom the Lord has once determined to snatch from this gulf of destruction," though God defers the rescue "until his own time" (3.24.10, 11). And so for disciples interacting with people they consider to be outside the Christian church, even the most apparently clear, reliable signs of reprobation — hostile opposition to Christianity, say, or callous inhumanity — are in fact no such thing. Only God knows who is marked with which destiny, and whose hearts will turn, like the crucified thief's, at the final hour: "For those who seemed utterly lost and quite beyond hope are by his goodness called back to the way; while those who more than others seemed to stand firm often fall" (4.1.8).[7]

Thus Calvin bars three doors to Christian judgmentalism, in effect situating Christian disciples within the bounds of a particular type of soteriological agnosticism. First, by casting faith as a matter of the whole human being, and in particular of the depths of the human heart, the inward persuasion of the Holy Spirit, and so on, Calvin denies that any disciple is in a position to know the destiny of any other. If God wills it, I may become convinced of my own salvation in Christ, but there I confront the limit of my soteriological knowledge; I cannot sort my neighbors into classes. Second, by teaching that even the "transitory faith" God grants to the reprobate may well appear to them, and so to others around them, as genuine faith, Calvin effectively chastens pilgrims to remain humbly dependent on God at every step along the way, continually welcoming the gift of salvation with gratitude at every turn, trusting it to be true, but never arrogantly claiming it as a possession.

---

7. A striking case in point here may be found in Calvin's 1564 letter to Princess Renee of France, duchess of Ferrara. The duchess's Protestant minister had declared that her late son-in-law, the duke of Guise, a notorious persecutor of Protestants in France, numbered among the reprobate — a declaration the duchess found objectionable. In his response, Calvin is quite critical of the duke (calling him "an avowed enemy of the truth of the gospel"), but then writes: "To pronounce that he is damned, however, is to go too far." In place of this kind of pronouncement, Calvin recommends "more moderation and sobriety," and moreover, that "the remedy for all that is to hate evil, without taking persons into the account, but leaving every one to his Judge." "Thus hatred and Christianity," Calvin continues, "are things incompatible. I mean hatred toward persons — in opposition to the love we owe them. On the contrary we are to wish and even procure their good; and to labor as much as in us lies to maintain peace and concord with everyone." See Bonnet DCLXIV, #4074, in OC 20:244-49; excerpted in Elsie Anne McKee, *John Calvin: Writings on Pastoral Piety* (New York: Paulist, 2001), pp. 310-12.

Doxology and Destiny

In other words, Calvin exhorts each believer to believe that God's mercy is personally meant for her, but also to guard against letting her faith become a cause for conceit or complacency, and instead to humbly persevere along the path God has prepared. This perseverance will by no means earn her salvation, of course, but rather merely manifest it along the way. In the meantime, disciples should live prospectively, faithfully relying on God under the training and tutelage of the Holy Spirit, continually refreshing and refining their faith through engagement with the Word and around the Lord's table — all the while bearing in mind that their call and their faith are theirs only as divine gifts. To lost and discouraged souls, Calvin cries, *Have faith!* To high and mighty believers, he cautions, *Even the reprobate may seem to have faith,* so "Let him who stands well take heed lest he fall" (3.2.40; cf. 1 Cor. 10:12; cf. 3.24.6).

Taken together, these first two barred doors are meant to orient disciples toward other Christians with a humble, circumspect, and finally charitable stance. By God's graceful persuasion, a disciple may become assured of her own salvation, but as to whether her Christian neighbor is destined for paradise or perdition, she cannot say. Her neighbor may appear to demonstrate faith in word and deed, but the secrets of his heart and the endurance of his faith are unknown to her: "to know who are His," Calvin writes, "is a prerogative belonging solely to God" (4.1.8). Strictly speaking, then, a disciple is properly agnostic about everyone's salvation but her own — and even with respect to her own, she can be fully and legitimately convinced only of her rescue, not of any supposed reprobation. For no matter how lost disciples may feel, no matter how ruined or undeserving, the Christian gospel proclaims to them in Scripture, preaching, and song that God has found them and will restore them, and in any case is perfectly capable of "making sheep out of wolves." Should God will it, the way of repentance is always open, and the idea that the Spirit will yet lead me in that direction can never be ruled out. Thus a disciple can come to know that God's parental love and mercy are meant for her, but on virtually every other soteriological question, she pleads ignorance. She remains agnostic. Are her fellow Christians also members of the elect? She may and should fervently hope so, Calvin contends, but finally and definitively, she cannot say. That question is not hers to answer, and therefore it is not even hers to ask: "For here we are not bidden to distinguish between reprobate and elect — that is for God alone, not for us, to do" (4.1.3).

155

Rereading the Institutio

A Church beyond Our Ken

How then should she treat her companions in the Christian church? Should her agnosticism about their destinies lead her to constantly hedge her bets as she interacts with them, choose her words carefully in conversation, or indeed nervously avoid the topic altogether? On the contrary, Calvin argues, a disciple's soteriological agnosticism should lead her into a generous, hospitable stance toward all, continually extending her fellow pilgrims the benefit of the soteriological doubt. For after all, in any given case, she has no grounds whatsoever to assume reprobation, and at least some circumstantial grounds to assume election: her neighbor's professed faith, for example, or indeed his affiliation with the church itself.

As a practical matter, then, Calvin counsels us to treat one another with "a certain charitable judgment whereby we recognize as members of the church those who, by confession of faith, by example of life, and by partaking of the sacraments, profess the same God and Christ with us" (4.1.8).[8] Of course, our neighbor's confession may be secretly insincere, his example secretly corrupt, or his sacramental life little more than a masquerade, but we are in no position to judge these matters, one way or the other. In fact, we are in no position to pursue or speculate about them at all.[9] The true church, that is, the church comprised of the elect, is invisible to us; it is "a church beyond our ken"

---

8. In this famous sentence, Calvin does not have in view three marks whereby genuine Christians can be identified; on the contrary, his governing subject in this section is that "God's eyes alone see the ones who are unfeignedly holy and will persevere to the very end," and so the three marks identify not those actually reckoned by God as "his children," but rather those whom disciples, for their part, should "count as his children" in the meantime, that is, prior to the eschaton. In other words, the marks establish a set of provisional, pragmatic working assumptions for Christian community, but these marks do not correspond to the marks of the elect, which "God's eyes alone see." Moreover, further underlining the strictly pragmatic, provisional character of these marks, Calvin explicitly characterizes them as less "certain" and less "plain" than the two institutional marks of the church: "the preaching of the Word and the observance of the sacraments." See 4.1.7-10.

9. For readers familiar with Calvin's emphasis on the importance of church discipline, the communal surveillance of the Genevan consistory, and so on, this may be surprising. But in fact, Calvin explicitly limits the jurisdiction of church discipline to external behavior capable of being "witnessed," and so excludes all sins that are by nature "completely hidden from men, as are those of hypocrites (for these do not fall under the judgment of the church)." See 4.12.6.

(4.1.3). Our role is decidedly not to ferret out and reveal its membership. Rather, our role is to recognize, with "charitable judgment," our ecclesial neighbors as members of the church, treating them as if they actually belong to Christ's body and therefore to the ranks of the rescued. Indeed, Calvin goes so far as to say that within ecclesial precincts, "we ought to treat like brothers and count as believers those whom we think unworthy of the fellowship of the godly" (4.1.9). On this side of paradise, then, for Calvin the church is a permanently mixed society, like "a net in which all kinds of fish are gathered and are not sorted until laid out on the shore" (4.1.13; cf. Matt. 13:47-58). On the sands of the eschaton, God will one day do the sorting. In the meantime, what remains for disciples is to live out a personally faithful, interpersonally charitable way of life.

Calvin's declared position is that the elect are a fraction of humanity, a remnant in which "a small and contemptible number are hidden in a huge multitude" — indeed, they are a fraction of the visible church, perhaps numbering something like one in five (4.1.2).[10] And yet, on the ground and in practice, this declared position has little or no bearing on proper ecclesial behavior, which in fact should be governed by a broad rule of mutually charitable reckoning. That is, Calvin contends that in their dealings with each other, disciples should reckon apparent faith as bona fide faith, apparent rectitude as actually being "clothed in Christ's sanctification," apparent sacramental observance as actual communion with Christ, and so on. So charitable should disciples be with one another, in fact, that they "ought to treat like brothers and count as believers" even those they would otherwise judge to be "unworthy of the fellowship of the godly," thereby treating as insiders those they would otherwise be tempted to regard as being on the outside.[11]

---

10. For "one in five," see 3.24.12, and above, pp. 149-50. Calvin explicitly characterizes this phenomenon as a "daily proof" of the fact that God predestines to destruction "those whom he has once condemned and deprived of participation in his light." Thus Calvin suggests that in a typical listening congregation, God "once condemned" approximately four out of five — and for Calvin, a listening congregation is a fair shorthand description of the visible church as a whole. Of course, with this remark Calvin by no means intends to suggest a hard-and-fast proportion or general rule, but at the very least, the passage does quite clearly suggest that as he imagines the elect within the larger visible church, he has a minority in mind.

11. To be sure, excommunication — that is, being "removed from the believers' fellowship" — is a chief use of church discipline for Calvin, but in the *Institutio* he sharply distinguishes between excommunication and "anathema": "Excommunication differs

In effect, then, among Christian disciples, Calvin means to quarantine the whole question of who does or does not belong to the ranks of the reprobate, and in that sense to bracket it from everyday ecclesial life. The possibility — even, in Calvin's estimation, the statistical probability — that my fellow Christian is a member of the reprobate properly plays no role whatsoever in my relationship with him, and in fact is put entirely in the shade by the radiant possibility that he is a member of the elect. In this latter light alone, I rightly regard and interpret and interact with him. Accordingly, I count him as a brother, a believer, a fellow Christian, and so for all practical purposes, the very idea of his reprobation recedes from my sight. After all, it is none of my business, and so is properly sequestered out beyond the horizon of what I even think about, much less claim to know. Even as a potential prospect, actual reprobation belongs to God alone. As far as I am concerned, my neighbor's eternal state is both "already decided" and beyond my ken. Accordingly, I attend to other things.

The broad, general concept of reprobation remains in view for me, of course, and may frequently or rarely play a role as a hortatory incentive, or a subject of edifying reflection, that is, it may function as part and parcel of the Spirit's persuasion of the church community as a whole and of individual disciples in particular: focusing the mind, clarifying the stakes, and so on. But as an enfleshed, definite, personified reality, a concept incarnated in an actual class of identified persons with faces and names and particular histories, reprobation recedes into the shadows outside of ecclesial life. Again, Calvin clearly believes that there is a reprobate class inside the visible church, and he suggests that it is legion, but he just as clearly denies that we can identify its ranks. So for all practical purposes, Christian disciples are to regard and relate to one another as if God has deigned to save the visible church as a whole.

Moreover, for Calvin, a version of this charity should also extend beyond the visible church — and here again is the third door to judgmentalism that Calvin attempts to bar, the passageway that leads to contempt or condescension toward those considered to stand out-

---

from anathema in that the latter, taking away all pardon, condemns and consigns a man to eternal destruction; the former, rather, avenges and chastens his moral conduct" precisely so that it may "call him back to salvation." Thus Calvin conceives excommunication as a corrective, reconciling tool, strongly censuring and thereby strongly encouraging an offender to repent, reform, and return to the church. "Moreover," Calvin adds, "anathema is very rarely or never used." See 4.12.2, 10.

side the visible church. For after all, if distinguishing between the reprobate and the elect is in fact "for God alone, not for us, to do," who can say that a given outsider is not a member of the elect, a person slated to be rescued, despite how that person may appear to us? Quoting Augustine, Calvin insists that when it comes to the visible church, "many sheep are without, and many wolves within." Who can say, then, encountering this or that particular person "without" the visible church, that she is not actually one of God's own sheep, destined for paradise? For God has "marked" as elect "those who know neither him nor themselves," and in the fullness of time the Spirit will draw them into the fold (4.1.8). On the ground and in practice, then, a Christian disciple never encounters a person she knows to be a member of the reprobate, either inside the church or outside it. In each and every case, no matter what the ostensible evidence, she encounters a potential member of God's elect and can only treat that person as such.[12]

---

12. At times in his work, Calvin does seem to suggest that under certain conditions, Christian disciples may identify members of the reprobate. For example, in a 1564 letter he refers obliquely to the possibility of "some certain and infallible mark of [a person's] reprobation" — though he leaves this mark unspecified. Or again, in a comment on Ps. 69, he writes, "We need wisdom by which to distinguish between those who are wholly reprobate and those of whose amendment there is still some hope," but his larger point in this passage is to attribute such wisdom to David insofar as he was "under the guidance of the Holy Spirit" as he composed Ps. 69 itself, and so this attribution may simultaneously be taken as a denial that such wisdom belongs to ordinary disciples in ordinary circumstances. And so on. On their face, such claims do contradict Calvin's otherwise consistent teaching that "we are not bidden to distinguish between reprobate and elect — that is for God alone, not for us, to do," but this tension may be mitigated, if not dissolved, by reading Calvin as simultaneously (1) ruling out all "distinguishing between reprobate and elect" for ordinary, individual disciples, and (2) nevertheless preserving this possibility for the church's prophetic office generally, and for rare, exceptional prophets such as David in particular. Indeed, Calvin's flicker of equivocation with regard to the church's use of "anathema" (the gesture by which the church "condemns and consigns a man to eternal destruction") may capture this twofold approach — and tension — quite nicely: "anathema," Calvin writes, "is very rarely or never used." That is, it is "never used" because identifying the reprobate is "for God alone, not for us, to do," but Calvin adds the phrase "very rarely," leaving the door ajar, so to say, or at least unlocked, so that the church as a whole, guided by the wisdom of the Holy Spirit, may take this exceptional step if necessary. Indeed, there are real tensions here in Calvin's thought, and between his thought and his work in Geneva, but the broad, prevailing gist of Calvin's writing on this subject is not dedicated to keeping anathema's door open or unlocked, but rather to closing it — and indeed to permanently locking it when it comes to a disciple's pragmatic, everyday life interacting with friends, enemies, and

today's prodigal sinner, after all, within or without the church, may be tomorrow's penitent: now wayward and lost, but nevertheless destined to come home.

In a comment on Psalm 109, Calvin sums up the implications for Christian life of this particular sort of soteriological agnosticism: "as we cannot distinguish between the elect and the reprobate," he writes, "it is our duty to pray for all who trouble us; to desire the salvation of all men; and even to be careful for the welfare of every individual."[13] Call it Calvin's practical, liturgical brand of universalism: precisely because disciples do not know whether or not this or that neighbor is one of God's elect, it becomes their "duty to pray for all," even and especially "all who trouble [them]" — and so in that sense "to desire the salvation of all." What we cannot engage epistemologically, we can and should engage liturgically and existentially, praying to God on behalf of even and especially our enemies, and if for them, then for all humanity with them. As we have seen, Calvin theologically defends a doctrine of limited salvation on both exegetical and experiential grounds, but with respect to Christian disciplines of prayer and desire, as it turns out, Calvin recommends a practical rule of charitable reckoning. A disciple should reckon no one a member of the reprobate, but rather should conceive all neighbors as potential members of the elect, and disciples as bona fide believers, engrafted into Christ's body.

In his chapter on prayer in book 3 of the *Institutio,* Calvin puts the same point this way: "Let the Christian man, then, conform his prayers to this rule in order that they may be in common and embrace all who are his brothers in Christ, not only those whom he at present sees and recognizes as such, but all men who dwell on earth. For what God has determined concerning them is beyond our knowing except that it is no less godly [*pium*] than humane to wish and hope the best for them" (3.20.38). Calvin pens these two sentences, please note, in a paragraph on intercessory prayer, the practice through which disciples love their neighbors by "commending them to the providential care of the best of fathers," and this love should extend to those beyond the visible church

---

strangers. See Bonnet DCLXIV, #4074 in OC 20:244-49; excerpted in McKee, *John Calvin,* p. 310; Calvin, *Commentary on Psalms,* 69:22; and Calvin, *ICR* 4.1.3; 4.12.10.

13. Calvin, *Commentary on Psalms,* 109:16. For a brief, excellent treatment of this and similar passages in Calvin's work, see John L. Thompson, *Reading the Bible with the Dead* (Grand Rapids: Eerdmans, 2007), especially pp. 64-66.

Doxology and Destiny

precisely because "what God has determined concerning them is beyond our knowing." As part and parcel of her *pietas,* then, in her daily prayer a disciple properly takes up a position "in common" with "all who dwell on earth," embracing them, commending them to God's care, and thus wishing and hoping the best for them — which is to say, wishing and hoping for their salvation.

Calvin was no universalist, of course. Indeed, in his comment on Psalm 109 he immediately adds, "At the same time, if our hearts are pure and peaceful, this will not prevent us from freely appealing to God's judgment, that he may cut off the finally impenitent."[14] In broad terms, then, Calvin's paradigmatic soteriological prayer was not for universal salvation, but rather for God to save the elect and "cut off" the "finally impenitent" — whoever they may be. But in pragmatic, everyday terms, since for all we know, even sinners and enemies today may be penitents and friends tomorrow, Calvin counsels disciples to pray not for their opponents' destruction but rather for "their amendment and reformation,"[15] and thereby "to desire the salvation of all."

This is an intriguing, suggestive tension in Calvin's work, and it points to a way in which his broad claims about the ranks of the reprobate may be challenged. On one hand, of course, the whole question of the reprobate boils down to the complicated exegetical task of interpreting biblical texts on salvation's scope that ostensibly seem to point in different directions, one batch apparently indicating limited salvation, the other apparently indicating universal salvation. On this subject, Calvin has made up his mind: like most of his predecessors and contemporaries, he reads the second batch through the lens of the first, and so contends that the Bible declares a limited salvation of the few. But Calvin buttresses his exegetical case with arguments from experience, and these latter claims stand in tension with his portrait of a disciple's proper agnosticism when it comes to distinguishing the elect and the reprobate.

For example, Calvin maintains that the varied response to Christian preaching indicates that God "does not touch the hearts of all" (3.24.15). But here we may ask, bearing in mind the epistemological lim-

---

14. Calvin, *Commentary on Psalms,* 109:16.

15. Calvin, *Commentary on Psalms,* 137:7. See also Calvin's comment on Ps. 109:6: "it may turn out that the man, who today bears toward us a deadly enmity, may tomorrow through that grace become our friend."

its drawn by Calvin himself: How do we actually know who has genuinely received a sermon with the "ready obedience of faith"? And moreover, how do we know that the one who rejects a sermon today will not, by the Spirit's gift, turn around and accept a sermon tomorrow? Indeed, even if we grant Calvin's claim that upon hearing a sermon four out of five congregants typically consider it "valueless, or laugh, or hiss, or loathe it," who can say that the Spirit will not supply all four of those critics the "eyes and ears" they require at some later date, indeed in the fullness of time according to God's own good pleasure (3.24.12; 3.22.10)? And finally, even for the most unsympathetic offender, how can we rule out the possibility that we are confronting someone akin to the crucified thief, that universally condemned man whose eleventh-hour conversion Jesus instantly receives with the breathtaking words, "Today you will be with me in Paradise" (Luke 23:43)?

For Calvin, in each and every individual case we come across in our daily lives, we cannot rule out this possibility. It remains permanently open. To be sure, outside the visible church, men and women neither confess Christian faith nor participate in Christian sacraments; but neither did any number of prestigious Christians before their conversions, and indeed, in Calvin's view, neither do any members of the elect before the Spirit's summons, as they "wander scattered in the wilderness common to all" (3.24.10). Even and especially with respect to precincts supposedly outside the visible church, then, realms likewise populated by both sheep and wolves, disciples cannot and should not distinguish between the reprobate and the elect. That is "for God alone, not for us, to do." Within the visible church or without it, disciples may testify to the Christian gospel as they understand it. They may proclaim the good news of life in Christ — and they do well to take heed to their own proclamation. Following Jesus, they may become fishers of people. They may work to repair and strengthen and recast the great net that is the Christian church. But they cannot sort the fish, neither the ones they catch nor the ones they don't. Only God can do that, and there is no telling "how far his secret judgments surpass our comprehension" (4.1.8).

Calvin's practical rule of charitable reckoning is decidedly, irreducibly pragmatic: it belongs to the sphere of interpersonal relationships, judgment, communal life, daily prayer, and the heart's desire. It proceeds from a modest soteriological agnosticism, that is, from the limits of our knowledge about God and about each other. Accordingly, it cannot be translated or abstracted into an ideological form of universalism, a general declaration that God saves all human beings — for that, too, is to claim to know too much. Wherever we draw the circle of God's saving grace, whether around all humanity or around some small fraction of it, the basic problem is the same: it is not our circle to draw. That is "for God alone, not for us, to do." But at the same time, as a practical matter and so as both a *lex orandi* and a *lex vivendi*, we can and should pray not only for our friends and favorites, but also for "all those who trouble us." We can and should "desire the salvation of all." We can and should treat even the most troublesome Christians with "charitable judgment," reckoning them as brothers and sisters, bona fide believers in Christ. And by a parallel principle, we can and should treat those outside the visible church with a similar style of generosity manifest in humble, hospitable, respectful forms of restraint: testifying clearly and winsomely to the good news that we have heard, but also always being more than willing to listen and learn, and never claiming to know the outer boundaries of the Spirit's saving work.

For Calvin, of course, all this sits side by side with his arguments from Scripture and experience that, in short, "many are called, but few are chosen" (Matt. 22:14). He perceives no difficulty in thinking and proclaiming that God has chosen to rescue only a marked minority of humankind, "a small and contemptible number hidden in a huge multitude," while at the same time insisting that disciples should treat the whole multitude with various forms of charitable judgment, including praying and wishing the best for their enemies and desiring the salvation of all. And indeed, strictly speaking, there is no contradiction or outright inconsistency here between these two claims, namely, that the church should pragmatically desire the salvation of all and doctrinally proclaim that God saves only an anonymous few. But there is at the least a practical tension here, one that puts the church's doctrines of God, prayer, and salvation under significant pressure. Key fundamentals of Calvin's case, however, open the door to another direction of theological development, one he never fully pursued himself, but which the rudiments of his doctrine of predestination make possible.

First, Calvin's particular brand of soteriological agnosticism — the idea that we can know our own destiny by the Spirit's inner persuasion but not the destinies of our neighbors — opens the door to a thoroughgoing Christian humility about the destinies of others. Second, Calvin's idea of "charitable judgment," which helps fill out how this humility looks in practice, opens the door to developing a practical stance that extends Christian agnosticism about the ranks of the reprobate to include agnosticism about whether those ranks include anyone at all. Indeed, the wide variety of biblical texts on the scope of salvation may be fruitfully read in just this way, that is, as properly forming disciples such that they never foreclose the possibility of universal salvation but at the same time never claim it finally and definitively. Reading and living this way, disciples may simultaneously guard against sectarian pride, presumptuous gossip, and losing sight of either the stakes involved or their own role — activated, empowered, and guided by the Holy Spirit — in God's saving and sanctifying work. In the end, on this view, the church's role is not to pontificate about universal salvation, but rather humbly and boldly to pray for it.

And third, the essence of Calvin's doctrine of predestination is that God saves not God's friends, but rather God's enemies. In short, God saves sinners — and for Calvin, as we have seen, sin is no mere neglect of duty. It is a posture and way of life oriented against God, a way of mistrust, ingratitude, idolatry, disobedience, and *impietas,* a disastrous mode of oblivion comprised "partly by ignorance, partly by malice" (1.4 title). The elect, Calvin contends, are no less sinners than the rest of humanity; they are not rescued because of their good works, but rather are granted the humbling privilege of doing good works, to the extent that they do them at all, because they are already rescued. The rescue itself, then, is entirely gratuitous, entirely free, entirely graceful. The elect may have been destined for paradise since before the foundation of the world, but they also fall, they also live and work under the shadow of sin, and so before their call, and indeed in a great many respects after it, they "do not differ at all from others" (3.24.10).

For Calvin, this doctrine properly functions to chasten and humble Christian disciples as they consider their own salvation. It reminds them that they are not rescued because of their own strength or piety or merit; instead, they are rescued despite their own weakness, insolence, and liability. In themselves, they "do not differ at all from others," and so they have no right to self-congratulation, which is to say, to self-directed doxology. On this much Calvin is quite clear. But his position here may be developed even further, for the basic idea that God saves God's enemies may also be understood to properly chasten and humble Christian disciples as they consider and relate to their neighbors, and in particular as they make claims not only about who does or does not belong to the ranks of the reprobate, but also about whether those ranks include anyone at all.

Precisely because in themselves they "do not differ at all from others," Christian disciples have no right to treat their neighbors with contempt or condescension. Even those who trouble us the most, even those who appear to us to be wolves, even our enemies may number among the elect. For God makes sheep out of wolves — and in fact has done so, Christians witness, in each and every case of Christian discipleship. Accordingly, when disciples behold someone they might consider God's adversary, they behold exactly the sort of person God saves. May it be, then, that God has predestined all to paradise and none to perdition? May it be that the set of sinners Calvin prays God will one day "cut off," that is, the set made up of those who are "finally impenitent," will at the last be an empty set? We cannot say. But by the same token, on this view, we cannot rule out this possibility, and it is in any case the scenario for which the Christian church properly longs, and calls, and hopes, and waits. For the church can only desire the salvation of all. And what's more, the church, of all people, should know only too well that God is a God of surprising, undeserved grace, and that grace makes all things new.

CHAPTER 9

Prayer and Communion

The two longest chapters in the *Institutio* are on prayer and the sacred supper of Christ, and sure enough, in Calvin's view, these two practices are at the heart of Christian life in God. As we have seen, for Calvin, a primary purpose of doctrine is to clarify and serve the paideutic, practical life of discipleship, and so to focus merely on doctrine without also embodying and practicing what that doctrine declares "would be of as little profit as for a man to neglect a treasure, buried and hidden in the earth, after it had been pointed out to him." In other words, doctrine may be an indispensable guide, but disciples, indwelled, empowered, and led by the Holy Spirit, still must roll up their sleeves and dig. However well instructed we may be that "whatever we need and whatever we lack is in God," it nevertheless "remains for us to seek in him, and in prayers to ask of him, what we have learned to be in him."[1]

Thus Calvin contends that while human salvation "begins" with doctrinal education, doctrine "must enter our heart and pass into our daily living, and so transform us into itself that it may not be unfruitful for us" (3.6.4). Properly and ultimately, doctrine pertains to something we *become*. It must "transform us into itself." And for Calvin, no disciplines of becoming are more important to this formation, and so to Christian "daily living," than disciplines of prayer and the sacred

---

1. John Calvin, *Institutes of the Christian Religion*, ed. John T. McNeill (Philadelphia: Westminster, 1960), 3.20.1 (hereafter cited as *ICR*; section references cited in parentheses in the text).

supper. In and through these key practices, Christ and the Spirit form disciples toward lives of intimate communion with God.

The Communion of Prayer

The practice of prayer is nothing less than "the chief exercise of faith," and since "faith is the principal work of the Holy Spirit," it comes as no surprise that for Calvin the Spirit plays a crucial role in Christian prayer (3.20 title; 3.1.4). Indeed, genuine prayer is principally accomplished in and through disciples by the Holy Spirit, "the Spirit of adoption," who "raises up our spirits to dare show forth to God our desires, to stir up unspeakable groanings, and confidently cry, 'Abba! Father!'" (3.20.1; cf. Rom. 8:15, 26). Likewise, we Christians pray "in Christ's name," since Christ is both our "mediator" and "our mouth" (3.20.17, 21). But insofar as God grants it, prayer belongs to human beings, too. It is also a human cry, human confidence, human groaning, and in this sense prayer is humanity's dialogue and intercourse with God. Indeed, at the outset of the *Institutio*'s chapter on prayer, Calvin describes the dialogue as "a communion of men with God," an intimate association "by which, having entered the heavenly sanctuary, they appeal to him in person concerning his promises in order to experience, where necessity so demands, that what they believed was not in vain" (3.20.2).[2]

In other words, for Calvin, God grants the communion of prayer precisely so that disciples may personally, consciously experience a taste of God's kindness, the fulfillment of God's promises, and thereby be assured that their trust is well placed. To be sure, prayer is also a form of asking God to fulfill our needs (the English word "pray" is an old way of saying "ask"), but according to Calvin, this is not prayer's foremost function in Christian life. In fact, when we pray, our interlocutor is someone who knows better than we do "both in what respect we are troubled, and what is expedient for us." When I ask, say, my neighbor for assistance, a significant part of what I am doing is informing her of my need — but not so with God. And so Calvin raises the question at the outset: Is prayer then "superfluous"? Or worse, does it con-

---

2. Cf. 4.17.45, where Calvin (quoting Chrysostom) refers to "the communion of prayer."

jure up a picture of God "drowsily blinking or even sleeping until he is aroused by our voice" (3.20.3)?

Not if we understand it correctly. Calvin defines prayer in the first place as a mode of communion with God aimed at providing disciples with an "experience" of assurance, a taste of God's capable, tender care. Accordingly, God ordains prayer "not so much for his own sake as for ours" (3.20.3). We may hear divine promises in Scripture and preaching, but through practices of prayer, Calvin maintains, we may also tangibly, persuasively experience their confirmation. Thus prayer properly functions for disciples as an "exercise of faith," a relational workout, a strengthening discipline that builds up their trust in God's fidelity and care.

For example, God promises to provide, and in the Lord's Prayer disciples ask for, daily bread: "give us this day our daily bread," we say, a line that would seem to presuppose, incidentally, a daily practice of prayer. As Calvin conceives it, we make this request not to inform God of our hunger, or to rouse God into action, but rather the better to experience — in and through the reception, touch, taste, enjoyment, and sustenance of whatever bread may subsequently come our way — the tangible reality of God's providential love for us. We ask for bread, then, not only so that we might receive it, but also and principally so that when we receive it, we might actually experience it as it is: a divine gift to us, and even more, an answer to our prayers. For in truth, Calvin insists, God does provide for us every day, precisely as our active, loving, attentive parent. But just as with human parents and children, we come to know and trust this kind of truth only through repeated experiences of asking and receiving, needing and enjoying, vulnerability and love.

Without this kind of experiential training, left to our own dull devices, we may well regard our daily bread as little more than just that: the same old daily bread, a humdrum prop in a bland or harried or thoughtless routine, or a more or less pleasing occasion for ungrateful satisfaction. Far too often, Calvin maintains, our attention lags or wanders in this way; we lose track of our actual situation as God's beloved children; and consequently our desires are anxious, paltry, self-absorbed, or unwise. We are amnesiac, and so need to be reminded. We are worried, and so need to be reassured. We are oblivious, "sleepy or sluggish," bogged down by "such great dullness," and so need to be awakened and revived. We are born for intimate communion with God, a relationship that calls for whatever "keenness of mind" and "affection

168

Prayer and Communion

of heart" we have at our disposal, but on both counts we "faint and fail, or are carried in the opposite direction" (3.20.3, 5).

And so we need to pray, Calvin contends, not only for our daily bread but also for all our needs and the world's needs besides, the better to remember, calm down, and wake up. In this sense, for Calvin, practices of prayer are ongoing disciplines of mindful attention, vigilance, and insight, always meant to shape how practitioners receive and interpret the world. The principal object of prayer, then, is by no means to inform God, who knows our needs in any case, but rather to inform and reform our hearts and minds. We really do ask God for divine gifts, and we do it so that we really may receive them as such. Accordingly, as we have seen, Calvin recommends a daily prayer cycle, in effect a laicized version of the monastic office, in which we pray "when we arise in the morning, before we begin daily work, when we sit down to a meal, when by God's blessing we have eaten, when we are getting ready to retire" (3.20.50).

Properly performed, this daily practice is no "superstitious observance of hours, whereby, as if paying our debt to God, we imagine ourselves paid up for the remaining hours." Rather, it functions as "tutelage for our weakness, which should be thus exercised and repeatedly stimulated" (3.20.50). That is, the daily office is formative, not transactional. With God's illumination and guidance, it strengthens us where we are weak, stimulates us where we are dull, and thereby restores us, little by little, toward intimate relationship with God — and thus to full humanity.

In a word, for Calvin, prayer is *paideia*. Throughout each day, woven through the comings and goings of ordinary life, "God admits us to intimate conversation," as Calvin puts, "gently summoning us to unburden our cares into his bosom" — a disarmingly personal, heart-to-heart form of companionship. By praying, "we invoke the presence" of divine "providence," "power," and "goodness": "in short, it is by prayer that we call him to reveal himself as wholly present to us" (3.20.2). Calvin understands God to be present to us in any case, of course, and conspicuously so in the shimmering details of creation around and within us. Again, the invocation here is fundamentally for our sake, to help dispel our dullness and make us more keenly aware of God in and through everyday life, thereby drawing us into more fully human lives of equanimity, thanksgiving, and praise. Calling on God to be present to us, we effectively call our own attention to God's presence, that is, to divine "providence," "power," and "goodness," and so to the fact that God is actually with us and for us all day long.

As we have seen, for Calvin, Christian life — the life of *pietas* — is largely dominated by two practical gestures: seeking every good from God, and crediting God with every good.[3] And so one way of approaching Calvin's account of prayer and its benefits is to ask the question: How does prayer advance these two basic tasks?

First, Calvin argues that through practices of prayer, the Holy Spirit helps practitioners "become accustomed in every need to flee to him as to a sacred anchor." In this sense, regular prayer properly trains disciples to seek every good from God, the actual source of those goods in any case. The primary point here is not that disciples should dutifully petition God for goods they could otherwise obtain elsewhere; rather, the point is that in fact, every good they receive is a divine gift, and through practices of prayer the Spirit makes them more mindful of this, their true situation. Thus they may live and act in ways more in tune with reality. In other words, through the daily prayer cycle, the Spirit accustoms disciples to turn toward God for all their needs, and so forms them toward a more humble, lively awareness of their daily reliance on what God provides, which is to say, their ongoing relationship to God as God's beloved children. At their best, practices of prayer clarify this relationship, and at the same time draw disciples toward deeper, more fully conscious participation in it (3.20.3).

And second, as we learn to relate to God in this way, we thereby become all the more "prepared to receive his benefits with true gratitude of heart and thanksgiving, benefits that our prayer reminds us come from his hand" (3.20.3). In this sense, prayer trains us to credit God with every good, again bringing us into closer touch with our actual circumstances. Prayer "reminds us." It prompts and stirs us. It provokes us to gratitude. This gratitude is less a question of mere good manners (though manners certainly play their part) and more a question of seeing our actual situation clearly, and so of being able to live and act accordingly.

After all, part of gracefully receiving a gift is receiving it gratefully; indeed, to a significant extent, gratitude constitutes the reception itself, since if no gratitude arises, we may well ask whether the gift was received

---

3. See, e.g., Calvin, *ICR* 1.2.1: Christians should "learn to await and seek all these things from him, and thankfully to ascribe them, once received, to him."

as a "gift" at all. Analogies abound in human affairs: If you generously give me bread to satisfy my hunger, and I simply devour it thoughtlessly, or conceive it as a *quid pro quo* for a favor I did for you yesterday, or as the front end of a bargain that tomorrow obligates me to "return the favor," as we say — then have I actually received the bread as a gift, that is, as a living symbol of your care for me? By no means. I have received it as plunder, windfall, or merchandise. But in the case of God's gifts to humanity, practices of prayer can help remind us that our daily bread finally "comes from God's hand," and so may help stimulate our thanksgiving not only to the "ministers," as Calvin calls them, through whom God makes the bread available (the shopkeeper, the baker, the farmer), but also and ultimately to God. Again, at their best, prayer practices help form and direct our praise, our thanks, and indeed our good manners, etiquette, decorum — all toward the graceful life on earth God calls us to live out.

How, then, may we practically, experientially come to know God's benefits, these goods that surround and pervade us that should induce us to *pietas* but instead so often go unnoticed? By praying for them without ceasing, Calvin replies, and in any case frequently and regularly, through a daily, disciplined, flexible regimen; and by allowing those prayers to remind us that every good thing we enjoy is in fact a blessing from God's own hand (3.20.7, 50). From this angle, we may see clearly what Calvin means when, in the title of the *Institutio*'s chapter on prayer, 3.20, he refers to it as the practice "by which we daily receive God's benefits." We may, of course, casually or obliviously seize and exploit these benefits, but to actually *receive* them as gifts, we have to be made conscious of them, to notice them and their provenance, and so to embrace them with "true gratitude of heart and thanksgiving." And this requires a Spirit-led, sanctifying discipline of mindfulness and attention, dialogue and intimacy.

Moreover, for Calvin, as we learn to interpret and gratefully receive the genuine goods in our lives as divine gifts, we may thereby learn to welcome and enjoy them with even "greater delight." After all, in Calvin's view, our daily bread is not only a good in itself. It is also a gift given directly to us by God, which is all the more reason to delight in it. And likewise, once this gift is set within the context of a disciple's ongoing life of prayer, she may recognize it as not merely a gift, but also and preeminently a *responsive* gift, a motherly, fatherly gift given in loving attention to her actual needs, which is to say, a gift given in answer to her prayers. Delight compounds delight.

For what does a present, active, loving parent do for her children? She provides for them, yes, but even more iconically, and therefore more reassuringly and persuasively, she hears their cries. She responds to them. She interacts with her children, relating and communing with them in freedom, familiarity, and love. She may very well know exactly what they need, and she may already have decided to provide it, but for their sake, so that they might even more vividly experience her care, she encourages them to ask for what they require. That way, her gifts may be seen and received for what they are. Thus she not only anticipates her children's needs, or provides for them in general, as if from afar. She also invites their requests, listens to them, and answers them, not always with the answers they expect or want to hear, but with kindhearted answers nonetheless. And she does all this for the sake of comforting, assuring, and delighting her sons and daughters, and so finally for the sake of her ongoing relationship with them. In the same way, God "is willing in turn to hear our groanings that he may the better prove his love toward us," thereby drawing us more deeply into a love and reverence of our own, which is to say, into *pietas* (3.20.3).

In Calvin's view, then, though God "watches and keeps guard on our behalf, and sometimes even helps unasked, still it is very important for us to call upon him." We should do so without reservation, so that "we learn to set all our wishes before his eyes, and even to pour out our whole hearts." This latter idea helps flesh out the "communion" Calvin has in mind between God and humankind, casting it in terms of intimate companionship. And yet, as this companionship unfolds, it has a normative, formative influence on a disciple's desires in the first place — just as frequently occurs in intimate relationships between human beings. As a child gets to know her parents, for example, she may take comfort in their unconditional care for her, and at the same time, indeed motivated in part by this care, she may strive to change and grow according to their example and instruction. In this way, for Calvin, learning to "set all our wishes" before God in prayer is simultaneously an exercise in building intimacy and a practical, sanctifying challenge, a discipline by which the Spirit, little by little, trains and reforms us so that "there may enter our hearts no desire and no wish at all of which we should be ashamed to make him a witness" (3.20.3). In short, disciples should both pour out their hearts to God and, for this very reason, strive to get their hearts into shape.

For Calvin, the Holy Spirit's sanctifying work on and with individual disciples — and for that matter, on and with the Christian church as a whole — is never finished this side of the eschaton, and moreover, in each and every case, progress in sanctification is at best strikingly modest. Indeed, the very idea that Christian life is *paideia,* an unfolding path of formative education and practical training, means that whatever else a disciple may be, she is always just that: a "disciple," a student, a learner, someone who stands in need of instruction and reformation, and so is enrolled in a remedial program. For Calvin, this remediation frames and defines her life, as it does the collective life of the church. To be sure, by the Spirit's gift she may make progress. She may improve. But even the most gifted disciples have a very, very long way to go; indeed, a sign of their giftedness is that they see their shortcomings quite clearly, and readily admit them. In short, though disciples may "climb upward" by God's grace, they nevertheless "remain suppliants" and sinners at every step along the way (3.20.14).

And so if disciples are supposed to "set all [their] wishes" before God in prayer, they properly do so in the hope that over time, and indeed through the frequent and regular "use and experience" of prayer itself, their hearts may be refashioned (3.20.3, 5). Christian prayer involves an ongoing reformation of desire. Living in and with God, little by little, we learn what to want. And accordingly, precisely because "we do not know how to pray as we ought," the Holy Spirit — "our teacher in prayer" — guides and instructs and trains us in how to want well, how to ask well, and therefore how to desire, long, and love well (3.20.5; Rom. 8:26). Indeed, so severe is our ignorance in this regard, that in and through our prayers we "commonly sin gravely" (3.20.5). Even the saints' prayers, even Abraham's and Jeremiah's, are each "a mixture of faith and error" (3.20.15).

Thus in Calvin's view, if prayer is a sanctifying challenge, that challenge arises precisely because the one who prays requires sanctification. Even as she improves, she remains both suppliant and sinner. In other words, she remains a penitent: "the beginning, and even the preparation, of proper prayer is the plea for pardon." Repentance is nothing less than "the key" with which disciples "open for themselves the door to prayer," a lesson "we learn from numerous passages in the Psalms" (3.20.9). Indeed, Calvin goes so far as to advise that in prayer, a disciple should continually "put away all self-assurance," humbly rely on God, and thereby continually "take the person and disposition of a beggar" (3.20.7).

That is, though my cupboards may be full, in and through practices of prayer — which is to say, by the Spirit's graceful guidance in and through those practices — I may recognize again and again that in truth, my hands are empty. Strictly speaking, I have no possessions of my own. I am a beggar. "And the rite of raising hands," Calvin adds, providing a glimpse into the physical arrangements of prayer in his day, "means that men remember they are far removed from God unless they raise their thoughts on high" (3.20.5). Poor and empty-handed, disciples reach and pray. No matter a man's ostensible wealth, "since he cannot enjoy a single morsel of bread apart from God's continuing favor, his wine cellars and granaries will not hinder him from praying for his daily bread" (3.20.7). And as the rich man prays for his daily bread in the shadow of his storehouses, he may thereby come to recognize himself as no "rich man" at all. Again and again, in prayer he takes up "the person and disposition" of a pauper. In this way, prayer properly functions for Calvin as a kind of equalizer among human beings, a discipline that "levels all haughtiness," dispels illusions of self-sufficiency, and returns disciples to the humble, grateful life that becomes them (3.20.8).[4]

In Calvin's view, this kind of humility is the bearing toward which the doctrine of predestination ought to form disciples, and so in this respect, at least, the two doctrines go hand in hand. But prayer practices should also encourage a bold confidence in God, Calvin insists — and here, too, he links prayer to predestination. On one side of this connection, "faith in election prompts us to call upon God": that is,

---

4. Calvin's position here is something of a double-edged sword, since on one side, it cuts against haughtiness, pride, and entitlement by emphasizing that my wealth is a divine gift, not a product of my own excellence or industry; and on the other side, for just this reason, the position may be taken to imply that the current distribution of wealth in society is beyond critique, since it is the one God intends. At times in the *Institutio*, Calvin himself seems to draw something like this latter conclusion (e.g., 1.16.6: "to each his condition is divinely assigned"). But as we will see in part III, other aspects of Calvin's work militate against this idea, and in any case, the idea presupposes that God providentially prefers social stasis over social change and development, a notion that may be challenged from a variety of angles, biblical, political, moral, historical, and so on. In brief: Israel has known God to assign both slavery in Egypt and liberation from it, and so in any given case, the discerning question is which sort of assignment is in play, confining or liberatory. The latter's dominant position in Israel's self-understanding would seem to recommend it as, at the very least, the default interpretive lens.

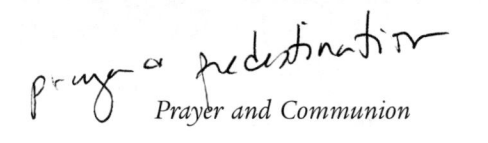

the more I am convinced that God has chosen to rescue me, the more I may turn to God in prayer, thanking and praising but also and preeminently trusting God, like a child taking refuge in her mother's arms. And in turn, Calvin writes, referring to the doctrine of election, "the practice of this doctrine ought also to flourish in our prayers." That is, whenever disciples pray, they properly ground their prayers in bold confidence that God has in fact already chosen to rescue and restore them as beloved children, for "it would be preposterous" for them to pray as if their salvation were somehow in doubt, as if to say, "O Lord, if I have been chosen, hear me" (3.24.5).[5]

Preposterous, Calvin contends, because prayer properly arises in the first place out of a disciple's confidence that God is her merciful parent, and so that she will be heard; in this sense, prayer takes election as its premise and foundation. In other words, the one who genuinely prays calls to God not because her prayer might be heard, or because it might make God more merciful to her. Rather, she calls precisely because she trusts that God has already elected to be merciful to her. In short, she prays because God is her loving, listening parent. She calls out on that basis. She pours out her heart as a child unburdens her troubles to her parents (3.20.12).[6]

Indeed, for Calvin, all prayer is the prayer of children, spoken from a child's stance and standing. Thus the paradigmatic Christian prayer begins, "Our Father," and thus Paul's shorthand for the Spirit's cry in human beings is "Abba!" Whenever disciples pray rightly (that is, whenever the Holy Spirit prays in and through them), they take up this stance and style, and are thereby formed to inhabit a filial way of life. And whenever this formative training takes place, they come to understand themselves more clearly as those God has already chosen to rescue, and is actively reforming even now. They pray because they understand themselves this way — and by praying, they understand themselves this way all the more. Prayer recalls them to who they are, and accustoms them to live accordingly.

Over the course of a life of prayer, then, with all its ebb and flow,

---

5. This is not to say, of course, that disciples should presuppose that the content of any given request is in keeping with God's providential plan for them; rather, the presupposition Calvin takes to underwrite all genuine prayer is the disciple's status as a member of the elect.

6. See also 3.20.34: "as children are wont to take refuge in the protection of the parents whenever they are troubled with any anxiety."

struggle and surprise, by the Spirit's gift disciples may come to see themselves more vividly as those God has saved and is saving from the oblivion of sin and death; has gathered and is gathering in Christ as the Christian church; has restored and is restoring to their true, original identity as children of God made in the image of God. This is the full triptych of human salvation, according to Calvin. It has to do with sin and atonement, to be sure, but also with incorporation into the church as Christ's body, and finally with restoration to full humanity in God's image.

The complete triptych, not any one panel in isolation, is the Christian gospel of "good news of great joy for all the people" (Luke 2:10). And on the basis of this good news alone, Calvin insists, disciples properly turn to God in prayer, assured and emboldened that God is their strong Mother and their gentle Father, their trustworthy savior and demanding teacher, their steady guide and graceful companion. Their destiny is communion with God, and in prayer they live out — and live into — that destiny. In this sense, prayer amounts to a "practice of predestination," both a practical manifestation of the bold humility — "Abba!" — to which divine election calls disciples, and a disciplinary latticework on which a disciple's companionship with God, ordained since before the foundation of the world, may live, grow, and develop (3.24.5).[7]

And so the one who prays, Calvin insists, prays humbly, but also boldly and faithfully. She repents, and also trusts. She admits what she has done and left undone, and at the same time believes that she will be heard, and forgiven, and remade. At stake here for Calvin is whether disciples are "content with God's promises," or, instead, whether they doubt those promises, in effect seeking some other source of consolation and assurance above or beyond them (3.24.5). In Calvin's view, of course, this kind of second-guessing is ungrateful and ungracious; it affronts God's generosity by rejecting the particular forms through which God has seen fit to accommodate and approach humanity: the Spirit's words in Scripture and preaching, and the Word made flesh in Jesus Christ.

Encountering these forms, then, a disciple's proper stance is at

---

7. For a treatment of this theme, see Charles Partee, "Prayer as the Practice of Predestination," in *Calvinus Servus Christi*, ed. Wilhelm H. Neuser (Budapest: Presseabteilung des Ráday-Kollegiums, 1988), pp. 241-56.

once humble enough to be "content with [God's] promises" and bold enough to believe them, including God's promise to hear our prayers. Accordingly, however much we may be "cast down and overcome by true humility, we should be nonetheless encouraged to pray by a sure hope that our prayer will be answered." In this way, both "repentance and faith" should be "present together" in our prayers, joined "by an indissoluble bond." We should turn to God as empty-handed beggars and at the same time as beloved children, fully and faithfully expecting to receive God's gifts, not on the basis of our own excellence or merit (for we are beggars), but rather strictly on the basis of God's abundant, graceful, parental love, and in particular, on the basis of God's promises to hear and provide (3.20.11).

Paraphrasing a passage from the book of James, Calvin opposes "faith" to "wavering," thereby casting faith as a species of resolve (3.20.11). How do we obtain this confidence, and keep it, and cultivate it? By the Spirit's gift, Calvin replies. But the form this gift typically takes is no bolt from the blue, no one-sided choreography in which human beings merely recline and collect. On the contrary, this gift takes a consummately participatory, holistic, engaging form: that is, the form of a lifelong practical path, framed by the "chief exercise" of prayer's intimate communion, day in and day out. This path begins with a "call," a divine call, typically heard (or at least confirmed) in the public reading and exposition of Christian Scripture; and likewise, the path leads to a call, a human call to God in prayer. Here again, Calvin's thought takes the shape of Paul's in Romans: "How will anyone call upon [God] in whom he has not believed? And who will believe unless he has heard? . . . Faith comes by hearing, and hearing from the Word of God" (3.20.11; cf. Rom. 10:14, 17). Indeed, for Calvin, a disciple's pilgrimage is constituted from the first by an ongoing cycle of invocation, of call and response, an "intimate conversation" wherein God calls to humanity through Scripture and the church's proclamation; humanity calls to God in prayer; God responds to these prayers through providential acts of love; humanity responds to this love through corporate and individual doxology; and so on.

Finally, if the relationship between God and humanity consists in this dialogue, this speech and song, this call and response, this conversation with and without words — how then should disciples interpret their experience when God seems to fall silent? What should we make of apparently unanswered prayer? Calvin candidly admits that God "seems to have neglected" many prayers, at least "in men's eyes," but despite appearances, he insists, God "is always present to us." In some cases, God is reticent in order to provoke and train us to speak: "our most merciful Father, although he never either sleeps or idles, still very often gives the impression of one sleeping or idling in order that he may thus train us, otherwise idle and lazy, to seek, ask, and entreat him to our great good" (3.20.3). In other cases, God's reticence is meant to form disciples toward patience, perseverance, and decorum, so that they may not be like those "who covenant with God only under certain conditions . . . as if he were the servant of their own appetites," or "who, carried away with their own ardor, so call upon God that unless he attends upon their first act of prayer and brings them help at once, they immediately fancy him angry and hostile toward them and, abandoning all hope of being heard, cease to call upon him." We need look no further than the Psalms to "see that David and other believers, when they are almost worn out with praying and seem to have beaten the air with their prayers as if pouring forth words to a deaf God, still do not cease to pray" (3.20.51).

In the end, Calvin denies that God actually neglects prayers, and so recommends that disciples interpret apparent disregard in other ways. For example, since God "does not always respond to the exact form of our request," what we think is no answer may in fact be an unexpected one. After all, even intimate conversations between human beings are significantly constituted by unforeseen twists and turns, including as many negative responses as positive ones along the way. Indeed, if it were otherwise, we would hardly learn and grow, and for Calvin, prayer is nothing if not *paideia,* the church's education of desire.

Moreover, Calvin maintains that "God, even when he does not comply with our wishes, is still attentive and kindly to our prayers," and so disciples ought to take heart in any case, "revived by the thought that God has regard for them and will bring an end to their present misfortunes" (3.20.52). Calvin calls this mode of consolation "deferring our hope with a well-tempered evenness of mind," trusting that whatever genuine goods are not provided today will be provided tomorrow, or in any event will be provided "on the Day of Judgment, when his Kingdom will be plainly manifested." In this way, Calvin finally frames the practice of prayer eschatologically, casting the day's provisions as what God has already granted, and the day's needs as what God has not yet granted, but will, we trust, one day — so that at the last, "all good things" will be revealed and enjoyed once and for all (3.20.51, 52).

To sum up: for Calvin, the practice of prayer is a form of communion with God, an intimate, developing dialogue in which pilgrims continually "pour out [their] whole hearts": petitioning God for gifts they need, thanking and praising God for gifts received. Each and every daily circumstance, bar none, is thus reframed as an occasion for intimacy with God, via either petition or praise, and so the whole pilgrimage is likewise reframed as a form of itinerant, evolving companionship. In this sense, Calvin casts prayer as a practice of *Immanuel*, we might say, of "God with us" at every step, a daily discipline by which the Spirit makes us aware that God "is always present to us," listening to us, providing for us, bringing us up as a mother brings up her children. Thus we may say that the purpose of prayer is not to inform God, but rather to reform disciples: to wake them up, alert them to their benefits and so to their benefactor, comfort their nerves, sharpen their senses, strengthen their faith, kindle their hearts — in short, to revive and restore them. And at the same time we may say that the purpose of prayer is precisely this ongoing interaction between God and human beings, this "intimate conversation" through thick and thin, this robust and challenging communal life. God the Spirit calls out in us, "Abba!" God the Son prays with us, "Our Father . . ." And the triune God — Father, Son, and Holy Spirit, one God, Mother of us all — unfailingly listens to us as we pray, in God's good time responding with "all good things."

For Calvin, then, the practice of prayer is fundamentally about keeping company with God — or rather, keeping alert and responsively alive to God's constant companionship. Calvin is quite clear that disciples are in no way exempt from suffering or difficulty, nor does prayer guarantee them special treatment. He explicitly rules out what is today sometimes called the "prosperity gospel," the idea that God showers material prosperity on the elect.[8] But he does maintain that if the Spirit

---

8. In the first place, when it comes to earthly goods, Calvin repeatedly extols the virtues of moderation, frugality, charity, and the like, and so advises disciples both to enjoy themselves within reasonable limits and "to indulge oneself as little as possible . . . cutting off all show of superfluous wealth" (see, e.g., 3.10.4-5). But even more fundamentally, Calvin contends that the inheritance granted to the elect is not a material inheritance, or even an earthly life of relative ease. On the contrary, in his treatment of the story of Isaac, Jacob, and Esau, for example, a story he takes to be a paradigmatic picture

wills it, a disciple's practice of prayer may fruitfully reframe her life, including whatever share of suffering and prosperity may come her way. By God's grace, though her material circumstances may or may not change, her regular prayer becomes a practical means by which the Spirit provides a sense of "abundance in poverty, and comfort in affliction," as well as a thankful posture of poise and humility in times of joy and plenty. God faithfully answers human prayer in expected and unexpected ways, like a caring parent answering her children. In and through all things, Calvin insists, God is with us, attentively, responsively, gracefully with us, and practices of prayer provide us with occasions to see and experience this companionship for ourselves. Indeed, Calvin goes so far as to call prayer not only the "chief exercise" of faith, but also "the chief part of [God's] worship." Alluding to Psalm 50, as he so often does, Calvin proclaims that in God's estimation, "to be called upon in the day of need is highest and precious above all else": "Call on me in the day of affliction; I will deliver you, and you shall glorify me" (3.20.13; Ps. 50:15).

The Sacred Supper

But prayer is not the only practical communion with God to which Calvin commends his readers. The other, of course, is the Lord's Supper. If the "communion of prayer" primarily pertains to divine accompaniment on the pilgrimage of discipleship, the supper's communion has to do with sustenance and strength for the journey, that is, how God has arranged "to nourish us throughout the course of our life," and at the same time "to assure us of this continuing liberality" (4.17.1).

---

of election, Calvin argues that the "right of primogeniture" Jacob receives pertains "to the age to come," not to any advantage whatsoever in the present age; indeed, if it were otherwise, that blessing "would be an empty and absurd kind of blessing, since from it [Jacob] obtained nothing but manifold hardships, troubles, sad exile, many sorrows, and bitter cares." Thus for Calvin, God wills for the elect a "spiritual election," not a material one, much less one manifest in money. The elect's true "treasure" is in heaven, Calvin insists, and as such, it is far more precious than gold. In the meantime, disciples should expect a life very much like their neighbors' in material terms, that is, a life riddled with both joys and trials. Indeed, so far is Calvin from a "prosperity gospel" that his approach at times suggests the reverse, an "adversity gospel" in which discipleship consists in an often challenging pilgrimage, by no means devoid of joy, but always undertaken in the shadow of the cross. See, e.g., 3.22.6.

For Calvin, the supper is a "spiritual banquet," a feast especially made for the human soul. The fare, of course, is Christ himself: "as bread nourishes, sustains, and keeps the life of the body, so Christ's body is the only food to invigorate and enliven the soul" (4.17.1, 3). Indeed, this basic "as . . . so" relationship captures what Calvin calls the "analogy or comparison" at the heart of the meal: "since the Supper is nothing but a visible witnessing of that promise contained in the sixth chapter of John, namely, that Christ is the bread of life come down from heaven, visible bread must serve as an intermediary to represent that spiritual bread" (4.17.14; cf. John 6:51).

And so while Calvin draws a clear distinction between the supper's "visible bread" and Christ's actual body, he also denies that the two can be separated, precisely because God has joined them together. That is, the liturgical bread and wine do act as "symbols," but by no means as "empty" ones: "by the showing of the symbol the thing itself is also shown," and so disciples should "think and be persuaded that the truth of the thing signified is surely present there" (4.17.10). In the midst of the worship service, then, as the bread and wine physically and actually nourish a disciple's body, so Christ's body and blood spiritually and actually nourish her soul. And for Calvin, since Christ's body now resides in heaven, the souls of disciples must somehow ascend to him to take part in the spiritual banquet, a choreography accomplished by the Spirit's "secret working" beyond human comprehension: "I rather experience than understand it" (4.17.31, 32).[9] Indeed, precisely because this spiritual feast is "by nature incomprehensible," God provides the earthbound, tangible, sacramental meal as a helpful "figure and image in visible signs best adapted to our small capacity." In this way, "even the dullest minds" may learn from this "familiar comparison": as common bread feeds the body, the bread of life feeds the soul (4.17.1).

Playing out this comparison, then, if physical food functions to "refresh, strengthen, and gladden" the body, the spiritual banquet likewise rejuvenates the soul, with Christ's flesh acting as both "fountain" and "channel" for receiving the whole plethora of Christ's benefits (4.17.9, 12). Calvin sums up the meal this way: "the Sacred Supper, where [Christ] offers himself with all his benefits to us, and we receive him by faith" (4.17.5). Receiving him, we receive what is his, and in this

---

9. Cf. 4.17.7: "nothing remains but to break forth in wonder at this mystery, which plainly neither the mind is able to conceive nor the tongue to express."

context, Calvin lays the emphasis not on Christ's righteousness that leads to our vicarious justification, but rather on Christ's life, the gift that leads, little by little, to our sanctification and restoration to full humanity.

To fully grasp Calvin's emphasis on divine life in his account of the supper, we may begin with a question: Why does the sacrament take the form of a *meal* — and an apparently cannibalistic meal at that? If the main idea in play here is that through the sacrament the church "faithfully receives Christ and his benefits," couldn't the appointed "figure and image" for this reception just as easily, and perhaps more clearly and pleasantly, be a robust confession of faith, a clear demonstration of catechetical knowledge, or indeed a symbolic, ceremonial embrace of the New Testament? Wouldn't that suffice? Let us accept and approve and even cling to Christ's flesh — but must we *ingest* it?

Calvin's answer boils down to his one-word summary of the supper's primary benefit for human beings: "quickening." That is, for Calvin, "we are quickened by the true partaking of [Christ]; and he has therefore designated this partaking by the words 'eating' and 'drinking,' in order that no one should think that the life that we receive from him is received by mere knowledge" (4.17.5). A fully engaged mind is essential to Christian life for Calvin, but that life is not reducible to intellectual work. It is by no means enough to receive Christ by way of cognitive assent, or by assiduously, earnestly holding the right opinions about him. Assent and right opinion have a role to play, of course, but in the end, by the Spirit's gift, a disciple must receive Christ with an ongoing, intimate, physical and spiritual openness, and at the same time a fundamental, thoroughgoing dependence. And in everyday human affairs, the best analogy for this kind of reception, as Calvin conceives it, is the practice of eating.

For without food, we die. It does us no good simply to think about food, or admire it, or extol its virtues, or even quite fondly embrace it. To live and thrive, we must eat it. We must count on it, utterly and basically, with unmatched vulnerability and trust. We must ingest it. Its body must enter our bodies, its life must pass over into our lives, indwelling and sustaining us as our own life and strength and spirit. "As it is not the seeing but the eating of the bread that suffices to feed the body," Calvin explains, "so the soul must truly and deeply become partaker of Christ that it may be quickened to spiritual life by his power" (4.17.5).

Prayer and Communion

And so the sacrament, Calvin contends, must take the form of a meal. Precisely as a "figure and image" meant to edify the church, a symbolic gesture inseparable from the spiritual reality it indicates, it must vividly and tangibly "teach" that, "by true partaking of [Christ], his life passes into us and is made ours — just as bread when taken as food imparts vigor to the body" (4.17.5). Moreover, in Calvin's view, this impartation of vigor is no mere enhancement of well-being, no mere boost of energy. Rather, just as in the parallel case of physical food and drink, whether or not one partakes of Christ is a matter of life and death — and it has always been so, even from the foundation of the world.

As we have seen, Calvin maintains that "in the beginning" all things were created in and through Christ: "what has come into being in him was life, and the life was the light of all people" (John 1:3-4) — a passage Calvin glosses to mean that Christ, "flowing even into all creatures, instilled in them the power to breathe and live." Accordingly, when humanity became "estranged from God through sin," it thereby "lost participation in life." In this sense, for Calvin, sinners — which is to say, every human being east of Eden — are the walking dead. It follows, then, that for them to be raised and restored to "participation in life," the Spirit must lead them back to the "communion of the Word" — and in Jesus of Nazareth, God provides human beings with the Word made flesh. Communing with this Word in the heavenly banquet, we come back to life: "when the Source of life begins to abide in our flesh, he . . . quickens our very flesh in which he abides." Indeed, Calvin goes so far as to suggest that the incarnation itself takes place largely for the sake of the reality symbolically manifest in the supper: "by coming down he poured power upon the flesh which he took [on] in order that from it participation in life might flow to us" (4.17.8). Christ is the "Source of life" for all things, and has been since the beginning; thus any deliverance from death, any "quickening," any resurrection requires a return to communion with him, which is to say, participation in him.

Put differently, Christ assumes human flesh precisely to render that flesh a clear and sure "channel" of new life for human beings: "the flesh of Christ is like a rich and inexhaustible fountain that pours into us the life springing forth from the Godhead" (4.17.9). From the fountain flows divine life; on the human side, Calvin returns to his image of "faith" as a kind of openness and receptivity, arguing that "the treasures of heavenly grace . . . avail and profit nothing unless received in faith. As with wine or oil or some other liquid, no matter how much you pour out, it will flow away and disappear unless the mouth of the vessel to receive it is open" (4.17.17). In this sense, participating in the supper, a disciple's own body is a living image of faith: an open, hungry vessel, receiving the nourishment of divine life, and "through this believers gain Christ abiding in them" (4.17.5).

Thus, at bottom, the supper is "that sacred partaking of his flesh and blood, by which Christ pours his life into us, as if it penetrated into our bones and marrow" (4.17.10). And by way of this indwelling, "Christ truly grows into one with us," communing with us from both without and within, we might say, and doing so more and more over time. Indeed, Calvin calls the meal "a help whereby we may be engrafted into Christ's body, or, engrafted, may grow more and more together with him, until he perfectly joins us with him in the heavenly life" (4.17.10, 33). Not surprisingly, then, Calvin condemns the practice of receiving the supper only once annually, and recommends instead a frequency of "at least once a week" and, ideally, "every time" Christians meet for worship (4.17.43, 44, 46). For the supper is the sacrament of "quickening," of spiritual strength and new life, of vividly and tangibly remembering "that the Lord's body was once for all so sacrificed for us that we may now feed upon it." Above all, for Calvin, the supper is the sacrament of "mystical union" with Christ, the mystery by which we "grow more and more together with him" (4.17.44, 4, 1; 3.11.10).[10] Given all this, Calvin advises disciples to receive the supper frequently, even as often as they hear the Word proclaimed (4.17.44, 45).[11]

At the same time, however, for Calvin, the sacramental rite itself does not so much effect a disciple's union with Christ as reflect it and, crucially, allow for her to feel it and take heart in it. So long as the Spirit grants a disciple the gift of faith, her communion with Christ takes place by way of that faith, whether or not she celebrates the ceremonial supper on any given day. The "quickening" symbolized in the supper is in fact "eternal," "we being ceaselessly nourished, sustained, and preserved throughout life by it." That is, the sacramental meal si-

10. Cf. 4.17.1, where Calvin calls the supper "this mystical blessing."
11. Here Calvin appeals to the authority of the early church, both to councils and to individual fathers who "decreed that those who enter the church and hear the Scriptures and abstain from communion should be removed from the church until they correct this fault."

multaneously points toward and participates in this larger, ongoing reality. It pictures and dramatizes it, calling and recalling a disciple's attention to the fundamental scenario of her life: namely, that in Christ God communes with her, nourishes her, gives her life, quickens her, raises her from the dead, and so restores her to her place as God's own daughter.

Again, this larger scenario is by no means dependent on the sacramental rite; rather, the rite is dependent on the larger scenario, reflecting it, clarifying it, and thereby helping to persuade disciples of it. Calvin puts the matter this way: "the Sacrament does not cause Christ to begin to be the bread of life; but when it reminds us that he was made of the bread of life, which we continually eat, and gives us a relish and savor of that bread, it causes us to feel the power of that bread" (4.17.5). At its best, the ceremony provides a "relish and savor" — a tangible taste — of the "bread of life" on which we "continually" feed in any case, inasmuch as we commune with Christ by the Spirit's gift of faith. That is, the bread of life nourishes disciples whether they feel it or not; the ceremony, insofar as the Spirit wills it, "causes us to feel the power of that bread." And when it does, it thereby reminds us that Christ is the source of everything on which we depend, not only sound doctrine (Christ as our Teacher), but also and preeminently our life and strength and sustenance (Christ as our Bread). In the beginning, "in him was life," and so for Calvin, in the end, to be truly and fully alive is to live in him, and for him to live in us. This is what "communion" ultimately means, on Calvin's account: as the bread of life itself, Christ lives in us; as members of his body, the community of the church, we live in him.

Christ quickens us. The sacramental supper does not make it so; but done well, it helps make it clear. It helps remind us. It helps us learn by doing. It helps us gain the kind of knowledge that comes only through experience, sensation, and practice. It helps us "feel in ourselves the working of that unique sacrifice," that is, Christ's sacrifice by which "he gave his body to be made bread" (4.17.1, 5). It helps us say of the supper, with Calvin, "I rather experience than understand it," and thereby be, in faith, "persuaded of what we do not grasp" (4.17.32; 3.2.14). Communing with Christ in the supper, then, disciples may better "feel his power in partaking of all his benefits," better trust that God will "nourish us throughout the course of our life," and therefore be better assured of "this continuing liberality" (4.17.11, 1). In this sense,

Calvin contends, God provides the sacred supper precisely so it might help fortify the church's faith.[12]

Again, for Calvin, the rite itself is no assemblage of "empty symbols," since God's own ordinance guarantees that "by the showing of the symbol the thing itself is also shown" (4.17.10). But in this case, "the thing itself" extends well beyond the bounds of the ceremony: indeed, "the thing itself" is a "continual eating" by which we are "ceaselessly nourished, sustained, and preserved throughout life." To be sure, disciples do actually commune with Christ during the ceremony, and they may "relish," "savor," and "feel" that communion in a heightened, clarified way, thanks to the Spirit's practical instruction and illumination in and through the rite. But the broader banquet is ongoing. Christ offers it "daily," indeed "continually," and "he seals such giving of himself by the sacred mystery of the Supper" (4.17.5).[13] In this way, Calvin refers to the sacrament of the Lord's Supper as a "seal," a "testimony," a "witness," and a "pledge" — in other words, a kind of synecdochic, participatory, promissory demonstration of a larger reality, namely, "sacred union with God," indeed the "mystical union" with Christ that "neither the mind is able to conceive nor the tongue to express" (4.17.10, 2, 33, 7).

If Calvin recommends that disciples frequently receive the supper, then, he does so not because the supper causes their communion with God, but rather because it clarifies and testifies to it: "Godly souls can gather great assurance and delight from this Sacrament," Calvin writes, since "in it they have a witness of our growth into one body with Christ such that whatever is his may be called ours" (4.17.2). In short, Calvin recommends frequent reception of the supper as a paideutic discipline, a crucial practice in their formative education. Christ is the quickening and sustaining "bread of life," whether or not the sacred supper is cele-

---

12. In Calvin's general discussion of the sacraments in the *Institutio*, he defines them as an "aid to our faith related to the preaching of the gospel," since "our faith is slight and feeble unless it be propped on all sides and sustained by every means." As such, Calvin continues, the sacraments are "aids to true piety [*pietas*]." See Calvin, *ICR* 4.14.1, 3, 19.

13. This basic pattern is consistent with Calvin's account of the sacraments generally: "a sacrament is never without a preceding promise" — here, the promise that Christ serves the faithful as "the bread of life" — "but is joined to it as a sort of appendix, with the purpose of confirming and sealing the promise itself, and of making it more evident to us and in a sense ratifying it. By this means God provides first for our ignorance and dullness, then for our weakness." See *ICR* 4.14.3.

brated on this or that occasion — or ever again, for that matter. The reason God institutes the supper, in Calvin's view, is that disciples, precisely as students, need to learn, to be reminded, to be assured, to physically and spiritually experience and in that sense to know that Christ is indeed the bread of life, continually given to them and for them. Thus they may "gather great assurance and delight." Thus their faith and *pietas* may be fortified. If the daily discipline of prayer reminds disciples that God accompanies them on their pilgrimage, and at the same time provides them with dialogic experience of that companionship, the supper likewise reminds them that God nourishes them along the way, and at the same time provides them a practical, visceral, memorable taste of that nourishment.

Call on me in the day of affliction. Take, eat — do this, and remember me. In this way, Calvin contends, through two of the most basic, everyday gestures of human life — language and food, word and flesh — a disciple may live out a life of communion with God. By the Spirit's gift and by way of this disciplinary, formative program, she may come to know God as the one who listens and feeds, answers and quickens. That is, little by little, she may come to know God as *Immanuel*, God with us, the one with whom, in whom, and by whom we live, and move, and have our being. And at the same time, she may thereby become more fully human: listening and eating, asking and living, and thus in her own way serving as a "figure and image" of the generous, graceful, loving God who made her, and walks with her, and will one day welcome her home.

PART III

On the Future of Protestant Theology

CHAPTER 10

Reforming Calvin

In part I of this book, I argued that for John Calvin, Christian life is properly formed by God in and through a particular suite of spiritual disciplines, a suite God bequeaths to the Christian church as its practical inheritance: a daily prayer office, extensive and intensive biblical study, frequent psalm singing, a qualified renunciation and embrace of "the world," regular reception of the sacred supper, and so on. This array of ecclesial and devotional practices is properly conceived, Calvin contends, as an immersive program toward a fully human life of genuine *pietas*, and finally toward an everyday mode of "mystical union" with God. Christian intellectual work, according to this view, properly serves this practical regimen at every turn.

In part II, as a way of fleshing out this basic idea, I reread several key themes in Calvin's *Institutio*, a text widely considered to be a monumental statement of Christian doctrine in the Reformed tradition. There I argued that across the theological board, from creation to Christology, from sin to Scripture, Calvin develops his doctrine for the sake of formational ends, and in particular, for the sake of the disciplinary suite just described. On one hand, then, I contend that Calvin's ideas cannot be well understood unless they are considered and engaged within their paideutic, formational context. And on the other hand, more generally, I contend that Calvin's theological approach frames doctrine itself as paideutic in the first place, that is, as edifying in its own right, and also as properly conceived, articulated, and interpreted for the sake of the church's broad program of practical formation.

Here in part III, I want to conclude prospectively, looking ahead

On the Future of Protestant Theology

to what implications this reading of Calvin's work might have for contemporary Protestant theology — and by ecumenical extension, for Christian theology at large. In what follows, then, I briefly outline a two-part assessment: first, a critical, constructive inventory of what I take to be some important hazards in Calvin's thought, that is, some aspects in need of reform; and second, in the next and final chapter, an account of what I take to be some of his work's most promising features, particularly for Protestants, features that may help chart new directions for Protestant theology today.

Calvin was nothing if not a bold, adventurous thinker, a caring pastor, and also a scholar with a taste for polemic, dispute, and prophetic indignation — and at times, it is not entirely clear whether his intellectual and rhetorical daring is courageous or simply brazen, even reckless. To be sure, the reputation he enjoys today as the Reformation's cold, lawyerly logician, the misanthropic prosecutor of our "total depravity," the gloomy champion of double predestination, and so on, is manifestly undeserved.[1] But at the same time, Calvin sometimes chose the severe, relatively complicated theological position over the more measured, relatively simple one, and he often embraced a rhetorical style of tacking dialectically between bold, ostensibly categorical claims (much as one of his rhetorical mentors, the apostle Paul, was wont to do), rather than steering directly down the moderate middle. This can make for exciting reading, of course, but by the same token, it can also make for some perilous thinking. Reading Calvin, one gets the sense that he wouldn't have it any other way. But the perils abound.

Let me mention three: quietism, masochism, and misanthropy. In sometimes subtle, sometimes obvious, and sometimes interlocking ways, these three dangers lurk in and around Calvin's thought, the first chiefly with respect to his doctrine of divine providence, the second with respect to human suffering, and the third with respect to human and worldly "depravity." In each case, I point toward not only a critique but also a potential theological remedy, either drawn from Calvin's work or broadly consistent with what I take to be its most important principles.

---

1. For example, in the wake of Geneva's 2009 quincentennial celebration of Calvin's birth, the *New York Times* first described Calvin as "best known for his doctrines about a depraved humanity and a harsh God predestining people to hell or heaven," and then, even more tellingly, referred in passing to "Calvin's dour philosophy," as if alluding to a settled matter of fact. See John Tagliabue, "A City of Mixed Emotions Observes Calvin's 500th," *New York Times,* November 4, 2009.

Quietism

Calvin's enthusiasm for his doctrine of divine providence is difficult to overstate: "nothing is more profitable," he writes, "than the knowledge of this doctrine."[2] Indeed, once a disciple understands that "not one drop of rain falls without God's sure command," a cascade of benefits and virtues follows: "Gratitude of mind for the favorable outcome of things, patience in adversity, and also incredible freedom from worry about the future all necessarily follow upon this knowledge" (1.16.5; 1.17.7). And yet, at the same time, Calvin is so keenly aware of the doctrine's potential for abuse and misunderstanding that he devotes a whole chapter of the *Institutio* to clarifying its "good and right use" — the only chapter of this explicit sort in the entire work (1.17.1). Like a physician's scalpel, the doctrine of providence can change lives for the better, or, if used in the wrong way, for the worse.

In fact, at least one of the many traps surrounding the idea seems to have ensnared Calvin himself. A person's socioeconomic class is "divinely assigned," he contends, and so "the poor" should cultivate patience, since "those who are not content with their own lot try to shake off the burden laid upon them by God" (1.16.6). When it comes to class, then, John Calvin, the great reformer and leader of social change, conceives God's providential hand as a fundamentally conservative defender of the status quo. On its face, this move may appear as an odd exception to the otherwise transformative work of divine providence, but in mid-sixteenth-century Europe, with bloody uprisings such as the German Peasants' War (1524-25) still a vivid memory, categorically casting poverty as a divinely assigned burden not to be "shaken off" was at least an understandable position, especially among the relatively privileged classes.

Understandable, but not theologically justifiable. Indeed, developing the doctrine of divine providence as an economically conservative idea contradicts what Calvin teaches elsewhere; in particular, a helpful counterpoint to his argument about poverty may be found in what he writes in the *Institutio* about "prudence" (1.17.4). Put briefly: against those who argue that, if all things happen by divine ordinance,

---

2. John Calvin, *Institutes of the Christian Religion*, ed. John T. McNeill (Philadelphia: Westminster, 1960), 1.17.3 (hereafter cited as *ICR*; section references cited in parentheses in the text).

On the Future of Protestant Theology

it is therefore "vain for anyone to busy himself in taking precautions," Calvin responds that the doctrine of providence is no cause for indolence or folly, for in any given instance, the foresight and energy to prudentially "take precautions" may well be part of what God provides (1.17.3). That is, though I may believe that my future is divinely determined, since that future is also unknown to me, I may just as well strive to shape it wisely and carefully, since for all I know, my very striving, wisdom, and care are themselves God's providential gifts, and are therefore part and parcel of God's providential plan.

In other words, divine providence need not and should not be understood in a fatalistic, quietistic, conservative way, as if endorsing things as they are or absolving humanity of its work in the world. Rather, the doctrine can and should be understood in ways that help us conceive our work as shot through with divine power and guidance: sometimes preserving things as they are, and sometimes changing them. Calvin puts it this way: "if the Lord has committed to us the protection of our life, our duty is to protect it; if he offers helps, to use them; if he forewarns us of dangers, not to plunge headlong; if he makes remedies available, not to neglect them" (1.17.4). Call it the "prudential principle" in Calvin's thought: far from absolving us of work, the doctrine of divine providence properly defines it, clarifying and framing it as always carried out from, with, and in God. And indeed, precisely as such, Calvin contends, our work should be vigorous and wise, bold and prudent, avoiding "dangers" and embracing "remedies" all along the way.

Critiquing Calvin's views of socioeconomic class, then, we need only include poverty — and more generally, severe economic inequality — among those "dangers" that threaten human life individually and socially, dangers from which it is, after all, our prudential duty to protect ourselves and each other. In other words, God may — and, if the exodus story is any indication, God paradigmatically does — provide deliverance from oppressive conditions in particular times and places, and so a belief in divine providence, far from endorsing the conservation of the economic status quo, is in fact perfectly consistent with its transformation. Indeed, the larger point here is that a robust doctrine of divine providence, according to which "not one drop of rain falls without God's command," by no means justifies the world as we know it, for God's unfolding plan may be to remake that world into something entirely new. After all, Christian preaching is nothing if not a herald's cry that God intends — and in fact has already, decisively begun — precisely this kind of renovation.

In this way, a disciple may indeed interpret her economic circumstances as providentially provided, but in practice, she may only carry out this interpretation according to what we might call a "retrospective" interpretive rule. That is, while past and present difficulties may be regarded as divinely ordained, the possibility is permanently open that God has also ordained present and future amelioration or deliverance from those very difficulties. In other words, viewed prospectively, economic transformation is always possible: an escape from a cycle of poverty, a wealthy family's decision to live on less, and so on. Disciples may retrospectively interpret their path as providential and paideutic, but the categorical assumption that in any particular sphere of life, economic or otherwise, God intends to preserve the status quo is an idea set squarely at odds with the Christian gospel. Looking backward, disciples may (or may not) discern the work of divine providence. Looking forward, however, they can only remain open and expectant, faithful and flexible, since God's work may well come as a surprising departure from the status quo — or rather, as a long-expected fulfillment of divine promises to deliver, nourish, and educate God's children.

A similar theological remedy may be applied to other problems in Calvin's thought related to divine providence. For example, in a variety of ways, Calvin maintains that since not only the joys but also the troubles of human life are divinely ordained, disciples should interpret even severe setbacks as paideutic, that is, as training meant to strengthen them, or corrective pedagogy meant to instruct them. The pastoral advantages of this view are profound and compelling, primarily because it can help make room for hopeful, empowering interpretations of otherwise debilitating circumstances. An afflicted person, for example, may make sense of what first appears to be a completely senseless situation by conceiving her difficulties as divine training or instruction, and so as part and parcel of her own maturation, development, and destiny. This tactic amounts to a theological version of an extremely common interpretive move in the face of catastrophe: recasting affliction as a key learning experience ("I never would have learned . . ."), a crucial turning point in the journey ("I never would have become . . ."), preparation for a subsequent challenge ("I never would have been able . . ."), an opportunity for new relationships ("I never would have met . . ."), and so on. Indeed, for some people in some situations, the only thing worse than the brute fact of suffering itself is that same suffering conceived as utterly arbitrary and meaningless, or as a sign that God has abandoned them, or as a chaotic, unbridled phenomenon taking place against God's will and power.

The clear and present pastoral risks here, however, are equally manifold, profound, and compelling. First, to interpret affliction as divine pedagogy may lead to quietism with respect to affliction, for who would dare cut short the divine lesson? And in fact, why not prolong it? As in the case of poverty, then, an important theological remedy here is to preserve and continually emphasize the point that conceiving suffering as paideutic in no way exempts us from our prudential duties to embrace divine deliverance: God may instruct us through difficulty one day, and instruct us through a rescue from that difficulty the next. From our point of view, then, we can only continue to strive to live wisely and fruitfully, neither seeking nor prolonging affliction, and no matter what difficulties arise, and no matter how edifying those trials may seem to us, if God "makes remedies available, not to neglect them."

In the second place, however, to attribute human suffering to God runs the risk of undercutting what for Calvin is the church's most important theological insight and proclamation: God's capable, active, parental love and mercy. Just as some people in some situations may be comforted or encouraged by the idea that their affliction is not against or outside of God's will, for others in other circumstances, the same claim only appears to cast God as a demon — and so it functions, in effect, as the very antithesis of the Christian gospel. In the face of genocide, for example, or incest, or chronic pain, or ecological ruin — or any number of other devastations — proclaiming divine *paideia* can be an unconvincing, repellent mistake.[3]

---

3. A similar point is a major theme — arguably *the* major theme, though it is often overlooked — of the book of Job, a text in which a strikingly large proportion of the narrative is devoted to the theological chatter of Job's friends, who assuredly insist that his suffering must be a divine sentence for some hidden sin. At the book's climactic close, of course, God rejects these theological theories out of hand, and metes out a corrective punishment not for Job (who has by then, incidentally, howled to heaven with lament bordering on blasphemy — see, e.g., 30:16-21), but rather for Job's prolix, know-it-all, no doubt quite theologically orthodox friends. Read this way, the whole book is a rebuke to the theological points of view the friends represent, and so to all presumptuous pronouncements about divine providence in the face of disaster.

And so it will not do to declare, flatly and categorically, that human affliction is divine pedagogy; nor will it do, however, even and especially in the most devastating cases, to rule out that possibility. Either way, we claim to know too much. As is so often true in theological reflection, we can only pursue these questions along the outer borders of human understanding, and so what we think and say should be determined as much by particular contextual constraints on the ground as by any abstract, general rule. In this sense, the doctrine of divine providence should function less as a one-size-fits-all description of the world as if surveying it from on high, and more as a formative habit of mind on the ground and in practice, a working assumption, a practical idea that shapes a disciple's bearing toward the world as she encounters it. That is, properly understood and lived out, the doctrine of divine providence is itself paideutic: it forms and reforms disciples, accustoms them to particular patterns of interpretation and experience. It trains and orients them so they may, when appropriate, undergo and understand whatever suffering they encounter as divine *paideia*, while at the same time, in cases where this approach is not possible, fitting, or wise, they remain supple enough to let other ideas come to the fore.

Indeed, it is no accident that the Psalter includes voices from across a wide range of perspectives on human suffering: some singers attribute their trouble to God, others attribute it elsewhere; some recognize purgative, pedagogical value in their affliction, others do not; some respectfully, devoutly request that God deliver them, others shake their fists in anger, demand rescue, accuse God of abandonment, or defiantly cry, "How long, O Lord?" This whole repertoire — Psalm 23, to be sure, but also Psalm 88 — is available to the Christian church at any given moment, and so which song to sing in which circumstance is finally a matter of case-by-case theological discernment.

In the background, of course, something like Calvin's doctrine of providence may remain in place. Even as we sing Psalm 88, Psalm 23 is still in the canon, silent but preserved — awaiting, perhaps, another day. Certain situations, however, preclude foregrounding any speculation about "God's will," never mind a solemn discourse about divine training or pedagogy. Misjudgments in this arena are often called "inept," "insensitive," or "tone deaf" — and that is exactly right. The whole matter turns on relational sensibility, tonal discernment, discretion, prudence, phronesis, tact: in short, knowing what to do when. Here we arrive at the limits of so-called "systematic," conceptual theological work, important as it is in Christian life. At the end of the day, all theological knowledge comes down to savoir faire: not only a conceptual, informational knowing-that, but also and ultimately a practical, relational knowing-how.

Calvin's work may itself be a rich resource in this regard, as I will argue in chapter 11. But when it comes to interpreting affliction, in the *Institutio* Calvin fails to take full advantage of the songs of lament scattered liberally throughout the Psalter, or indeed the laments and lament-like gestures scattered throughout the Christian Bible as a whole. At times, these songs suggest, a disciple's life in God involves various forms of struggle, including crying out precisely because we do not — and for the life of us, cannot — see how particular instances of human suffering are consistent with God's promises to protect, sustain, and care for God's people. Again, on the ground and in practice, this kind of lament is perfectly consistent with a broad, everyday interpretive approach of conceiving affliction as divine training or corrective pedagogy: that is, a disciple may at once interpret many or most of her trials as paideutic and nevertheless lament the most severe or enigmatic burdens among them. But a full portrait of this unfolding, case-by-case, relational form of discipleship requires a more robust theology and practice of Christian lamentation than Calvin provides in the *Institutio* — and so his work on divine providence may be fruitfully reformed and developed in this direction.[4]

Thus by appealing to Calvin's ideas about "prudence" on one hand and biblical traditions of lament on the other, we may hold at bay two important perils of Calvin's teaching on divine providence: first, the risk of fatalism, and therefore of a quietism that flows from a false sense of powerlessness; and second, the risk of a blithe, repellent optimism with respect to suffering, and therefore of a quietism that flows from a false sense of sanguinity. Both kinds of quietism erode Christian life — and in fact, both risks may be most acute in connection with the Christian cross, and particularly in connection with Calvin's teach-

---

4. Calvin gives more attention to lamentation in his commentaries on the Psalms, for example, and in his sermons on Job. But even there, his work requires critique and development. See, e.g., Herman J. Selderhuis, *Calvin's Theology of the Psalms* (Grand Rapids: Baker Academic, 2007), especially pp. 179-94, 220ff.; and on divine hiddenness, see Brian Gerrish, "'To the Unknown God': Luther and Calvin on the Hiddenness of God," in *The Old Protestantism and the New: Essays on the Reformation Heritage* (Chicago: University of Chicago Press, 1982), pp. 131-49.

ing on how "bearing the cross" is fundamental to Christian discipleship. That is, intensified in the soteriological context, the twin threats of quietism shade into the threat of masochism.

Masochism

In a key passage, Calvin puts his case this way: "the more we are afflicted with adversities, the more surely our fellowship with Christ is confirmed! By communion with him the very sufferings themselves not only become blessed to us but also help much in promoting our salvation" (3.8.1). As in the case of divine providence, Calvin's doctrine of "bearing the cross" runs the distinct and permanent risk of being understood as a summons to suffering, a rationale for accepting, seeking, or extending pain and hardship — though this time, the stakes are arguably even higher, since now not only learning a divine lesson but also "promoting our salvation" allegedly hangs in the balance. "Fellowship with Christ" is, after all, the fulcrum of human salvation according to Calvin, and if "the very sufferings themselves" increase that fellowship, why not endeavor to increase that suffering?

To be sure, this masochistic conclusion is a misreading of Calvin's thought overall. But on the other hand, in passages like this one, he does not explicitly address or sufficiently guard against it, and so his work requires clarification and development. For example, building up from his ideas, today's theologians do well to clarify that when disciples interpret human suffering and its relationship to the Christian cross, Calvin's prudential principle still applies, as does the retrospective interpretive rule. That is, we should always recall that while already-existing afflictions may be regarded as a form of "communion" with Christ's passion and death, further affliction is by no means to be prospectively pursued or prolonged. Like Jesus in the garden of Gethsemane, disciples are not to seek suffering, but rather are repeatedly to pray, "Let this cup pass."

Indeed, when it comes to "bearing the cross" in Christian life, a similar proviso follows theologically from two other ideas: first, the idea that Christ's suffering and death are utterly sufficient in themselves, and so require no additional suffering on our part;[5] and second,

---

5. Cf., e.g., Heb. 9:25-26; 10:10, 14.

the idea that in and through the Christian cross, Christ joins us in our affliction, and so we have no need to turn around and attempt to join him in his. He is already with us, precisely as *Immanuel*. The "communion" of suffering between Christ and his disciples, then, is choreographically asymmetrical: to be sure, it is our communion with Christ, but most fundamentally and decisively, it is Christ's communion with us. The initiative and dynamism are his. We do not, by suffering, ascend to him; rather, with compassionate love, he descends to us in our affliction, meets us there, comforts us, testifies that he is with us, and so assures us that his companionship, his righteousness, and above all his resurrected life are and will be ours.

In this sense, Christ suffers with us and for us. And so in practice, day in and day out, we may rightly interpret the suffering we encounter as "promoting our salvation" only in the sense that, in and through the cross, Christ joins us in our affliction. Precisely when and where we feel most alone, most forgotten, most forsaken by the protective, providential, parental love of God — Christ meets us there. Christ reassures us. Christ suffers with us, engrafting us into his broken body, so that we may rise in and with him at the last.

Put another way: the Christian gospel in this context is not that Christ's cross is itself so remarkably unique, and that our task is therefore to seek out and take up a cross of our own so that we might participate in his passion. On the contrary, by virtue of both our sin and our finitude, we already bear our own crosses, each in her own way. Every one of us will suffer and die, and every one of us, to one degree or another, will endure one or more varieties of affliction: a grueling physical or emotional trial; a heartbreaking sense of failure or fault; a deadening experience of betrayal, scorn, shame, or desertion. Moreover, regardless of personal biography, every one of us will become aware, to one degree or another, that others near or far from us suffer in these ways every day. Indeed, the world over, crosses are as common and as countless as they were in the decades before Jesus was born in occupied Judea: thousands upon thousands of them, lining the thoroughfares running in and out of Rome.

The remarkable thing, then, is that when the Son of God comes and dwells among humanity, he bears a cross, too, and thereby joins the rest of us. Even the Lord of hosts will suffer and die. "God with us" extends even and exactly to the place that God, by all conventional accounts, does not go: the wasteland of weakness, humiliation, disgrace, and death. The suffering involved in Christ's passion — physical and emotional, social and spiritual — is a mirror, not a model. That is, the point is not that our suffering must be identical to his, but rather that whatever ails us, he is with us nonetheless, and so we nonetheless participate in him. Precisely where we feel most lost — there, we are found. Precisely where intimate communion with God seems most imperceptible and dubious — there, God communes with us. Indeed, even at the apparent outer limit and breaking point of human relationship with God, the anguished cry of a godforsaken human being, God not only hears us, but also joins us in the cry (Ps. 22:1; Mark 15:34).

Thus the Roman imperial cross, arguably the most appalling, abysmal object in the world, is co-opted and transformed into the Christian cross, a site of promised divine solidarity and love precisely where it is least expected or obvious — and in that sense, for Christians at least, the most beautiful, hopeful object in the world. God gracefully accomplishes this co-optive, loving solidarity quite apart from human works; it requires no additional suffering from us. And yet, insofar as we do suffer, we may interpret our affliction as part and parcel of Christ's communion with us. We may say: even now, even here, in the valley of the shadow of death, God is with us, remaking what otherwise would be destructive into something creative, what otherwise would be humiliating into something humanizing (cf. Ps. 23:4ff.). Or, paraphrasing Joseph's remark to his brothers at the close of the book of Genesis: though the forces of suffering apparently arrayed against us may very well intend to do us harm, God works through even these forces for good. Indeed, this is the basic theme not only of the Joseph cycle but also of the New Testament passion narratives: God's secret providence working its way in and through all things, even human conflict and suffering, "in order to preserve a numerous people, as he is doing today" (Gen. 50:20).

To sum up, it is as if Jesus says this to us: do not pursue or prolong affliction — but insofar as you do suffer, fear not, for I am with you, and your affliction will serve as sanctification. Pray for deliverance from your troubles as continually and fervently as the psalmist, and never for a moment neglect the help God provides — but insofar as you do suffer, fear not, for I am with you, and your troubles will serve as training, your pain as *paideia*. In this way, paideutic interpretations of affliction may be preserved in Christian life, even as religious masochism is emphatically ruled out. Clarifying and correcting Calvin's position on this subject are, I contend, a second important direction for Protestant theology today.[6]

Misanthropy

Finally, a tangle of difficulties surrounds Calvin's notorious work on human and worldly "depravity." As we have seen, Calvin understands humanity's fall into sin's "miserable ruin" to have completely corrupted human nature, so much so that our attempts to save ourselves only deepen the trouble. And likewise, for Calvin, humanity's corruption is matched by the world's: "what else is the world," he writes, "but a sepulcher?" (3.9.4). Taken alone, as they so often are today, these ideas

---

6. The degree to which Calvin's position needs to be clarified in this respect, and the degree to which it needs to be corrected, is a complicated question. As we have seen, Calvin is quite clear that (1) Christian life includes lifelong repentance; (2) repentance involves "mortification of the flesh"; and (3) this mortification "depends upon participation in [Christ's] cross" (2.16.13) — a chain of ideas at least open to the conclusion that to live an excellent Christian life, a disciple should seek out affliction so that she might participate all the more in Christ's cross. But on the other hand, by itself, the claim that our mortification "depends upon participation in his cross" need not entail the notion that a disciple should pursue even one iota of suffering beyond the considerable share she will endure without any special pursuit. Further, when Calvin discusses "mortification" directly, he frames its practical form not in terms of suffering per se, but rather in terms of putting aside narrow self-interest in and through "the duties of love": genuine love, he writes, is how mortification "takes place in us" (3.7.7). Similarly, in his chapter on crossbearing, Calvin gathers three crosses — (1) the cross on which Christ died, (2) what Calvin calls the "perpetual cross" of Christ's "whole life," and (3) the figurative cross borne by each disciple in and through her own "adversities" — all under a single pedagogical banner: like us, Calvin contends, Christ had to "learn obedience through what he suffered" (3.8.1). Again, this way of putting things opens the door to supposing that, if my suffering enables my obedience, then to obey more, I need to suffer more. And so on. But again, the starting point of conceiving adversity as pedagogical in character need not lead to masochistic conclusions, provided the adversity in question is consistently clarified as, from the human point of view, involuntary and incidental, never pursued or prolonged. Indeed, the gist of Calvin's overall approach frequently points away from spiritual masochism: for example, he criticizes "the ancients" for their "excessive severity" with respect to practices of church discipline and repentance, recommending instead that a "spirit of gentleness" infuse and temper the church's practical life (e.g., 3.3.16; 4.12.8). Nevertheless, his language is too often ambiguous or unprotected in these respects, and so requires, at the very least, more explicit theological safeguards against the potentially destructive interpretations outlined here.

appear misanthropic and world-loathing. And yet, as we have seen, elsewhere in his work Calvin extols the human being as "a rare example of God's power, goodness, and wisdom," and the world as a "dazzling theater," "school," and "mirror in which we can contemplate God, who is otherwise invisible" (1.5.3, 8, 1).[7] A principal problem here is not that Calvin cannot make up his mind between, say, misanthropy and philanthropy, but rather that his dialectical rhetorical style can be misleading, particularly when considered only in part.

In fact, in terms of substance, Calvin's views on human nature and "the world" are much more moderate than his reputation would suggest. Like a speed skater moving across the ice, or a sailboat tacking across a lake, he moves crisply and decisively to his left, and then crisply and decisively to his right — with the overall effect of moving forward along what amounts to a relative *via media*. To be sure, partly because many of the great theological controversies of his day turned largely on questions of whether human beings could to some extent "merit" salvation by their own efforts, Calvin repeatedly underscores human "dullness," "depravity," "corruption," and so on. But he also insists on the dignity of human nature as created by God for life in God, and in his doctrine of sanctification he argues that, through the Spirit's ongoing fellowship, Christ's ongoing communion, and the church's society of ongoing practical formation, God is restoring fallen sinners, little by little, to that original integrity.

Reading the *Institutio*, then, we may tack in one direction during key passages on "depravity" — and in the other direction during key passages on creation, or *pietas*, or sanctification. Indeed, even Calvin's well-known moral and devotional expectations of (and demands upon) Christian behavior are themselves dialectical counterpoints to his emphasis on human "depravity," since they imply that, with God's sanctifying help, human beings are perfectly capable of honorable, devout conduct. And if someone objects, for example, that making divine assistance the linchpin of human decency is still basically a misanthropic position, since it preserves the idea that without God, humanity is hopelessly corrupt and inept, Calvin's reply, in effect, is to dispute the critic's working definition of humanity. We are not, he insists, independent agents in the first place. On the contrary, in the first place we are symbiotic, commensal agents in relationship with God, fully alive only

---

7. Calvin, *Commentaries on Genesis* (Grand Rapids: Baker, 1981), p. 60.

insofar as we participate in divine life: feeding on the divine "bread of life," conspiring with the one Paul calls the "Spirit of life," and so on.[8] That is, we are made to live in God and with God, and so our full humanity emerges only insofar as, by God's graceful gift, that primordial, intimate, quickening relationship actually takes place.

Given this account of human being, then, we should be neither surprised nor insulted that, apart from our gracious divine host and companion, we are indeed corrupt and inept — just as a mosaic is corrupt without its proper design and designer, or a sailboat is inept without the wind and sea. After all, as Calvin puts it in the *Institutio*'s opening paragraph, "our very being is nothing but subsistence in the one God" (1.1.1). Any attempt to live against or away from this subsistence — that is, any oblivious disregard for our actual situation — puts nothing less than "our very being" in jeopardy, arranging us in the consummately awkward, contorted posture of self-sabotage. In short, we fall from grace, and so from the gracefulness for which we are born. Thus in Calvin's view, we are indeed "depraved" in the root etymological sense of the term (Latin *de-*, "completely" + *pravus*, "warped" or "crooked") — which is to say, in the fundamentally *formational* sense of the term. Without God, we are malformed and mixed up, distorted and disordered. As such, we require reformation, training, a new order, a rehabilitation program, a remedial rule of life. With God, however — or rather, in and through *Immanuel*, "God with us," and led by the enveloping, indwelling Holy Spirit — we embark on that recuperative road, that lifelong pilgrim's way of restoration and return.

In this sense, though Calvin does move crisply and decisively to one side when he writes of human "dullness" and "depravity," he does not thereby endorse what is sometimes called a "low anthropology." On the contrary, his view of genuine human being as such — that is, the human being living with and in God — is quite high. As Calvin portrays her, the true human being is nothing short of a marvel: a humble, dig-

---

8. For "Spirit of life," see Rom. 8:2. There are three types of symbiosis (Greek *symbiosis*, "living together"): mutualism, where both parties benefit; parasitism, where one party benefits and the other is harmed; and commensalism, where one party benefits and the other is unharmed. Strictly speaking, then, the type of symbiosis most fitting as a figure for Calvin's account of human life vis-à-vis God is commensalism, a term made even more felicitous for use in Christian theology (and in particular, in eucharistic theological anthropology) by its etymological origin: from the Latin *com-*, "together" + *mensa*, "table," that is, "eating at the same table."

nified, reverent, loving, creative creature made in God's own image, indeed "the noblest of all [God's] creatures," fashioned for a life of filial *pietas* toward God the Father and Mother through ongoing, intimate communion with Christ and the Holy Spirit (2.1.11). For Calvin, this is what being human means. In sin's "miserable ruin," of course, we abandon this birthright and vocation; we contradict and confine ourselves; we turn away from God, the one on whom we symbiotically, commensally rely; we betray our own humanity. And in sanctification's gradual recovery, Calvin contends, God reforms and restores disciples to their original beauty, that is, their *imago Dei*, with full recuperation realized not in this life, but rather in the heavenly life to come.

Thus Calvin's anthropology amounts to a threefold vision: a high doctrine of humanity as such; a robust, thoroughgoing doctrine of sin; and an ambitious doctrine of Spirit-led, Christ-centered sanctification, grounded in the church's historic inheritance of practical disciplines. To focus on the "depravity" panel of this triptych in isolation from the other two is to misread not only what Calvin has in mind about humanity, but also what he has in mind about "depravity" itself. For on one side, human depravity is dialectically qualified and colored by Calvin's high doctrine of genuine human being — a doctrine culminating, of course, in Calvin's Christology, since in Christ genuine humanity is revealed once and for all. In this sense, Calvin contends, humanity as we know it is in fact an exceedingly good thing, albeit one gone terribly wrong. On the other side of the triptych, human depravity is likewise dialectically qualified and colored by Calvin's ambitious doctrine of sanctification, his account of how God is paideutically restoring human beings to their original beauty and dignity. In this sense, Calvin contends, humanity as we know it is a good thing gone wrong that is, little by little, returning to form in and through the practical community of the Christian church. Bearing in mind all three of these panels, then, we may summarize Calvin's anthropology this way: a disciple is a ruined masterpiece, but a masterpiece nonetheless, and one currently in the process of being restored by the master himself.

In the same way, Calvin's account of the world's depravity must be understood in its dialectical context. Calvin does call the world a "sepulcher," but he does so in contrast to heaven's new life, and with the explicit goal of forming disciples such that they are "freed from too much desire" for the "present life," as he puts it, the better to desire "the life to come." In the same passage, when he considers the world apart from this comparison, he insists that it is "rightly to be counted among those blessings of God which are not to be spurned," especially since "we begin in the present life, through various benefits, to taste the sweetness of the divine generosity in order to whet our hope and desire to seek after the full revelation of this." In other words, the stance Calvin recommends vis-à-vis the world is indeed a version of *contemptus mundi*, but one at no point inconsistent with gratitude for the world itself as a divine gift: "let believers accustom themselves to a contempt of the present life that engenders no hatred of it or ingratitude against God." That is, Calvin aims to cultivate in his readers not a hatred of the world, but rather a particular kind of detachment from it that is nonetheless thankful for it as an incomparable blessing: a "dazzling theater" of divine glory and an immersive "school" for sanctification. Receive the world with all its delights, Calvin seems to say, but do not hold to it so tightly that you cannot, when the time comes, let it go (3.9.3).

In this way, Calvin seeks to form disciples dialectically, and so his emphases on human and worldly "depravity" are properly understood, first, in dialectical, tensive relationship with their counterpoints, and second, always within the larger framework of this formative project. To make more humble, hopeful disciples, Calvin underscores both the depravity of fallen humanity and the excellence of created and, ultimately, sanctified humanity. And likewise, to make more dignified, delighted disciples, Calvin underscores both the depravity of the world and the character of the world as a divine blessing — both glorious theater and sanctifying school. Calvin takes each of these claims to be true, of course. But he rhetorically arranges them in keeping with what he takes to be their principal and proper function in Christian discipleship, that is, their contribution toward forming more humble, hopeful, dignified, delighted disciples.

Some of the difficulties associated with Calvin's work on human and worldly "depravity," then, arise when this dialectical rhetorical arrangement is overlooked or misread. But some of these difficulties derive directly from that arrangement itself: at times, Calvin's rhetoric obscures his own case. For example, in the *Institutio* Calvin makes the fatal — and explicitly rhetorical — decision to describe humanity's "miserable ruin" as "natural," the better to emphasize its congenital character: "we call it 'natural' in order that no man may think that anyone obtains it through bad conduct, since it holds all men fast by hereditary right" (2.1.11). Careful readers will pick up that Calvin actually has in mind two "natures" here, created human nature and fallen human nature, with the second being a thoroughgoing, self-inflicted deformation of the first.[9]

But by using the term "natural" on both sides of this crucial divide, Calvin rhetorically obscures precisely what should be continually made clear. For according to his own account, humanity is corrupt "by nature" only in a secondary, deformational sense; and indeed, since in its primary sense "nature" is created by God, sin's corruption is in fact antinatural, consisting, after all, precisely in human nature's "miserable ruin." To characterize the ruin of nature as itself "nature," and what is actually unnatural or antinatural as itself "natural," is at best confusing, and at worst runs the risk of inviting an (often unwitting) misanthropic collapse of "humanity" and "depravity" from which a multitude of mischief may follow.

For example, in Christian liturgies of confession and reconciliation, disciples who learn to conceive their sin as "natural" to them, indeed as what we might call "second nature," may thereby lose sight of their first nature, their genuine nature, the true identity for which they were born. This distinction lost, they may come to understand their sin, regrettable as it is, to be a function or feature not of their fallen human nature but rather of their human nature *simpliciter*. Accordingly, they may quite earnestly take up the habit of asking God, in effect: *Forgive me for my humanity*. In the first place, this misguided, finally misanthropic prayer flattens out the disciple's sense of sin itself: no longer a tragic fall from nobility to depravity, sin becomes merely an inborn condition, a natural state, a lamentable but "all too human" fact of life. And moreover, the same prayer may well imply that God's gift of sanctification is no restoration and return to full humanity, but rather an escape from it, a transcendence of it, an event in which we leave our humanity behind and become something else, something better.

---

9. Calvin puts it this way: "we declare that man is corrupted through natural vitiation, but a vitiation that did not flow from nature." Or again: "depravity and malice ... do not spring from nature, but rather from the corruption of nature." In effect, Calvin's argument is that humanity's depravity is "natural" only in the sense that human nature is its locus, not its origin. Depravity is originally "adventitious" to human nature, but thereafter it is intrinsic to it. This is a subtle, conceptually rigorous, uncommon use of the word "natural" — and precisely as such, I argue, it only too easily ends up contributing to an ambiguous rhetorical muddle. See 2.1.11; 1.14.3.

Again, the point here is not that Calvin approves these views or would endorse this prayer. In the *Institutio* Calvin makes quite clear that for him, the human being as such is "the noblest of all creatures," sin is a fall from nobility to depravity, and sanctification is a restoration and return to full humanity, the *imago Dei* according to which humanity was originally made. The point, then, is that by using the terms "nature" and "natural" to characterize both God's creation and sin's depravities, Calvin rhetorically obscures his own case, leaving open the door to interpretations of his work — by friends and critics alike — that lead to fundamentally misanthropic ideas and practices.

Likewise, Calvin's derogatory flourishes elsewhere are at times open to challenge. For example, when he dismisses the world's secular songs as "empty," "stupid," and "vile," and calls for their wholesale replacement with psalms and other similar music, he betrays a totalizing impulse at odds, I contend, with other aspects of his work: namely, his emphasis on Christian humility, and the related idea that God providentially works in and through all manner of things, even outside the visible (and audible) church.[10] Indeed, to the extent that Calvin's vision for Geneva included categorical, coercive participation in Christian life (mandatory worship, citywide consistorial regulation, and so on), twenty-first-century Protestants will and must demur — not only because we have long since left behind the world of sixteenth-century Geneva, but also because the very idea of compulsory Christianity, civic, musical, or otherwise, is theologically mistaken.

Or again, we may ask: In practical terms, can disciples really interpret the world as both a "sepulcher" and a "dazzling theater" of divine glory, a crypt and a sanctifying school? Can they really conceive the human body as both a "prison," as Calvin puts it, and "a workshop graced with God's unnumbered works," including "their individual members, from mouth and eyes even to their very toenails" (3.9.4; 1.5.4)? Perhaps. But the negative poles in these dialectical pairs ("sepulcher," "prison," and so on) are so severe that they threaten to throw the overall rhetorical arrangement out of balance — and in any case, for twenty-first-century Reformed theologians, Calvin's widespread reputation today may be all the evidence needed to submit his work, in so many respects substantively sound, to rhetorical reform.

---

10. See Calvin, "The Form of Prayers and Songs of the Church," translated by Ford Lewis Battles, *Calvin Theological Journal* 15 (1980): 165.

Formational language may help. Terms such as "nature" and "natural" may leave the impression that the intrinsic qualities of humanity — our very stuff, substance, or essence — are at stake when it comes to sin and depravity; metaphors of contamination and contagion, which are legion in Calvin, can have a similar effect. A contaminated food, for example, is typically thrown away, not restored; likewise, calling a person "bad-natured" is shorthand for suggesting that he is beyond rehabilitation. But formational language, by contrast, may open up different lines of thought, even while still preserving the indispensable Reformed idea that sin's effects are thoroughgoing and, for fallen humanity alone, irreversible. That is, formational language may frame both human depravity and its divine remedies not in terms of stuff and substance, but rather in terms of act and form, practice and *paideia*, choreography, relationships, *pietas* — and so, finally, in terms of ways of life. Moreover, as we have seen, formational language is not only quite common in Calvin; it frames and orients his whole theological project. From his sermons to his commentaries, his *Institutio* to his ecclesial, civic work in Geneva, Calvin's governing goal was always that disciples learn and grow, little by little becoming formed to true piety (*formarentur ad veram pietatem*).[11]

Like any project of similar complexity and scope, Calvin's work requires revision, and in this chapter I have proposed three directions for critique and development: the first with respect to his doctrine of divine providence and the dangers of quietism; the second with respect to human suffering and the dangers of masochism; and the third with respect to his accounts of human and worldly "depravity" and the dangers of misanthropy. This list is not exhaustive, of course. But it does represent, if only partially, the range of vulnerabilities that attend Calvin's work. Any attempt to constructively appropriate that work must bear these risks in mind at every turn, and actively guard against them. But at the same time, Calvin's project, and in particular his fundamentally formational understanding of theology, is also a profoundly promising resource for Protestant communities today. In the next and final chapter, I briefly sketch this promise in more detail.

---

11. Calvin, *ICR*, "Prefatory Address to King Francis I of France," p. 9.

CHAPTER 11

Life in God

For most of his theological career, Calvin wrote in sixteenth-century Geneva, but he also wrote for other times and places. After all, he was himself a religious refugee in a city teeming with refugees, living in one place but often thinking of another; moreover, as Geneva's reputation spread as a model reformed city, the widening reach of Calvin's work became increasingly clear.[1] In terms of time, Calvin understood himself to stand at the outset of a new chapter in God's book of history. He looked around, but he also looked ahead. As he revised and polished the final 1559 edition of the *Institutio*, he certainly hoped and expected that it would outlive him and, to some degree at least, help shape the new emerging era. And though he could not possibly have imagined, say, twenty-first-century North American readers and readings of his work, it is in the nature of such writing that a text's addressees are, to a greater or lesser extent, unknown to the author. In this sense, disciples today may justly read the *Institutio* as a book written for them and, however remotely, addressed to them, as heirs or friends or critics of the tradition — that is, the reformed, catholic Christian tradition — that Calvin sought to represent, clarify, strengthen, and pass down to generations he would never meet.

To close this book, then, I want to point toward three broad fea-

1. In Calvin's lifetime, the *Institutio* appeared in Spanish (1540), Italian (1557), Dutch (1560), and English (1561); it became the best-selling Reformed theological text of the sixteenth century. See David Steinmetz, *Calvin in Context* (New York: Oxford University Press, 1995), p. 18, and Philip Benedict, *Christ's Churches Purely Reformed: A Social History of Calvinism* (New Haven: Yale University Press, 2002), pp. 90-91.

tures in Calvin's thought that might hold special promise for Protestant theology today: first, the particular substance and arrangement of his key doctrines; second, his overall approach to Christian life — and to doctrine itself — as fundamentally formational; and third, the way his work emphasizes and supports practical disciplines, while at the same time situating them within a critical framework. In these and other ways, the great reformer may yet speak to us today, even across five centuries. Indeed, it may well be the distance between the sixteenth century and the twenty-first, between his world and ours, that provides us with a fresh angle of vision, a helpful paradigm, or a promising direction for further research.

Calvin's Ideas

In the first place, as we saw in part II, fresh readings of Calvin's key doctrines may fruitfully provoke twenty-first-century theological thinking — particularly in Protestant quarters, but also across ecumenical lines. Take, for example, the idea that the world is an ongoing work of divine rhetoric, paideutic instruction, and, above all, loving consolation, a radiant theater and sanctifying school replete with "innumerable benefits, from the enjoyment of which [we] might infer the paternal benevolence of God."[2] This approach to the world in all its physical and historical detail may helpfully recast everyday life as a dynamic, dialogic engagement with God at every turn — as opposed to, say, a merely material engagement with divinely manufactured goods, or a basically secular journey into which God may or may not occasionally "intervene." Indeed, these latter views, insofar as they portray the world (or significant swaths of it) as a landscape without God in the first place, may in practice function to promote a more or less veiled form of deism in Christian communities today. Fresh appropriations of Calvin's work on creation and divine providence, then, may help counteract de facto deism wherever it takes hold or lurks in the background, presumed or implied by other claims.

Similarly, Calvin effectively reverses what for many in the late modern West is a central theological problem: the question of how to ground belief in a supposedly imperceptible God, particularly since

---

2. Calvin, *Commentaries on Genesis* (Grand Rapids: Baker, 1981), p. 115.

"supernatural" evidence appears to be, by definition, a crude exception to the credibility rules we play by in the everyday, "natural" world. Calvin's reversal here is to argue from the outset that in fact, if we only had eyes to see, we are continuously surrounded, indeed thoroughly saturated and overwhelmed, by clear signs of God's presence and love. In this sense, for Calvin, God is perfectly perceptible to us, in our own "bodies and souls" no less than in the world around us, but we are tragically, inexcusably oblivious to these signs. If we spend our time solemnly or skeptically seeking after intricate proofs or extraordinary evidence of God's existence or benevolence, we are like miners doggedly digging for a scrap of precious metal (any scrap will do!), though in fact we burrow through a mountain made of gold, with silver shovels in our hands.

As far as perceiving God goes, then, in Calvin's view, humanity's key problem is by no means a dearth of evidence confirming divine presence and parental love (we need look no further than "our daily bread"), nor is it the famous difficulty of believing Christian claims in a grim, lonely, inscrutable world. On the contrary, Calvin sees our key problem as our inability to notice, properly interpret, trust, and respond to the brilliant signs of God's loving presence around and within us. As the old hymn has it, we are blind until — by the Spirit's light and Christ's life — we see; or, to return to Calvin's other favorite term, we are "dull" until God sharpens our awareness and insight, waking us up, bringing us back to our senses. This basic theological move is by no means unique to Calvin, but his distinctive version of it may yet serve Protestants (and others) today, not least because it frames Christian life as a Spirit-led, Christ-centered *paideia,* a reformation not only of morals but also of sensibility. And at the same time, Calvin thereby frames the world as, among other things, a marvelous, challenging training ground for that reformation, an unfolding divine work of immersive instruction, shimmering with the glory of God.

According to this line of thought, the Holy Spirit provides us with Scripture, sacraments, the church, and so on, not because the world is insufficiently radiant and clear as a revelation of divine love, but because we have become so dull as to require remedial training in order to see and sense the world as it truly is. If our minds and sensoria were properly formed and engaged, we would require no special sermon on Sunday morning. The whole world is a sermon, indeed a Great Sermon composed of countless smaller ones: even "infants," Calvin insists, "while they nurse at their mothers' breasts, have tongues so eloquent to preach [God's] glory that there is no need at all of other orators."[3] No need, that is, except for our dullness and oblivion. As it happens, then, we do have need for other orators, a pressing need in fact: first, so we may hear God's word eloquently addressed to us, and second, so we may learn to discern the divine eloquence all around and within us. In short, as disciples in training, we need nothing so much as a good sermon, last Sunday morning and next. There God speaks to us, we hope and trust, and there we may learn to hear and see and believe the Great Sermon, creation itself, this symphonic, ongoing work of God's providential love, even here, even now.

Moreover, as with preaching, so too with Scripture, the church, theology, prayer, worship, and so on: properly conceived, these objects, institutions, and practices are humbling, remedial tools in our formation, training, and development. They are ways to understand and experience a divine benevolence that should already be quite clear. Were we fully awake, alert, and perceptive, we would need only to listen to the cooing of an infant; since we are not, we need sermons, Scripture readings, sacraments, and churches. Understood this way, our use of these aids continually marks us as neophytes, convalescents, beginners, learners, disciples — not as spiritual experts, moral exemplars, or master technicians. That is, these aids are exercises in humility, and should be understood and practiced as such. If they indicate wisdom, they do so only in the Socratic sense of "knowing that we do not know." In other words, they are testimonies and reminders that we are children of God who require upbringing, formation, training — in a word, *paideia*. "Truly I tell you," Jesus said, "unless you change and become like children, you will never enter the kingdom of heaven"; and in the ancient world, a child was first and foremost a beginner, a "humble" human being, as Jesus goes on to put it, an unlearned creature in need of formative education (Matt. 18:3-4).

The community of the church is thus a community of learners following Jesus, an assembly set neither above nor apart from the world. Disciples may strive to live a life of renouncing the world's iniquities, but they thereby gain no advantage over their non-Christian

---

3. John Calvin, *Institutes of the Christian Religion*, ed. John T. McNeill (Philadelphia: Westminster, 1960), 1.5.3, 4 (hereafter cited as *ICR*; section references cited in parentheses in the text).

neighbors. For disciples, too, are sinners. Disciples, too, individually and collectively, are at best a questionable mix of good intentions and hypocrisy, dignity and pride. If they are justified before God in Christ, it is none of their doing, but rather an astonishing, unmerited gift. If they are being sanctified by God in the Holy Spirit, it is by divine grace, and in any event, their progress is both strikingly modest and paralleled by a progressively keen sense of how far they have to go. Moreover, properly understood, their formative, ecclesial practices are not ends in themselves, but rather epitomic illustrations of how their whole lives ought to be. Thus they have no cause to look down on their neighbors with contempt or sympathy. If anything, they have ample cause to look up to them, precisely from the christological posture of a servant.

Accordingly, Calvin develops his key doctrines in formational terms, and with formational ends in view. Retrieving his doctrines of creation and providence, theologians today may rethink, for example, the familiar theme of ecological "stewardship" to include not only humanity's cultivation and care of the world, but also and crucially its practical reception of it as an unfolding gift — that is, as a living, tangible symbol of God's parental love — through regular, paideutic disciplines of thanksgiving and doxology. In this sense, so-called ethics and so-called liturgics are inseparable, even indistinguishable, in Calvin's thought, and theologians today do well to pick up and develop this basic approach.[4] Or again, another fruitful locus may be Calvin's portrait of the human being as a creature in the first place made for intimate, commensal life in God; in the second place a sinner oblivious both to

---

4. For relatively recent examples of work at once liturgical and ethical, see William Cavanaugh, *Being Consumed: Economics and Christian Desire* (Grand Rapids: Eerdmans, 2008), *Theopolitical Imagination: Discovering the Liturgy as a Political Act in an Age of Global Consumerism* (London: T. & T. Clark,, 2002), and *Torture and Eucharist* (Oxford: Blackwell, 1998); Brian Brock, *Singing the Ethos of God: On the Place of Christian Ethics in Scripture* (Grand Rapids: Eerdmans, 2007); Samuel Wells, *God's Companions: Reimagining Christian Ethics* (Oxford: Blackwell, 2006), and *Improvisation: The Drama of Christian Ethics* (Grand Rapids: Brazos, 2004); E. Byron Anderson and Bruce T. Morrill, eds., *Liturgy and the Moral Self: Humanity at Full Stretch before God* (Collegeville, Minn.: Liturgical Press, 1998); Miroslav Volf, *Exclusion and Embrace: A Theological Exploration of Identity, Otherness, and Reconciliation* (Nashville: Abingdon, 1996); Don E. Saliers, *Worship as Theology: Foretaste of Glory Divine* (Nashville: Abingdon, 1994); Geoffrey Wainwright, *Doxology: The Praise of God in Worship, Doctrine, and Life* (New York: Oxford University Press, 1980); and Alexander Schmemann, *For the Life of the World* (Crestwood, N.Y.: St. Vladimir's Seminary Press, 1963).

this vocation and to God's radiance within and around her; and in the third place, in and through the Christian church, a child being formed and restored by Jesus Christ and the Holy Spirit to her original integrity. This anthropological triptych, with its dialectical tensions on both sides of the middle image of human "depravity," may help reframe, fill out, and correct Protestant theologies of sin and salvation.

Likewise, Calvin's account of Christian Scripture as a primary means by which the Holy Spirit dispels our oblivion, and so in that sense as "spectacles" for seeing God more clearly in and through the world, may serve as a fresh paradigm for disciples studying the Bible, and in particular, for preachers and teachers expounding it. Similarly, Calvin's accounts of prayer as a discipline of mindfulness and delight, the Lord's Supper as a discipline of recognition and quickening, salvation as a matter not only of atonement but also of participation in Christ, the doctrine of predestination as an intellectual condition of continual, humble doxology — in each of these areas, Calvin may make a congenial, provocative conversation partner for today's theologians. At every turn, Calvin gives the lie to the supposed distinction between so-called systematic and so-called practical theology: for him, doctrine is always already practical, that is, oriented toward the church's disciplinary program of practical formation, which itself takes place for the sake of fully human life in God.

Calvin's Approach

Protestant theologians who take this formational starting point and framework seriously in the twenty-first century will produce a different kind of theology than the one that typically dominated Protestant circles in the nineteenth and twentieth centuries.[5] The church's signature prac-

---

5. For relatively recent examples of formational approaches to Christian theology, see, e.g., David Ford, *Christian Wisdom: Desiring God and Learning in Love* (Cambridge: Cambridge University Press, 2007); Craig Dykstra, *Growing in the Life of Faith: Education and Christian Practices*, 2nd ed. (Louisville: Westminster John Knox, 2005); Kevin Vanhoozer, *The Drama of Doctrine: A Canonical-Linguistic Approach to Christian Theology* (Louisville: Westminster John Knox, 2005); John Witvliet, *Worship Seeking Understanding* (Grand Rapids: Baker Academic, 2003); Miroslav Volf and Dorothy Bass, eds., *Practicing Theology: Beliefs and Practices in Christian Life* (Grand Rapids: Eerdmans, 2002); Ellen Charry, ed., *Inquiring after God* (Oxford: Blackwell, 2000), and Ellen Charry, *By the Renewing of*

tices will come front and center, for starters, as will their paideutic purposes, and this will set the stage for reconsidering the whole gamut of Christian doctrine, from creation to eschatology. In terms of genre, the closest analogue discourse will not necessarily be philosophy or science, as it so often was in major nineteenth- and twentieth-century Protestant texts, but rather other forms: scriptural commentary (or other biblically saturated genres); devotional-liturgical speech; literary, musical, and dramaturgical arts; and so on — all without for a moment surrendering theology's place as a critical, analytical mode of intellectual rigor. Indeed, part of the point here is that the widely presumed association of these latter genres with less critical or uncritical thinking is a specious and, for the Christian church, self-defeating association, since it effectively demotes everyday ecclesial forms of discourse to a second-class (or third-class) status. In the end, the key task is not only to insist that elements of Christian life commonly categorized as "spirituality" are as potentially important and intellectually legitimate as those elements commonly categorized as "theology." The key task is to call this very distinction into question and, when necessary, to oppose and dismantle it.

All this implies a broader understanding of theological knowledge than often prevails today in Protestant circles, among others. According to the reading of Calvin outlined here, while theological knowledge does involve conceptual, informational forms of knowing-that or knowing-about ("orthodoxy" in the sense of "right opinion"), it ultimately culminates in practical, relational forms of knowing-how. That is, it culminates in knowing how to act and live in light of our commensal, symbiotic relationship with God; how to graciously respond in and with God to divine gifts; in sum, how to live a fully human life of genuine *pietas,* a life of reverent love, service, thanks, and doxology ("orthodoxy" in the sense of "right praise").[6] In this sense, again, all theological knowledge comes down to savoir faire: know-how, knack, phronesis, practical wisdom.

Your Minds: The Pastoral Function of Christian Doctrine (New York: Oxford University Press, 1997); Andre LaCocque and Paul Ricoeur, eds., *Thinking Biblically: Exegetical and Hermeneutical Studies* (Chicago: University of Chicago Press, 1998); Dorothy Bass, ed., *Practicing Our Faith: A Way of Life for a Searching People* (San Francisco: Jossey-Bass, 1997); and Margaret Miles, *Fullness of Life: Historical Foundations for a New Asceticism* (Philadelphia: Westminster, 1981).

6. "Orthodoxy," from the Greek *ortho,* "right, true, straight" + *doxa,* "opinion" or "praise."

Life in God

To be sure, right opinions are often indispensable to savoir faire. Ideally, they help constitute the intellectual framework within which wise judgments and gestures take place. But just as in any other practical discipline — say, carpentry or cooking or diplomacy or sport — theology's ideas exist not for their own sake, but for the sake of skillful, creative action. For example, knowing "about" God has its place in Christian life, but only insofar as it helps us know how to relate to God and with God, and thereby helps enable us to do so. Indeed, from this angle, theological knowledge is finally relational knowledge, savoir faire culminating in *savoir vivre*, "knowing how to live" — which is to say, in Calvin's view, knowing how to live in and with God.

Analogies here abound in ordinary human life. Think of the relational knowledge between spouses, or between parents and children, or between friends. In each case, holding the right opinions about the other person has its crucial part to play, but the main thing is to be together gracefully, to live as intimate companions, to connect, to love. Doing these things well means employing a particular set of skills with agility, versatility, fluency, and tact. It means exercising discernment and finesse. It means doing the right thing at the right time, and moreover, it means doing it with the right tone, style, and demeanor. It means living in and through the particular dispositions that best suit the given situation. It means street smarts, savvy, decorum, grace. In a word, it means convenance: social aptness or propriety, from the Latin *convenire* (literally "to come together").

And to pull all this off, to "come together" with God and neighbor in the ways that constitute genuine Christian life, disciples need practice. They need to cultivate the appropriate dispositions and develop the appropriate capacities. They need mentors, companions, and regular disciplines through which to learn and grow. That is, they need to train, to work out, and thereby to strengthen their fitness, dexterity, and poise. After all, in carpentry or cooking or diplomacy or sport, how are excellence and gracefulness typically learned and maintained? Through practice, of course: experience and exercise that form particular habits and aptitudes, thereby affording disciples, little by little, with both a repertoire of skills and the seasoned judgment to use them wisely.

As we saw in part I, the basic outline of this approach is by no means unique to Calvin, and even today, virtually every Protestant theologian — indeed, every Christian theologian — would agree in principle that theological doctrine is ultimately for the sake of theological life. The trouble is that in too much Protestant theology, this connection is relatively attenuated, de-emphasized, or underdeveloped; and even when it is quite clear, it is too often worked out in terms of the particular ethical positions and actions allegedly implied or entailed by Christian doctrine. If we hold this or that theological opinion, the argument goes, we should also hold this or that ethical opinion, and our lives (our politics, our activism, and so on) should reflect our ethics. So goes a great deal of modern Protestant theological work.

But this approach effectively bypasses, or at any rate sidelines, what is central for Calvin: the work of Jesus Christ and the Holy Spirit in and through the transformative disciplines of the church's practical inheritance. To be sure, scriptural study, daily prayer, psalm singing, the Lord's Supper, and so on may well appear in modern doctrinal or "systematic" Protestant theological texts, but in most cases, disciplinary formation is hardly their dominant or organizing theme. And so in bookstores, publishers' catalogues, and classroom syllabi, books focus-

---

7. For example, Ellen Charry, in her superb study *By the Renewing of Your Minds*, leans in this general direction. She defines her interpretation of Calvin as "aretegenic," that is, as concerned with "the moral shaping function" of his doctrine, and so leaves the impression that for her, formation principally means "character formation," the shaping of particular moral virtues in particular moral subjects. To be sure, Calvin was quite interested in morals, virtue, "righteousness," and so on, but moral formation is not, in his view, the organizing telos toward which Christian life should be oriented. Rather, as we have seen, that telos is intimate communion with God, a relationship that entails a return to full humanity in God's image. To be sure, as Calvin understands it, becoming fully human involves reformation of character (the development, say, of virtues of humility, fidelity, and so on), but at the same time, it also involves a reformation of sensibility, ongoing participation in God, and so on. And precisely because this restoration to full humanity is so multifaceted and fundamentally relational, for Calvin it will not do if disciples simply engage the right ideas, or even develop the right virtues. In addition to these, they ideally engage a holistic, relational, practical formative program, complete with intellectual, sensorial, moral, emotional, somatic, and dialogic aspects, among others, all with an eye toward union with God. Indeed, a striking omission from Charry's discussion is any treatment of the disciplinary *paideia* Calvin envisions for Christian disciples. Of course, Charry's declared subject is not "Christian practices" but rather "the pastoral function of Christian doctrine," but the point is that for Calvin, neither "doctrine" nor "pastoral function" is thinkable apart from the church's practical program. Nevertheless, Charry's work on Calvin, and in particular her emphasis on the fundamentally formational character of his thought, represents a profoundly important step forward. See Charry, pp. 19, 199-221.

ing on these practices are typically classified not under "theology" but rather under "church and ministry," "worship," or "spirituality." This now familiar arrangement seems harmless enough on its face, but it both reflects and perpetuates a significant category mistake, leaving the impression that "theology" is principally an exercise in conceptual clarification and logical rigor at some significant remove from the church's practical life. Theologians may and do insist that their work is indirectly or even directly related to that life, but the link typically takes place across a considerable distance — and at times, the link is difficult to discern at all.

Dividing Christian life in this way, with "theology" or doctrine on one hand (or shelf, or syllabus) and practical formation on the other hand (or shelf, or syllabus), would have been virtually unintelligible to Calvin — and that, in a nutshell, is another reason why revisiting his work may be so helpful for theologians today. As we have seen, for him, theology is indeed an exercise in conceptual clarification and logical rigor, but at the same time it is properly conceived, oriented, and articulated in the service of the church's broad program of practical formation. In other words, in Calvin's view, ultimately and fundamentally, theology is meant to help produce not texts, or ideas, or opinions, but people.

To be sure, texts, ideas, and opinions may be of great help to this formative process, and so an important part of what theologians do is write and think and opine, with clarity and precision (God willing!). But the goal of this thinking and writing, the telos that gives it its overall form and direction, is to provide intellectual support for a mission that both includes and exceeds intellectual life: namely, the church's mission to help produce a particular kind of human being, and a particular kind of human community. What kind? A human being fully alive, as Irenaeus of Lyons famously put it; and a human community that, in the prophet Micah's vision, loves kindness, does justice, and walks humbly with God. Or, in Calvin's terms, a human being in the image of God, conformed to Christ, indwelt by the Holy Spirit, and flourishing in and through genuine *pietas;* and a human community that serves as both a sanctifying school and a vivid witness to Christian life together.[8]

---

8. At first glance, this position may seem to bear some resemblance to the one laid out by Stanley Hauerwas and William Willimon in, e.g., *Resident Aliens: Life in the*

Typically at least, such individuals and communities do not simply appear fully formed in a flash of light or repentance or sincerity.

Christian Colony and *Where Resident Aliens Live: Exercises for Christian Practice*, but key differences are worth noting. When Hauerwas and Willimon claim that the Christian church is a "colony of heaven," "an island of one culture in the middle of another," a community that "confronts the world with a political alternative the world would not otherwise know," "a visible people of God," "the visible, political enactment of our language of God," and so on, they draw their contrasts too sharply, and blow the trumpet of triumph too soon. In fact, Calvin's response to "certain Anabaptists" of his day, parallel as it is to his critique of monasticism and "double Christianity," is instructive here: the Holy Spirit, he insists, is indeed leading the church on a path of perfection, but "we are purged by [the Spirit's] sanctification in such a way that we are besieged by many vices and much weakness so long as we are encumbered with our body. Thus it comes about that, far removed from perfection, we must move steadily forward, and though entangled in vices, daily fight against them" (*ICR* 3.3.14). For Calvin, the visible church, like the world around it, is riddled with "vices and weakness," and even its marks of apparent holiness may or may not be bona fide. As such, the visible church is "far removed from perfection," and so cannot rightly be described as a colony of heaven, a sacred island in the midst of a more or less profane sea. To be sure, God willing, the church is a pilgrim band *on its way to heaven,* or better, a community expectantly calling and watching for heaven to arrive, foretasting heaven here and there, and hoping, praying, and boldly trusting that heaven will one day be their home, along with the whole human family — but that day has not yet arrived, to put it mildly. And so for the time being, the contrast between "church" and "world" is simply not as clear and crisp as Hauerwas and Willimon suggest. The act of crossing the threshold into a church is not an act of stepping up onto higher ground; nor is it a bracing event in which, as Hauerwas and Willimon put it, we "strike hard against something which is an alternative to what the world offers." On the contrary, from Calvin's point of view, the world is too replete with divine glory, and the church too replete with worldly patterns, protocols, and people, for that kind of contrast to be theologically tenable (never mind empirically clear!). The church does not withdraw from, transcend, or surpass the world: not geographically, but also not in terms of virtue or political organization, and so certainly not in the sense of being a heavenly outpost set off from its earthly environment, a diamond shining in the dust. No, this side of the eschaton, even as the church's sanctification takes place, it remains, like the wider world, besieged and entangled by vices and weakness. Indeed, as John of Patmos styles it, the New Jerusalem itself is the heavenly settlement destined to descend to earth (Rev. 21), whereas today's church, by contrast, is a rather motley, often flawed, sometimes beautiful, and in the end quite ordinary crew of wayfarers and witnesses to that coming day. This is no cause for quietism; Calvin's ecclesial standards, after all, are by no means lax or low. But he does not claim success in the way Hauerwas and Willimon's rhetoric would imply. This debate is as old as Christianity, of course, and it fundamentally has to do with striking the right balance between Christian boldness and Christian humility, and with gauging the degree of eschatological realization the church may properly proclaim. At stake here ecclesiologically, I contend, is the de-

Life in God

Rather, even in cases where a sudden conversion is involved, they must be trained and formed over time, raised and coached and strengthened through an immersive, paideutic program. They must be remade and restored. They must be sanctified. And so for John Calvin, Christian life is a disciplined life, a life of discipleship formed largely in and through a particular suite of practical disciplines. Accordingly, at every turn in his theological and reforming work, Calvin sought to serve this governing goal.

And yet: putting things this way means coming face-to-face with a permanent temptation, a spiritual trial for any variety of Christianity, but especially for varieties oriented toward practices. That is, bringing practical disciplines to the center of Christian life and thought carries with it the lure of thinking that our salvation is our own work to do, our practice to practice, our feat of spiritual athleticism to accomplish through our own training, self-discipline, and exertion. In other words, if Christian discipleship is at bottom a kind of sanctifying *paideia*, the clear and permanent danger is that disciples themselves might conceive their sanctification as a result of their own striving and technique. Indeed, as many sixteenth-century reformers emphasized, spiritual pride is so insidious in human life precisely because it characteristically cloaks itself in ostensibly reputable, good-mannered, apparently humble forms. Thus even and especially the fervent, earnest critique of "works righteousness" can and does become, with only a subtle twist of tone and spirit, a proud, supposedly self-justifying piece of work.

And so any turn toward practical disciplines in Christian theology must be accompanied by a clear, constant, humble, and humbling critique of works righteousness, self-justification, and spiritual pride — and this kind of critique is precisely what the Reformed theological tradition, at its best, has to offer. In fact, from this angle, it is possible to argue that Reformed theology provides exceptionally promising ground on which a more robust integration of doctrinal theology and practical disciplines might take root, not least because Reformed thought may so

---

gree to which the practical community of the church will be a centripetal society, oriented inward, pointing toward itself as, say, a "colony of heaven," and the degree to which it will be a centrifugal society, oriented outward, pointing toward itself but also distinctively beyond itself to creation as a whole, and above all to Christ and the coming kingdom of heaven all around (Matt. 4:17). See Hauerwas and Willimon, *Resident Aliens: Life in the Christian Colony* (Nashville: Abingdon, 1989), pp. 11, 12, 41, 82, 171, 94; and *Where Resident Aliens Live: Exercises for Christian Practice* (Nashville: Abingdon, 1996).

readily situate practices within a critical theological framework. And in just this respect, John Calvin may help show the way forward.

Reforming Formation

In the first place, one of Calvin's signature theological moves is his emphasis on "sanctification" (or "regeneration"), a phenomenon he clearly distinguishes from "justification" in his soteriology. In short, for Calvin, the elect are "justified" — that is, "reckoned righteous in God's judgment" — not because of their good work, but rather despite their ongoing sin. Their salvation is wholly undeserved, and so completely depends on God graciously incorporating them into Jesus Christ (3.11.1). Whatever practices they may or may not carry out, then, have nothing whatsoever to do with effecting their justification before God — and indeed, without this justification and the reconciliation with God it involves, those practices can only function as presumptuous, counterproductive extensions of their "miserable ruin."

Thus in principle, at least, Calvin clearly rules out any practice of daily prayer, for example, that unfolds as an alleged exercise in self-justification, and to the extent that this principle functions as a critical check on the church's practices, Calvin's soteriology may help ground the proper performance of daily prayer and other ecclesial disciplines. That is, Calvin calls justification "the main hinge on which religion turns," and it turns not just apart from a disciple's good works, but also expressly in spite of them. Strictly and solely on Christ's account, the elect are "reckoned righteous," "reconciled to God through Christ's blamelessness," and so on. Their "sanctification," on the other hand, is something else altogether, a kind of second, inseparable, parallel movement in this choreography of salvation, and so a disciple's good works — including her formative exercises — are properly and strictly conceived underneath this second rubric. According to Calvin, the church's practices — scriptural study, daily prayer, and so on — do not and cannot justify. They contribute not one whit to a disciple's being "reckoned righteous" by God. Indeed, Calvin's work on sanctification can be understood as, among other things, a strategy for inheriting the church's practical treasury while at the same time cordoning it off — again, at least in principle — from the idea that such practices justify their practitioners.

Life in God

Moreover, in his account of sanctification, Calvin describes the disciplines of regeneration as divinely activated, empowered, and directed at every step along the way. That is, disciples may and do perform these sanctifying practices, but their performances are themselves divine gifts, and they take place properly and fruitfully — that is, in ways that produce genuine humility and insight for them and for others — only by way of divine accompaniment and power. For example, disciples read Scripture only by way of the Holy Spirit's illumination and Christ's instruction; pray by way of the Spirit's voice and in Christ's name; gather at the communion table by way of the Spirit's prompting and Christ's hospitality; and so on. Most fundamentally, then, disciplines of regeneration are divine acts freely accomplished in and through human beings, and as such, they are no cause for human boasting, but only for humility and gratitude. Thus following Calvin, we may reframe "spiritual practices" as in the first place works of the Holy Spirit and Jesus Christ, the sanctifying, regenerating, restorative labor of God with us and in us.[9]

In this way, Calvin's approach effectively relativizes and reorients the common definition of a human "practice," and thereby builds up a significant rampart against the possibility of spiritual pride. Each of the church's key practices is still something human beings do, but they do it neither alone nor as the act's primary agent. Rather, in and through the practice, they participate in divine work. They take part in God's body and life. They live — but not "in themselves," not intrinsically, not as a closed, supposedly self-sufficient system, and not for their own sake alone. Rather, they live in God, extrinsically and commensally open, for their own sake and their neighbor's sake and above all for God's sake. To paraphrase Paul: they live, not they, but Christ in them (Gal. 2:20). Or, as Jesus puts it: "Abide in me as I abide in you" (John 15:4).[10]

Calvin calls this mutual indwelling "mystical," but he does not thereby mark it as exceptional, rare, or set apart from everyday life — and this move, too, functions as a potential safeguard against Christian pride (3.11.10). For Calvin, a human being's whole life is properly a life

---

9. On the theme of divine agency in and through human liturgical and devotional action, see John Witvliet, "Images and Themes in John Calvin's Theology of Liturgy," in *Worship Seeking Understanding*, pp. 127-48, especially pp. 145ff.

10. For a full discussion of this theme in theological anthropology, see David Kelsey, *Eccentric Existence: A Theological Anthropology* (Louisville: Westminster John Knox, 2009).

of union with God, and in that sense is properly a "mystical" life. With this in mind, then, if the church's formative practices are events of intimate collaboration in which disciples participate in divine work, they are on that account by no means exceptional or extraordinary. On the contrary, ecclesial disciplines serve as participatory examples, remedial illustrations of divine-human intimacy, models of what should be common and ordinary. That is, the church's practices epitomize the whole of human life in its genuine form. Properly discharged, they are mnemonic, synecdochic, experiential instances of what our lives ought to be — and in many, often unnoticed respects, already are.

In short, the church's key disciplines are indeed "practices." They are rehearsals, training, participatory object lessons meant to help make broader performances possible. As such, they are part and parcel of Christian *paideia,* a lifelong program of formation, and so each practice is carried out not only as an end in itself, but also and preeminently as a means toward building and living a whole Christian life. The disciplines themselves are properly centrifugal, not centripetal; they are oriented out and beyond their own limits in time and space. Reading God's book of scripture, for example, is a practice not only for its own sake, but also for the sake of reading God's book of creation. A daily prayer cycle is not only an end in itself, but also and ultimately an aid to a whole life of prayer without ceasing. The sacred supper is not only itself a nourishing, "quickening" meal; it also gives us a revealing, reassuring taste of how Christ, the bread of life, quickens us always and everywhere. And so on. For Calvin, we might say, Sunday morning is for the sake of the entire week, not the other way around. Or again, in Jesus' terms: "The sabbath was made for humankind, and not humankind for the sabbath" (Mark 2:27).[11]

> 11. In passages like this one in Mark, the object of Jesus' critique is not the practice of Sabbath keeping itself, but rather a distorted, contemptuous style of observing the practice that loses sight of its governing telos, namely, the nourishment and protection of life, and in particular, human life. And in the midst of this controversy, Jesus provides a compact theology of religious practices, and so for our purposes here, we may paraphrase his approach this way: *Ecclesial disciplines are made for humankind, not humankind for ecclesial disciplines.* That is, the church's practical treasury is provided for the sake of life abundant ("to save life," as Jesus pointedly goes on to put it [3:4]), and should always be performed with that end in view, so that in any trade-off scenario, life should flourish at the practice's expense, not the other way around. Properly understood, then, Sabbath keeping is a life-giving discipline "made for humankind." And in passages such as this one, so far from casting Jesus as a critic of Sabbath keeping per se (or, even more

Life in God

And this brings us to one other way in which the Reformed tradition may prove to be particularly fruitful ground for both emphasizing practical disciplines and situating them within a critical framework. The controversies over Sabbath practices in the Christian Gospels belong to a larger set of episodes in which Jesus critiques and clarifies particular religious practices of his day (prayer, fasting, almsgiving, worship, and so on), such that the need for vigilance against the dangers of such disciplines emerges as an important theme in his teaching. Ever since, of course, would-be reformers of Christianity have taken up this basic critical mantle in their own various ways, and the leaders of the sixteenth-century European reformations are no exception.

Indeed, these reformers appear on the scene first and foremost as critics of religious practices, which is to say, as critics of many prevailing, normative forms of religion in the world as they knew it. What most concerned Martin Luther, for example, was not abstract or generic human pride, but rather *spiritual* pride, pride in its patently religious, practical forms, what he called the attempt "to obtain righteousness in the sight of God" through "brotherhoods, indulgences, orders, relics, forms of worship, invocation of saints, purgatory, Masses, vigils, vows, and the endless other abominations of that sort."[12] Calvin, too, in the opening chapters of the *Institutio,* spells out human degeneration not as a fall into avowed atheism or outright rebellion vis-à-vis God, but rather as a fall into a specious "shadow" of religion, a sham, a counterfeit *religio* in which fallen human nature functions as little more than a "perpetual factory of idols" (1.11.8). In other words, these reformers understood the chief threat to Christian life to emanate not from outside the camp, but from within it, honorably cloaked in its most exalted gestures and accoutrements. The devil comes, they were convinced, disguised as an angel of light (2 Cor. 11:13-15).[13]

---

broadly, of ascetic practices per se), the Gospel writers actually portray him as an advocate and reformer of key Jewish disciplines, clarifying their proper purpose, character, and spirit.

12. *Luther's Works,* ed. Jaroslav Pelikan and Helmut Lehmann (St. Louis: Concordia, 1960-74), 26:231, 222. Or again, Luther once remarked, "For where God built a church, there the Devil would also build a chapel. . . . Thus is the Devil ever God's ape" (*Table Talk* 53).

13. For a full discussion of this theme in Reformed theology, and a brief systematic theology built up from it, see my *God against Religion: Rethinking Christian Theology through Worship* (Grand Rapids: Eerdmans, 2008).

On the Future of Protestant Theology

Thus, potentially at least, a basic skepticism toward religious practices was built in to the Reformed theological tradition from its inception, at its best both a vigilant guard against Christian arrogance and a humble sense for the ways in which even and especially the very best of religious life can serve the very worst human beings can do. Our most earnest cultivations of humility, for example, can function as a cause for pride, and so for contempt toward those we judge to be not quite so humble as we are. The most eloquent, ostensibly unassuming prayer can function as a mercenary gambit, a more or less veiled attempt to secure or maintain divine favor. And so on. Indeed, the "protest" from which Protestantism takes its name was originally directed against what reformers regarded as corrupt religiosity masquerading as holiness, and just this kind of critique may serve as a crucial counterpoint for any theological turn toward practices and practical formation.

This potential for theological self-criticism is not unique to Protestantism, of course, nor is its full realization guaranteed (or even especially common!) in Protestant quarters. Reformed arrogance is at least as legion as Roman Catholic arrogance, or Orthodox arrogance, and so on. But there are distinctive resources within the historic reformation traditions that theologians today should develop in relation to practical formation, and the characteristically Protestant tendency toward theological critiques of religious institutions and disciplines is certainly among them. That is, distinctively *Protestant* accounts of ecclesial practices will situate them within a critical framework, continually pointing toward the dangers that attend them, including self-deception and spiritual pride. The reality of human sin, Protestant theologians will insist, does not somehow go on hiatus simply because an idea or practice is "biblical" or "liturgical" or "devotional" or "spiritual." Indeed, Protestant traditions shaped by Calvin's clear emphasis on sin's thoroughgoing, often pseudoreligious "miserable ruin" may be especially well positioned to press this particular point, calling for heightened scrutiny and discernment when it comes to the church's disciplines of formation.

Following Calvin, then, Protestants may insist that ecclesial practices have nothing to do with effecting human justification, everything to do with human sanctification, and — most important and decisive of all — everything to do with divine agency and power. The practices I carry out do not and cannot gain me entrance into God's good graces. Rather, at best, they are in the first place already graceful divine works carried out in and through me. Thus they are not human techniques for "getting closer to God." They are not little towers of Babel. Indeed, insofar as they are helpful at all, they are divine techniques — enacted in and through human beings as fully divine, fully human work — for bringing us closer to our own true humanity, which is to say, closer to the life in God for which we are made. Accordingly, I properly conceive my own practical work as reassuring, humbling indications that God is already graciously working in me and on me, forming me, training me, little by little rebuilding my "miserable ruin" toward full humanity in God's image. In other words, at best, the church's practices are fundamentally divine works of descent and accommodation, not human works of ascent and transcendence.

To be sure, Calvin uses the language of human ascent and human action throughout the *Institutio*, but only in a secondary sense: ecclesial disciplines first of all involve, as Calvin puts it in his account of the Lord's Supper, "the manner of descent by which [Christ] lifts us up to himself" (4.17.16).[14] The human ascent is quite real, but it is secondary; the divine descent is prevenient and primary all the way along. We rise, we might say, but only by way of the Spirit's lead and Christ's resurrection and ascension, that is, only as members of his body. In the same sense, as we have seen, the church's formative practices are human acts only insofar as God grants us participation in prevenient, primary divine acts of interpretation, prayer, communion, and so on. Again, we do act, but only by way of divine action. In sum, when it comes to the church's key disciplines, God provides them not once and long ago, but every day afresh, practicing them in us, through us, and with us.

Moreover, for Calvin, this radically intimate, collaborative, asymmetrical agential arrangement is true of everything we do: "whatever you undertake, whatever you do, ought to be ascribed to [God]" (1.2.2). Thus what distinguishes the disciplines of the church's practical inheritance — scriptural study, daily prayer, the singing of psalms and spiritual songs, the Lord's Supper, and so on — is not that they involve acting in and with God, or rather, God acting in and with us. What sets them apart is their function as the church's *paideia*, the immersive, formative program for restoring disciples to fully human life, which is to say, life lived consciously and gracefully in communion with God.

---

14. For an extended discussion of the theme of ascent in Calvin's work, see Julie Canlis, *Calvin's Ladder: A Spiritual Theology of Ascent and Ascension* (Grand Rapids: Eerdmans, 2010).

Through these particular acts and patterns of life, the church learns to be human in all times and places.

Reforming Church

Thus for those Protestants today who find a renewed recovery of ecclesial disciplines to be an appealing prospect (or indeed for those who experience it as a salutary development already well under way), Calvin's approach may provide a helpful, critical framework. On the other hand, however, Protestantism's signature drumbeat against "works righteousness" has made many twenty-first-century Protestants wary not only of the potential hazards of spiritual practices, but also of those practices themselves. And moreover, a third camp within Protestantism is largely indifferent to such disciplines, since in their view the Christian church is primarily a society of right opinion and, by extension, right ethics. For this third group, it is less than clear why a daily prayer cycle, say, or frequent reception of the Lord's Supper, is a necessary or even particularly helpful feature of Christian discipleship. Teach me the outlines of the scriptural message and the historic confessions, this group contends, and preach to me occasionally about the moral implications of Christian opinions, and I'll be satisfied.

For these latter two Protestant camps — those wary of spiritual practices and those basically indifferent to them — fresh retrievals of Calvin's work may be especially provocative and fruitful, opening up new avenues for ecclesial life and, ultimately, ecclesiological reform. For Calvin, being continually, critically alert to the perils of "works righteousness" should by no means entail an aversion to "works" per se. In fact, Calvin understands the church's disciplinary inheritance as indispensable for the sanctifying formation that, alongside justification, constitutes the "double grace" of human salvation. Right opinion has its place in ecclesial affairs, of course, but ultimately, in Calvin's view, the church is a kind of gymnasium: a society of formation and development, gathering occasionally for guidance and inspiration, but then sent out into the world to exercise all week long, at home and in the fields, day in and day out. A good deal of this formation involves training a disciple's intellect, of course, but it also trains her heart, her sensibility, her moral compass, her relational skills — in short, it trains and develops her *savoir vivre*, her "knowing how to live" with and in God.

Indeed, seeing through Calvin's eyes, we may describe what ails many Protestant churches today as follows: having inherited a treasury of formative exercises, we practice them only here and there, now and then — and still expect and even claim to be getting in shape. Or, we expect no such thing, instead interpreting the treasury as a collection not of exercises meant to form us, but rather of activities meant to express, demonstrate, or symbolically establish ourselves as believing Christian beliefs, belonging to a Christian crowd — or simply accomplishing some supposedly Christian task (obtaining a divine favor, for example, or meeting with divine approval).

But this is, at bottom, another category mistake. We take a yoga mat and frame it on the wall. We resolve to run a marathon and enroll in a training program of short runs two or three Sunday mornings a month. We dream of mastering the piano but only rarely sit down at one, and even more rarely practice our scales. We are like a community to which a benefactor bequeaths a warehouse full of fitness machines and related equipment. In our wisdom, we resolve to keep the machines in the warehouse, gather there once a week (or less) for an hour or two, lightly engaging the machines, and spending a good portion of the time watching a few of us exercise on behalf of the whole group (we sent them to exercise school, you see, so they are the experts).

If someone objects that a light workout once a week (or less) is hardly enough to produce the transformation our benefactor likely had in mind, we may insist — rather oddly — that what really count are our *ideas* about the exercises, the machines, the benefactor, and so on. Or, we may explain that the real purpose of the equipment is not to help us get into shape, but rather to help us express our worldview, or demonstrate our affiliation, or confirm our place in the community — tasks for which participating at a rate of once a week (or less) is, after all, perfectly sufficient. Or, more likely, we simply don't dwell much on the objection. We block it out, change the subject, and hope for the best. Wittingly or unwittingly, we live out the idea that, most fundamentally, the Christian church is no gymnasium but rather a social club, an ethical society, a creedal clan — in short, an organization in which participating a few times a month (or even a few times a year) poses no real problem for membership.

Calvin would have none of this, of course. For him, the church is indeed a social, moral, and creedal association, but underlying and determining each of these other dimensions, the church is a gymnasium, a training ground, a school, a community of preparation and practice enrolled (we hope and pray) in God's sanctifying, transformative *paideia*. That is, the church is a circle of disciples, of learners, of children being raised by God our Father and Mother. As such, the church is constituted not by its ideas alone, but by its disciplines — which is to say, by its distinctive intellectual, moral, social, sensory, somatic practices and patterns of life. To the extent that disciples accomplish these disciplines fruitfully, they do not accomplish them alone. Rather, God accomplishes them in, through, and with disciples, activating, empowering, and directing each practice at every step along the way, and thereby restoring God's children, little by little, to their full humanity in God's image.

Accordingly, in his reforming work in Geneva, Calvin envisioned an immersive, comprehensive regimen of practical, experiential instruction, a Christian *paideia*, a formative program complete with a daily prayer office, twice-daily domestic worship, twice-weekly public worship, frequent celebration of the sacred supper, and so on. And to serve this embodied education, Calvin wrote intellectually vibrant, scripturally saturated Christian doctrine — and today's Protestant theologians, I argue, should follow suit. The particular paideutic details of the overall program itself will (and should) vary, of course, as will the twenty-first-century ecclesial contexts within which such programs may take place. But the basic theological orientation should be the same: doctrinal theology conceived, oriented, and articulated — sometimes implicitly, often explicitly, but always clearly — for the sake of practical formation, and thus ultimately for the sake of human life in God.

Finally, to the extent that Protestant theologians today take up this approach, a range of promising, ongoing conversations may better flourish across religious, ideological, and disciplinary lines. For example, in recent decades, thinkers in philosophy, anthropology, critical theory, ritual studies, and other disciplines have turned toward practices as fundamental forms through which human communities and human beings are shaped and reshaped, made and remade.[15] Forma-

---

15. For example, see Michel Foucault's work on "technologies of the self," that is, patterns of practice through which "the self" is at once articulated and produced — a set of ideas Foucault develops, in part, through his study of Christian monastic asceticism. Pierre Hadot, while critiquing Foucault's position as "focused far too much on the 'self'" and not enough on the ways in which the self is transcended in certain respects

tional approaches to Christian doctrine will help theologians engage these discussions more deeply and critically, and in turn, these discussions may provide theologians with analytical tools for understanding and developing Christian formation.

Not all paideutic work in Protestant theology should proceed by way of an interdisciplinary method, of course. Some texts, like the pres-

---

through "spiritual practices," nonetheless shares the view that such exercises, in the ancient philosophical world no less than the subsequent Christian one, were meant to transform a person's whole "way of being." That is, for Hadot, the schools of ancient Greek and Roman philosophy each functioned in their own way as "an art, style, or way of life," and this fundamental approach was preserved and passed down through a particular Christian current: "that current, namely, which defined Christianity itself as a philosophy." (Indeed, Calvin refers to "the Christian philosophy" in the *Institutio*; see, e.g., 3.7.1). Further, anthropologist Talal Asad has problematized a familiar view — familiar, that is, among Western anthropologists, but also among many Christian liturgists and theologians — that both religious "ritual" and "religion" in general are best described as, to borrow Clifford Geertz's famous phrase, "a system of symbols," and therefore primarily as a kind of code to be deciphered, a text to be read. This way of thinking, Asad argues, is itself a product of Western modernity, and so is foreign both to many premodern forms of Christianity and to other contexts across the religious world today where a rite is less a text to be read and more a discipline to be done, less something that makes a particular point and more something that makes a particular person. Further, from a different angle, in ritual studies, Catherine Bell — developing the work of J. Z. Smith, Pierre Bourdieu, and others — contends that "ritualization" is a widespread, varied phenomenon by which agents are produced and endowed with particular forms of "ritual mastery." Similarly, Adam Seligman, Robert Weller, Michael Puett, and Bennett Simon have examined *Xing Zi Ming Chu* ("Nature Emerges from the Decree"), a fourth-century B.C.E. Chinese text, as itself a source of ritual theory. They highlight the text's category of "propriety," that is, the capacity, learned through ritual practices, for "responding to things properly" — a concept with fascinating comparative potential vis-à-vis Calvin's thought. Finally, in his influential essay "Walking in the City," Michel de Certeau cites Erasmus's phrase *magnum monasterium* as a way into the complex tensions of the modern urban scene, the institutional strategies and individual tactics that together constitute what Certeau calls "the practice of everyday life." And so on. See Michel Foucault, "Le combat de la chasteté," *Communications*, no. 35 (1982); *The Care of the Self*, vol. 3 of *The History of Sexuality* (New York: Pantheon Books, 1986); and *Technologies of the Self: A Seminar with Michel Foucault* (Amherst: University of Massachusetts Press, 1988); Pierre Hadot, *Philosophy as a Way of Life* (Oxford: Blackwell, 1995), pp. 207, 127; Talal Asad, *Genealogies of Religion: Discipline and Reasons of Power in Christianity and Islam* (Baltimore: Johns Hopkins University Press, 1993); Catherine Bell, *Ritual Theory, Ritual Practice* (New York: Oxford University Press, 1992), p. 141; Adam B. Seligman et al., *Ritual and Its Consequences: An Essay on the Limits of Sincerity* (Oxford: Oxford University Press, 2008), pp. 32-33; and Michel de Certeau, *The Practice of Everyday Life* (Berkeley: University of California Press, 1984), p. 93.

ent one, will principally consist in close, constructive readings of the formational designs underpinning classic works of Christian doctrine. Still others will engage Christian Scripture afresh, building up new doctrinal accounts on behalf of ecclesial disciplines and discipleship. But whatever the particular approach, the most promising future for Protestant theology, I contend, lies in this general direction: Christian ideas, conceptually rigorous and clear, worked out and spelled out in ways that concretely, conspicuously serve the church's practical program.

No Protestant theology, past, present, or future, stands completely detached from Christian life. In any given theological text, sermon, or system of thought, tangible connections with everyday discipleship may be implicit, or peripheral, or cryptic, or undeveloped — but they are there. The trouble is, they are too often implicit, peripheral, cryptic, or undeveloped. And moreover, the crucial task before us is not to trace out the implications of doctrine for practice (or vice versa), as if the two categories are distinct spheres of life. Rather, the task is to debunk and discard that distinction, to think the two at once, *lex orandi, lex credendi,* to write and preach and practice what Calvin would call *pietatis doctrina,* doctrine of *pietas,* teaching for the sake of life in God: in short, a newly imagined, reformed Christian *paideia* for a dark and dawning day.

Bibliography

Anderson, E. Byron, and Bruce T. Morrill, eds. *Liturgy and the Moral Self: Humanity at Full Stretch before God.* Collegeville, Minn.: Liturgical Press, 1998.
Asad, Talal. *Genealogies of Religion: Discipline and Reasons of Power in Christianity and Islam.* Baltimore: Johns Hopkins University Press, 1993.
Athanasius. *The Life of Antony.* Translated by Carolinne White. Early Christian Lives. London: Penguin Classics, 1998.
Barth, Karl. *The Theology of John Calvin.* Grand Rapids: Eerdmans, 1995.
Bass, Dorothy, ed. *Practicing Our Faith: A Way of Life for a Searching People.* San Francisco: Jossey-Bass, 1997.
Battles, Ford Lewis. "God Was Accommodating Himself to Human Capacity." In *Interpreting John Calvin,* edited by Robert Benedetto. Grand Rapids: Baker, 1996.
———. *The Piety of John Calvin.* Phillipsburg, N.J.: P&R Publishing, 2009.
Bell, Catherine. *Ritual Theory, Ritual Practice.* New York: Oxford University Press, 1992.
Benedict, Philip. *Christ's Churches Purely Reformed: A Social History of Calvinism.* New Haven: Yale University Press, 2002.
Billings, Todd J. *Calvin, Participation, and the Gift: The Activity of Believers in Union with Christ.* Oxford: Oxford University Press, 2007.
Boulton, Matthew Myer. *God against Religion: Rethinking Christian Theology through Worship.* Grand Rapids: Eerdmans, 2008.
Bouwsma, William. "Calvin and the Renaissance Crisis of Knowing." *Calvin Theological Journal* 17, no. 2 (1982).
Bradshaw, Paul F. *Early Christian Worship: A Basic Introduction to Ideas and Practice.* Collegeville, Minn.: Liturgical Press, 1996.
———. *The Search for the Origins of Christian Worship: Sources and Methods for the Study of Early Liturgy.* New York: Oxford University Press, 2002.

Bibliography

———. *Two Ways of Praying*. Rev. ed. White Sulphur Springs, W.Va.: OSL Publications, 2008.
Brock, Brian. *Singing the Ethos of God: On the Place of Christian Ethics in Scripture*. Grand Rapids: Eerdmans, 2007.
Brooke, Christopher. *The Age of the Cloister: The Story of Monastic Life in the Middle Ages*. Mahwah, N.J.: Paulist, 2003.
Cabaniss, Allen. "The Background of Metrical Psalmody." *Calvin Theological Journal* 20 (1985).
Calvin, John. *Articles for Church Organization*. In Calvin, *Theological Treatises*, translated by J. K. S. Reid. Library of Christian Classics, vol. 22. Philadelphia: Westminster, 1954.
———. *Calvin's Commentaries*. Grand Rapids: Baker, 1981.
———. *Commentary on Seneca's "De Clementia"* (1532). Edited and translated by Ford Lewis Battles and André Malan Hugo. Renaissance Text Series, vol. 3. Leiden: Brill, 1969.
———. "The Form of Prayers and Songs of the Church." Translated by Ford Lewis Battles. *Calvin Theological Journal* 15 (1980).
———. *Institutes of the Christian Religion*. Edited by John T. McNeill. Philadelphia: Westminster, 1960.
———. *Letters of John Calvin*. Edited by Jules Bonnet. New York: B. Franklin, 1973.
———. *The Mystery of Godliness and Other Sermons*. Morgan, Pa.: Soli Deo Gloria Publications, 1999.
Canlis, Julie. *Calvin's Ladder: A Spiritual Theology of Ascent and Ascension*. Grand Rapids: Eerdmans, 2010.
Cavanaugh, William. *Being Consumed: Economics and Christian Desire*. Grand Rapids: Eerdmans, 2008.
———. *Theopolitical Imagination: Discovering the Liturgy as a Political Act in an Age of Global Consumerism*. London: T. & T. Clark, 2002.
———. *Torture and Eucharist*. Oxford: Blackwell, 1998.
Certeau, Michel de. *The Practice of Everyday Life*. Berkeley: University of California Press, 1984.
Charry, Ellen. *By the Renewing of Your Minds: The Pastoral Function of Christian Doctrine*. New York: Oxford University Press, 1997.
———, ed. *Inquiring after God*. Oxford: Blackwell, 2000.
Chitty, Derwas J. *The Desert a City: An Introduction to the Study of Egyptian and Palestinian Monasticism under the Christian Empire*. London: Mowbrays, 1977.
Clark, R. Scott. "Election and Predestination: The Sovereign Expressions of God." In *A Theological Guide to Calvin's Institutes*, edited by David W. Hall and Peter A. Lillback. Phillipsburg, N.J.: P&R Publishing, 2008.
Cohn, Henry J. "Changing Places: Peasants and Clergy 1525." In *Anticlericalism in Late Medieval and Early Modern Europe*, edited by Peter A. Dykema and Heiko A. Oberman. Leiden: Brill, 1993.

Bibliography

Cunningham, Lawrence S. *Francis of Assisi: Performing the Gospel Life.* Grand Rapids: Eerdmans, 2004.

Dykstra, Craig. *Growing in the Life of Faith: Education and Christian Practices.* 2nd ed. Louisville: Westminster John Knox, 2005.

Elwood, Christopher. *Calvin for Armchair Theologians.* Louisville: Westminster John Knox, 2002.

Erasmus, Desiderius. *The Correspondence of Erasmus.* Translated by R. A. B. Mynors and D. F. S. Thomson. Toronto: University of Toronto Press, 1982.

Farley, Edward. *Theologia: The Fragmentation and Unity of Theological Education.* Philadelphia: Fortress, 1983.

Ford, David. *Christian Wisdom: Desiring God and Learning in Love.* Cambridge: Cambridge University Press, 2007.

Foucault, Michel. *The Care of the Self.* Volume 3 of *The History of Sexuality.* New York: Pantheon Books, 1986.

———. "Le combat de la chasteté." *Communications,* no. 35 (1982).

———. *Technologies of the Self: A Seminar with Michel Foucault.* Amherst: University of Massachusetts Press, 1988.

Garside, Charles, Jr. "The Origins of Calvin's Theology of Music: 1536-1543." In *Transactions of the American Philosophical Society.* Vol. 69. Part 4. Philadelphia: American Philosophical Society, 1979.

Gerrish, Brian. "Calvin's Eucharistic Piety." In *Calvin Studies Society Papers 1995, 1997.* Grand Rapids: Calvin Studies Society, CRC Product Services, 1998.

———. *Grace and Gratitude: The Eucharist in John Calvin's Theology.* Minneapolis: Fortress, 1993.

———. "Theology within the Limits of Piety Alone." In *The Old Protestantism and the New: Essays on the Reformation Heritage.* Chicago: University of Chicago Press, 1982.

———. "'To the Unknown God': Luther and Calvin on the Hiddenness of God." In *The Old Protestantism and the New: Essays on the Reformation Heritage.* Chicago: University of Chicago Press, 1982.

Gordon, Bruce. *Calvin.* New Haven: Yale University Press, 2009.

Grumbach, Argula von. *Argula von Grumbach: A Woman's Voice in the Reformation.* Edited by Peter Matheson. Edinburgh: T. & T. Clark, 1995.

Hadot, Pierre. *Philosophy as a Way of Life.* Oxford: Blackwell, 1995.

Hauerwas, Stanley, and William Willimon. *Resident Aliens: Life in the Christian Colony.* Nashville: Abingdon, 1989.

———. *Where Resident Aliens Live: Exercises for Christian Practice.* Nashville: Abingdon, 1996.

Hill, Christopher. *The World Turned Upside Down: Radical Ideas during the English Revolution.* New York: Viking Press, 1972.

Jaeger, Werner. *Early Christianity and Greek Paideia.* Cambridge: Harvard University Press, 1961.

Bibliography

———. *Paideia: The Ideals of Greek Culture.* New York: Oxford University Press, 1943-45.
Jones, Serene. *Calvin and the Rhetoric of Piety.* Louisville: Westminster John Knox, 1995.
———. "Glorious Creation, Beautiful Law." In *Feminist and Womanist Essays in Reformed Dogmatics,* edited by Amy Plantinga Pauw and Serene Jones. Louisville: Westminster John Knox, 2006.
Jussie, Jeanne de. *The Short Chronicle: A Poor Clare's Account of the Reformation of Geneva.* Chicago: University of Chicago Press, 2006.
Kelsey, David. *Eccentric Existence: A Theological Anthropology.* Louisville: Westminster John Knox, 2009.
———. *To Understand God Truly: What's Theological about a Theological School.* Louisville: Westminster John Knox, 1992.
Kingdon, Robert M. "Worship in Geneva before and after the Reformation." In *Worship in Medieval and Early Modern Europe: Change and Continuity in Religious Practice,* edited by Karin Maag and John Witvliet. Notre Dame, Ind.: University of Notre Dame Press, 2004.
———, ed. *Registers of the Consistory of Geneva in the Time of Calvin.* Grand Rapids: Eerdmans, 2000.
———. *Transition and Revolution: Problems and Issues of European Renaissance and Reformation History.* Minneapolis: Burgess, 1974.
LaCocque, Andre, and Paul Ricoeur, eds. *Thinking Biblically: Exegetical and Hermeneutical Studies.* Chicago: University of Chicago Press, 1998.
Lee, Sou-Young. "Calvin's Understanding of Pietas." In *Calvinus Sincerioris Religionis Vindex: Calvin as Protector of the Purer Religion,* edited by Wilhelm H. Neuser and Brian G. Armstrong. Sixteenth Century Essays and Studies, vol. 36. Kirksville, Mo.: Sixteenth Century Journal, 1997.
Luther, Martin. *Luther's Works.* Edited by Jaroslav Pelikan and Helmut Lehmann. St. Louis: Concordia, 1960-74.
———. *Method of Confessing* (1520). In *Dr. Martin Luthers Werke,* 6:167ff. Weimar: Böhlau, 1883-1993.
———. *On Monastic Vows* (1521). In *Dr. Martin Luthers Werke,* 8:564-669. Weimar: Böhlau, 1883-1993.
———. *Topics on Vows* (1521). In *Dr. Martin Luthers Werke,* 8:313-66. Weimar: Böhlau, 1883-1993.
Maag, Karin. "Change and Continuity in Medieval and Early Modern Worship: The Practice of Worship in the Schools." In *Worship in Medieval and Early Modern Europe: Change and Continuity in Religious Practice,* edited by Karin Maag and John D. Witvliet. Notre Dame, Ind.: University of Notre Dame Press, 2004.
MacCulloch, Diarmaid. *The Reformation: A History.* London: Penguin Books, 2003.
Markus, R. A. *The End of Ancient Christianity.* Cambridge: Cambridge University Press, 1990.

Bibliography

Marrou, H. I. *A History of Education in Antiquity*. New York: Sheed and Ward, 1956.

Matheson, Peter. *The Imaginative World of the Reformation*. Edinburgh: T. & T. Clark, 2000.

———, ed. *Reformation Christianity*. Minneapolis: Fortress, 2007.

McKee, Elsie Anne. "Exegesis, Theology, and Development in Calvin's *Institutio*: A Methodological Suggestion." In *Probing the Reformed Tradition: Historical Studies in Honor of Edward A. Dowey, Jr.*, edited by Brian G. Armstrong and Elsie A. McKee. Louisville: Westminster John Knox, 1989.

———. *John Calvin: Writings on Pastoral Piety*. New York: Paulist, 2001.

———. "Reformed Worship in the Sixteenth Century." In *Christian Worship in Reformed Churches Past and Present*, edited by Lukas Vischer. Grand Rapids: Eerdmans, 2003.

McNeill, John T. Introduction to *Institutes of the Christian Religion*, by John Calvin. Philadelphia: Westminster, 1960.

Melanchthon, Philip. *Loci Communes Theologici*. In The Library of Christian Classics, Volume XIX: *Melanchthon and Bucer*. Edited by Wilhelm Pauck. Philadelphia: Westminster, 1969.

Mentzer, Raymond A. "The Piety of Townspeople and City Folk." In *Reformation Christianity*, edited by Peter Matheson. Minneapolis: Fortress, 2007.

Miles, Margaret. *Fullness of Life: Historical Foundations for a New Asceticism*. Philadelphia: Westminster, 1981.

Muller, Richard. *After Calvin: Studies in the Development of a Theological Tradition*. New York: Oxford University Press, 2003.

———. "Directions in Current Calvin Research." In *Calvin Studies IX: Papers Presented at the Ninth Colloquium on Calvin Studies*, edited by John H. Leith and Robert A. Johnson. Davidson, N.C.: Davidson College, 1998.

———. *The Unaccommodated Calvin*. New York: Oxford University Press, 2000.

Parker, T. H. L. *Calvin's Doctrine of the Knowledge of God*. Edinburgh: Oliver and Boyd, 1969.

———. *John Calvin: A Biography*. Louisville: Westminster John Knox, 2006.

Partee, Charles. "Calvin's Central Dogma Again." In *Calvin Studies 3*, pp. 39-46. Davidson, N.C.: Davidson College, 1986.

———. "Prayer as the Practice of Predestination." In *Calvinus Servus Christi*, edited by Wilhelm H. Neuser. Budapest: Presseabteilung des Ráday-Kollegiums, 1988.

Reinburg, Virginia. "Liturgy and the Laity in Late Medieval and Reformation France." *Sixteenth Century Journal* 23 (1992).

Reymond, Robert L. "Calvin's Doctrine of Holy Scripture." In *A Theological Guide to Calvin's Institutes*, edited by David W. Hall and Peter A. Lillback. Phillipsburg, N.J.: P&R Publishing, 2008.

Richard, Lucien. *The Spirituality of John Calvin*. Atlanta: John Knox, 1974.

Saler, Benson. "*Religio* and the Definition of Religion." *Cultural Anthropology* 2, no. 3 (August 1987).

Bibliography

Saliers, Don E. *Worship as Theology: Foretaste of Glory Divine.* Nashville: Abingdon, 1994.

Schmemann, Alexander. *For the Life of the World.* Crestwood, N.Y.: St. Vladimir's Seminary Press, 1963.

Schreiner, Susan. *The Theater of His Glory: Nature and the Natural Order in the Thought of John Calvin.* Durham, N.C.: Labyrinth Press, 1991.

Selderhuis, Herman J. *Calvin's Theology of the Psalms.* Grand Rapids: Baker Academic, 2007.

———. *John Calvin: A Pilgrim's Life.* Downers Grove, Ill.: IVP Academic, 2009.

Seligman, Adam B., Robert P. Weller, Michael J. Puett, and Bennett Simon. *Ritual and Its Consequences: An Essay on the Limits of Sincerity.* Oxford: Oxford University Press, 2008.

Smith, Jonathan Z. "The Bare Facts of Ritual." In *Imagining Religion: From Babylon to Jonestown.* Chicago: University of Chicago Press, 1982.

Smith, Wilfred Cantwell. *The Meaning and End of Religion.* San Francisco: Harper and Row, 1978.

Steinmetz, David. *Calvin in Context.* New York: Oxford University Press, 1995.

Tagliabue, John. "A City of Mixed Emotions Observes Calvin's 500th." *New York Times,* November 4, 2009.

Taylor, Charles. *A Secular Age.* Cambridge: Harvard University Press, Belknap Press, 2007.

Thompson, John L. *Reading the Bible with the Dead.* Grand Rapids: Eerdmans, 2007.

Vanhoozer, Kevin. *The Drama of Doctrine: A Canonical-Linguistic Approach to Christian Theology.* Louisville: Westminster John Knox, 2005.

Volf, Miroslav. *Exclusion and Embrace: A Theological Exploration of Identity, Otherness, and Reconciliation.* Nashville: Abingdon, 1996.

Volf, Miroslav, and Dorothy Bass, eds. *Practicing Theology: Beliefs and Practices in Christian Life.* Grand Rapids: Eerdmans, 2002.

Wainwright, Geoffrey. *Doxology: The Praise of God in Worship, Doctrine, and Life.* New York: Oxford University Press, 1980.

Weber, Max. *The Protestant Ethic and the Spirit of Capitalism.* London: Routledge, 1992.

Wells, Samuel. *God's Companions: Reimagining Christian Ethics.* Oxford: Blackwell, 2006.

———. *Improvisation: The Drama of Christian Ethics.* Grand Rapids: Brazos, 2004.

Willis, David. "Rhetoric and Responsibility in Calvin's Theology." In *The Context of Contemporary Theology,* edited by Alexander McKelway and David Willis. Atlanta: John Knox, 1974.

Witvliet, John. *Worship Seeking Understanding.* Grand Rapids: Baker Academic, 2003.

Zachman, Randall C. *John Calvin as Teacher, Pastor, and Theologian.* Grand Rapids: Baker Academic, 2006.

Index

Anabaptists, 16n., 220n.
Articles for Church Organization (Calvin, 1537), 33-34
Asad, Talal, 231n.
Athanasius, 9, 24-25
Augustine, 14-19, 20-21n., 46, 48, 55-56, 139, 143, 149, 159

Barth, Karl, 7n., 52n.
Bass, Dorothy, 215-16n.
Battles, Ford Lewis, 46, 71n., 103n., 208n.
Bell, Catherine, 231n.
Benedict, Philip, 32n., 33n., 37n., 210n.
Bible. *See* Scripture
Bouwsma, William, 5n.
Bradshaw, Paul, 25n.

Calvin, John: anthropology, 50n., 62-70, 87, 91-95, 112-17, 128-37, 205-7, 214; early life, 12; epistemology, 61-82; as formational thinker, 45-58; governing goal(s), 52, 66, 78, 84, 105, 156n., 209, 221; and the Psalter, 33-37; reforming, 191-209. *See also* Monasticism; *and individual doctrinae and titles of individual works*
Canlis, Julie, 227
Certeau, Michel de, 231n.

Charry, Ellen, 7n., 54n., 215n., 218n.
Church: architecture, 103; beyond our ken, 153-54, 156-65; and Christ, 41, 121-23, 132-33, 176, 203, 208, 213; danger of, 68; early, 24, 27-28, 35, 51, 102, 205; and formation (and/or disciplines), 2-4, 7, 13-22, 31-34, 43, 49, 51, 54, 58, 75, 99, 102, 120, 137-38, 141, 156-65, 176-78, 191, 202n., 205, 213, 215-42; and late medieval Europe, 29-30, 42; as "microcosmic temple," 101; and monasticism, 2-4, 13-22, 120; and mystical union *(unio mystica)*, 41, 132; in Reformed worship, 31-32, 35, 43; role of, 2, 102, 105, 213; and role of *Institutio*, 54n.; and sacraments, 182-86; and sanctification, 172-73; as school, 110; and theology, 215-20. *See also* Geneva; *Pietas*; Psalter; *and individual doctrinae*
Clark, R. Scott, 139n.
Cohn, Henry J., 26n., 27n.
Commentary on 1 Timothy (Calvin), 50, 128
Commentary on Genesis (Calvin), 96-103
Commentary on Psalms (Calvin), 160-61, 198n.
Commentary on 2 Timothy (Calvin), 67

Index

Commentary on Seneca's "De Clementia" (Calvin), 45
Communion: life in, 50, 82, 120n., 121-24, 137, 141, 146, 157, 166-87, 199-205, 218n., 223, 227. See also Lord's Supper
Creation: doctrine of, 5, 58, 86-88, 140, 148; as gift, 95; and knowledge of God, 55, 58, 76-87, 169; as paideutic, 79, 82, 212; as rhetoric, 107, 117, 212; as school, 99-102, 112, 212; as theater, 84, 91, 97-104, 109-10, 203, 206, 208, 211
Cunningham, Lawrence, 21n.

Dialectic, 192, 203, 205-8, 215
Doctrina (doctrine): and formation, 6-8, 50-58, 82, 140-41, 154, 163, 166, 210-32. See also individual doctrinae

Election, 115, 132, 139-40, 142, 148-76, 179-80n., 222. See also Providence
Elwood, Christopher, 57
Erasmus, Desiderius, 20n., 22n., 27, 28n., 36, 56n., 57, 231n.

Ford, David, 46, 103n., 208n., 215n.
"The Form of Prayers and Songs of the Church" (Calvin), 37n., 208n.
Foucault, Michel, 230-31n.

Garside, Charles, 37-38n.
Geneva, 2, 4, 11-43
Gerrish, Brian, 8n., 47n., 49n., 53n., 55, 72n., 198n.
Gordon, Bruce, 16n., 31, 40n., 56n.

Hadot, Pierre, 230-31n.
Hauerwas, Stanley, 16n., 219n.
Hill, Christopher, 27n.

Institutio Christianae Religionis: and governing theme, 52, 108, 209; and human knowledge, 61-82; role of, 50-53, 54n.; and Scripture, 105-11; structure of, 61; translation of title, 56-57. See also individual doctrinae

Jaeger, Werner, 23n.
Jesus Christ: as abiding, 184, 223; and communion with, 5n., 23, 41-43, 48, 79-82, 122-24, 136, 141, 156, 166-67, 181-87, 199-200, 205, 224, 227; dialectical relationship to sin, 205, 215; and "double grace," 135-38; and faith, 131-37, 150, 214; as giver of gifts, 2; image of, 4, 117, 128-32, 138, 147, 219; intimacy (and solitude), 124; and knowledge, 61, 63, 76-79, 82, 132, 182; as mediator, 28, 77-78, 117-29, 167; and new life, 145-46, 162; and providence, 89, 200; and salvation, 57, 92, 149-50, 154, 199-200, 215, 222; and sanctification, 157, 205, 219; as teacher, 136, 185, 223; word made flesh, 176. See also Lord's Supper; Prayer; Sanctification
Jones, Serene, 8n.
Justification, 125, 128-29, 132, 134-35, 138, 140, 182, 193-94, 214, 221-22, 226, 228

Kelsey, David, 23n., 223n.
Kingdon, Robert M., 12n., 31n., 32n., 33n., 40n.

LaCocque, Andre, 216n.
Liturgy, 24, 28n., 29-42, 54-56, 74n., 102-3, 136, 160, 181, 207, 214, 216, 223, 226
Lord's Supper: and commensalism, 204n.; and formation, 4, 24, 75, 80, 136, 164-65, 180-87, 215, 218, 227-30; in Geneva, 40-43; in late medieval Europe, 29-30, 42; and mystical union (*unio mystica*), 27-28, 43; and nourishment, 87, 180-87, 224
Luther, Martin, 1, 12, 28n., 34, 56n., 225

Maag, Karin, 31n., 36n.

240

Index

MacCulloch, Diarmaid, 22n., 34
Markus, R. A., 21n., 25n.
Marot, Clement, 36
Marrou, H. I., 23n.
Matheson, Peter, 1n., 3n., 26n., 31n., 32n., 38n., 39n., 44n.
McKee, Elsie Anne, 5, 6n., 31n.
McNeill, John T., 56n., 73n.
Melanchthon, Philip, 20n., 56n., 139
Mentzer, Raymond A., 31n., 35n., 41n.
Monastery. *See* Monasticism
Monasticism, 2-29, 35, 39, 49, 50, 55-56, 74n., 102, 120, 169, 220n., 230-31n.
Muller, Richard, 5, 6n., 45n., 56n., 61, 106n.

Paideia: Christ-centered, 212; Christian life and formation, 4, 22-28, 35, 42, 49-51, 58, 66, 75, 82, 90, 102, 109-10, 119-23, 136-37, 141-47, 166, 169, 173, 178, 186, 191, 195-98, 209-32; *Institutio,* 42, 50-53, 57-58, 61-187, 191; monasticism, 22-28; in New Testament, 23, 67; and prayer, 169, 178, 201; restorative, 79, 97-99, 136-38, 141-46, 205, 221-23; and sanctification, 138. *See also Doctrina;* Geneva
Parker, T. H. L., 28n., 37n., 61n.
Partree, Charles, 5n., 54n., 176n.
Pietas (piety): alternative title to *Institutio,* 57; and Christ, 117, 127-28; and creation, 115-16, 127-31; and doctrine, 46, 51-58, 66, 82, 88, 90, 191, 203, 216, 232; and Geneva, 5, 9-26, 36; *Institutio* as guide to, 6n., 45-58; and knowledge, 46-49, 53, 62, 65-67, 70-83, 88, 95; and Lord's Supper, 43, 186n.; and music, 36-37; and practice, 48-50, 57-58, 66, 73-74, 80, 82, 109, 209, 232; and prayer, 17-72, 87; providence, 143, 147, 161, 164, 170; and sin, 85, 91, 95, 114-16, 127; and thanksgiving (or gratitude), 46-48, 65-68, 72
Prayer: as "chief exercise of faith," 39, 167, 177, 180; of children, 175-76;

communion of, 167-80; daily, 2, 13, 24, 26 35, 39, 43, 51, 75, 108-11, 136, 162, 166-80, 187, 191, 218, 222; as dialogue, 167-68; and formation, 28, 43, 49-57, 102, 108-11, 121-22, 160-80, 213, 215, 218, 222-30; *lex orandi,* 54, 163; Lord's, 146-47; and monasticism, 9, 14-24, 27, 169; and for mystical union *(unio mystica),* 27; and practical knowledge, 75, 79-82; and reforming Calvin, 199-201, 207-8; and scriptural language, 110-11; singing, 34-39; unanswered, 177-79; for universal salvation, 160-65. *See also* Jesus Christ; *Paideia;* Prayer; Providence
Predestination, 138-64. *See also* Providence
Providence: and church, 88; governed by, 92, 104; as a host, 107; and knowledge of God, 72n., 77, 83, 88-90; and masochism, 199-201; and misanthropy, 208-9; and *pietas,* 88, 90; and prayer, 88, 146, 160, 168-79; and predestination, 145; and quietism, 174n., 192-99; reforming the doctrine of, 208-14; and sin, 88-90; in web of doctrines, 140
Psalms: *Commentary on,* 160-61, 198n.; as instructive, 173, 178; singing, 24, 27, 30, 33-38, 42, 123
Psalter, 33-37. *See also* Psalms

Richard, Lucien, 8n.

Sanctification: and affliction, 201; and Christ, 118, 128-38, 140, 150-53, 157, 191, 214, 221; and depravity, 205, 208; as doctrine, 140, 203; and formation, 2, 4, 24-27, 49, 70, 164, 171-73, 220-30; and knowledge, 69-70; and monasticism, 2, 24-27, 220n.; and prayer, 173, 207; and providence, 45-46; Psalms, 38; and restoration, 205, 220-23; school of, 82,

241

144, 206, 208, 211, 219; and Scripture, 111. *See also* Geneva; *Pietatis*
Schreiner, Susan, 16n.
Scripture: correction to "dulling," 51n., 92-93n., 96-111, 107; education, 6n., 32-33, 51, 80, 110, 136, 141; *Institutio* as a guide to, 45n., 52-53, 96-111; and monasticism 18-19, 24, 27; and *paideia*, 23, 51, 53, 57, 79; and *pietatis*, 53-58; in liturgical setting, 38, 42, 44n., 110, 136, 187, 213; and practices, 2, 24, 27-30, 43, 96-111, 191, 224, 232; proper role of, 104; as remedial, 76, 79; as spectacles, 79, 97, 105, 108-12, 141; and the Spirit, 97-105, 176, 212, 215, 223. *See also* Psalms
Selderhuis, Herman, 39, 198n.
Sin: as bar to judgmentalism, 153-54; book of Job, 196n.; and depravity, 83-84, 203-9, 215; dying to, 119-23; and ingratitude, 26, 77, 91, 93, 112, 114, 118, 144, 164, 206; "miserable ruin," 65, 76, 83, 109, 112, 115, 128-29, 135, 143, 202-7, 226; and "nature," 207; and oblivion, 84-85, 89-95, 104, 115, 127, 176; and shame, 77, 112; us without God, 112-17. *See also* Creation; Jesus Christ; Providence; Scripture

Smith, Jonathan Z., 102, 231
Smith, Wilfred Cantwell, 55-56n.
Steinmetz, David, 13-14n., 210n.

Tagliabue, John, 192n.
Taylor, Charles, 7n.

Universalism, 160-64

Weber, Max, 7n.
Witvliet, John, 35, 36n., 215n., 223n.
Worship: and Christ, 121, 136; domestic, 110, 136; and formation, 4, 24, 33, 42, 49-51, 75, 102-3, 109-11, 121, 136, 213, 225, 230; and Geneva, 29-44, 110, 208, 230; and knowledge, 65, 75, 81, 86; in late medieval Europe, 30, 42; and Lord's Supper, 181, 184; and monasticism, 4, 24, 102; and Nuremberg, 1; and *pietas*, 46, 55-56, 66n., 74n., 81; and prayer, 180; and the Psalter, 33-35, 38n.; and "the sanctuary," 43; as "sermon," 32; and theology, 208, 219

for book

starting knowledge from rt brain to left (McGilchrist)
how to talk about P's pr-communic'n of Xn life in way that gives
knowledge of? So using new categories - to link language to its
source in body, bodily experience by Θ & us, by us

if X reveals true humanity (307), reveals it as second-person relatedness
that is, participatory - & more, relatedness as participation
across boundaries / like to like

Then perhaps reveals sin-relatedness as false rela - pseudo,
hollow (or worse than that - predatory relation b/ sin & humanity)

Themes - primacy of θ's agency
     humans return, but doesn't
     just X's work,
     practices grounded in grace

p 307 re. depravity as de-formation, not intrinsic to humanity

p 300 re suffering - X joins us already in our suffering → don't one
                                                          to join his

(compare Fowl & Calvin on paideia   (189)
 getting paideia to the laity - democratization
                               (Fowl misses this - Calvin)

215 - no dist b/ systematic & practical theol.
216 - analogue discourses for 'theol'
      " theological knowledge

232 dist b/ just'n & sanctif'n - see Hampton on this
discuss esp. reforming 'practice'

fr p 220-21   for AAR on apoca church

I outline of Calvin's reforming work
II 7 key loci
 reg reports ofo   — theol. knowledge — goal pietas 66
 refunctioning of self   creation, providence, sin
                    scripture
                    xtology
                    predestination
                    prayer
                    Lord's supper

III constructive proposal for retrieving
     Calvin — theol/ doctrine for
     sake of church

theol knowledge has goal of pietas — 66 — doctrine must be
'useful' — how relate to sheer gratuity of grace

28 — atonement a participation — or grafted
    knowledge of vs knowledge about — incorporated

93 — Calvin's anthropology

(122 III) 103 divine participation

194 prudential principle

To discuss:
  ascetic way as departure for self – p 26
     from own senses p 9?–92
  sin as inhuman act / oblivion 90 ff
(C's anthropology p 93

(dismantling dist of sacred & secular p 32
  cf 219-20, n. 8 {see Hammuwas ch v's world

p 90 trusting providence – how teach this in S. Sudan?

dis junction bef 'ideal' & practice p 40 – what is 'perfect'
  46 – 'piety' as goal

piety alone constitutes xn life – p 50
  57 needs H5 – ok

54 – re Foxley – (alium exemplified theologia that now
       (acc 7) is lost.
  63 – re reciprocal knowledge | Θ & self — respect
                                                  intersubjectivity
no divide bef theory & practice at 54

  84 ff (sin)

(incorporation p 78
(184 – support a somatic knowledge,
                     bodily cognition